Jordan L. Harding

COLLECTION

Class of
1950

Doctor of Laws (Honorary)
2002

SHENANDOAH UNIVERSITY

EXPERIMENTS IN FORM

Henry James's Novels, 1896-1901

EXPERIMENTS IN FORM

Henry James's Novels, 1896-1901

WALTER ISLE

HARVARD UNIVERSITY PRESS
CAMBRIDGE, MASSACHUSETTS
1968

© Copyright 1968 by the President and Fellows
of Harvard College

All rights reserved

Distributed in Great Britain by Oxford University Press,
London

Library of Congress Catalog Card Number 68-27086
Printed in the United States of America

Quotations from *The Awkward Age*, *The Spoils of Poynton*, and *What Maisie Knew* are reprinted with the permission of Charles Scribner's Sons from Volumes IX, X, and XI of THE NOVELS AND TALES OF HENRY JAMES. Copyright 1908 Charles Scribner's Sons; renewal copyright 1936 Henry James.

To Brenda

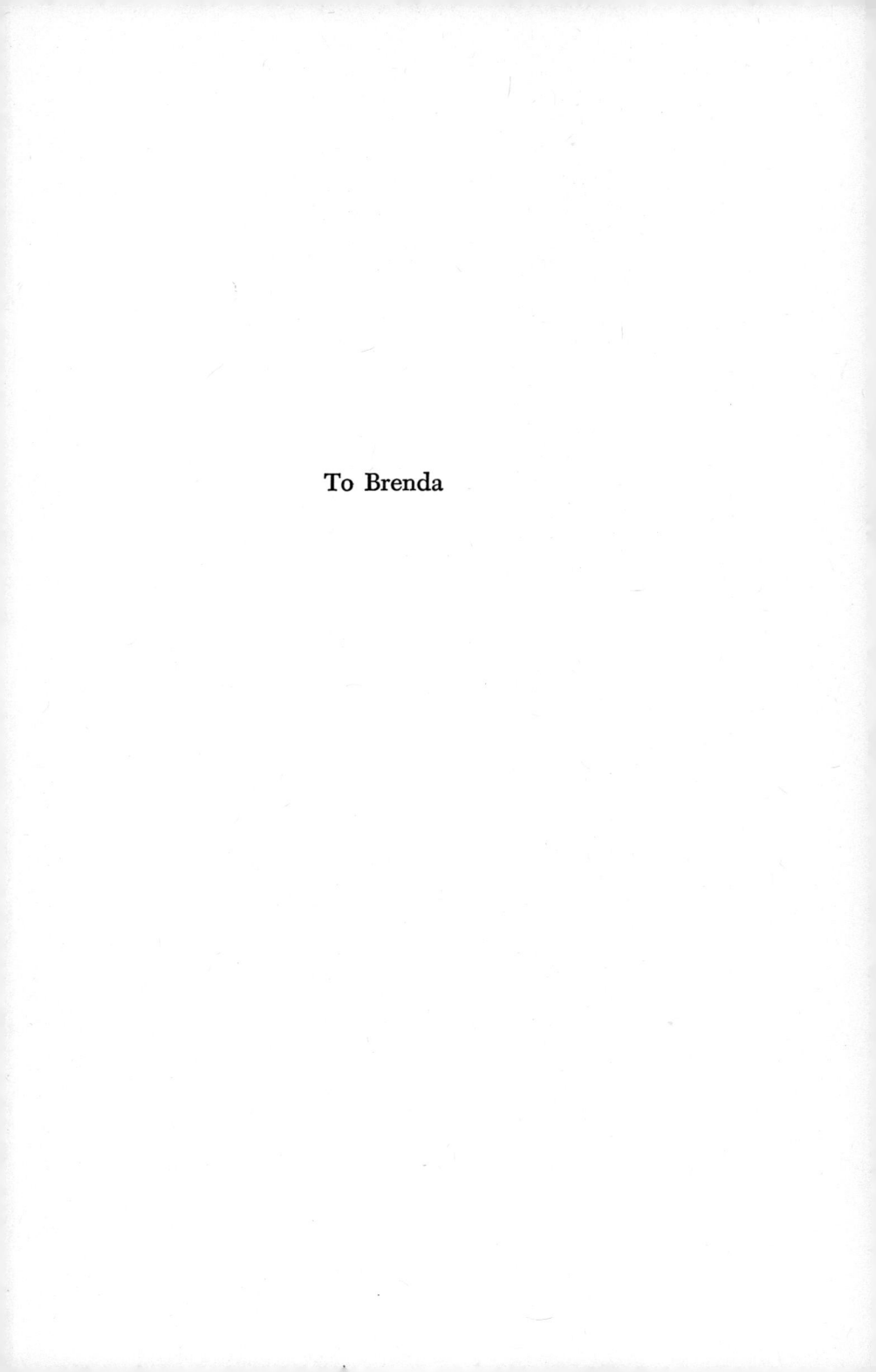

PREFACE

SEVERAL interests combined to suggest this study of five novels and a short period in Henry James's career. I was first interested in novelistic techniques, especially the more radical departures of Joyce, Woolf, and Proust. Out of this came an historical interest in the development of the novel toward a writer like Joyce. A separate interest in James's novels led me to a study of technique and to his prefaces and notebooks as conscious records of technical preoccupation. In following James's career I began to see a pattern of development from the long novels of the 1880's through the drama and the novels of the 1890's to the long novels of the "major phase," after the turn of the century. The pattern seemed to reflect in miniature many of the general changes from nineteenth-century to twentieth-century fiction, or rather vaguely, from "Victorian" to "Modern."

The period of the 1890's, especially, appeared more significant in James's career than had been noted by critics and historians and the novels of greater value and worth more detailed comment than they had been given. I found the five novels representative in various ways of the general historical changes and I thought several of them excellent. After he had stopped writing plays James returned to the novel, and it seemed to me that he was consciously trying out or experimenting with new fictional techniques which pointed ahead more than they continued previous achievements. I decided to analyze these experiments in as much detail as I could.

The broader concerns nevertheless remain important. In this study I have tried to keep several contexts present in varying degrees: the general history of the novel as background, the period of the nineties in relation to James's career, and, most importantly, the novels themselves as representative experiments. I have not tried to write a history of the novel, or even to go fully into James's career. There are many developments and interests I have left out of this study. The general context of "the novel" I have only tried to suggest, directly in the first chapter, more implicitly in the later chapters. Again, James's full career has not been treated. I have pointed to what seemed the essential relationships and developments from one period to the next in the first and second chapters and have tried to keep James's other novels in mind throughout the rest of the study. The method of the book is to move from general considerations about the novel, especially the novel as experiment, and James's career in the first chapter to more immediately relevant parts of that career, particularly the drama, in the second chapter. Then I devote a chapter of detailed analysis to each of the five novels published between 1896 and 1901. Chapter One can serve as an introduction and perhaps, in its more general aspect, as a conclusion.

PREFACE

The body of the study is in the analysis of the individual novels. I do not feel that I can now generalize too effectively about the history of the novel. I have offered a few tentative suggestions, but these are restricted mostly to some remarks on experiment and some brief indications of the placement of this period and these novels in a more general scheme of what comes before and after. There is perhaps little that is new in this, but I hope that it will provide background for the analyses of the separate novels.

In a sense every novel is an experiment. Some experiments are more radical departures from an established mode than others. I have focused on what James was doing in this period of experiment because I believe it reveals not only James's own development but something about the nature of the novel. I am here interested both in James and in novels and I hope that the analyses will illuminate both. Close attention to one author's experiments in form should help us to distinguish more clearly forms constructed by other, perhaps very different, novelists.

The method of analysis I have chosen seems to me the most natural. It arises partly from my own more general critical interests and partly from the nature of this particular subject. It is a critical commonplace that it is impossible to hold a novel completely in the mind; in this imperfect memory of the reading experience the formal elements are perhaps the most difficult of all to retain. James's technical experiments, however, force one's attention on just this aspect and my analyses must therefore concentrate on structure and technique. This cannot, however, even in considering experiments in form, be an exclusive concern. The nature of any novel seems to me to direct critical attention to three very general areas: characters and characterization, technique and structure, themes and meaning. Character is a way into a novel; structural features and technique give the novel form and are the area of experiment; themes and meaning give substance to form; and the form and meaning considered together provide a summation of the critical experience and a test for unity and achievement in the novel.

Any consideration of a novel which does justice, as it must, to all three areas will be lengthy. A long analysis, though risking tedium, also allows the critic to incorporate as much detail as possible from the novel. A long critical analysis permits a fullness, an attention to detail, to patterns, and to cross-references among all the novels of the period. Given my own bias toward technique and structure, I have tried to provide as balanced an analysis as possible. I have attempted to combine close attention to the text and the unique formal characteristics of each novel with the more general human subjects and "ideas" that have arisen in my reading of the novels. My method may at times, then, seem eclectic; I have used whatever material in the novel seemed to me significant and whatever critical approach seemed useful at that point. In each analysis, however, I have organized the material around the major areas of character, structure, and meaning. This organization is, I hope, not arbitrary. The material seemed naturally to fall that way. This method of analysis seems to me the most effective and comprehensive way I can give faithful critical representation to the reading experience of an entire novel.

Consequently the reader will find rather long exegetical chapters on novels like *The Other House* and *The Spoils of Poynton* which, though interesting, cannot be valued as highly as the two following novels, *What Maisie Knew*

PREFACE

and *The Awkward Age*. Any novel by James is worth examining closely and, moreover, since one emphasis of this study is on the whole period, a careful reading of these first novels is necessary to the analysis of the techniques with which James was experimenting. They are the first events in the story of experiment, and the cruder experiments must be seen clearly before the more refined ones in the later novels can be apprehended. *The Sacred Fount*, with all its ambiguities and radical departures, marks the furthest limit of experiment in the period and points ahead. All the experiments in all the novels, in fact, point to later achievements by James or even by other novelists. But that's another book.

It is impossible to acknowledge all the help I have received in studying Henry James and the novel. I have taken too many courses, taught too many students, read too many critics even to begin to list the ones I remember. Most specific critical debts are acknowledged in the footnotes, but more general obligations to critics like R. P. Blackmur, Kenneth Burke, Mark Schorer, Ian Watt, and others are hard to specify.

I would like to thank by name all those who have read the manuscript fully or in part, at one stage or another of its development. Thomas Moser started me on it and guided me through the first drafts. I owe him the most. Professors Yvor Winters, David Levin, and Richard Poirier also read and made valuable comments on an early version. Mrs. Barbara Hardy read, made suggestions, and helped in many ways during a year in England. Michael Millgate was extremely helpful in reading the whole manuscript and commenting on both style and ideas. My colleague at Rice, J. A. Ward, has taught me much about

James and read part of the manuscript in a late form. The unknown reader for the Harvard University Press was very generous and through his criticism enabled me to formulate better the purposes and limits of this study. All errors in fact or interpretation are of course my own.

I have also been aided materially by a Fulbright Scholarship for a year's study at the University of London, and by several summer research grants generously provided by Rice University which gave me time to write and rewrite and also paid for typing.

W.I.

Contents

1
Introduction: The Context of Experiment
page 1

2
The Early Nineties and the Drama
page 18

3
The Other House
page 39

4
The Spoils of Poynton
page 77

5
What Maisie Knew
page 120

6
The Awkward Age
page 165

7
The Sacred Fount
page 205

Experiments in Form:
Henry James's Novels, 1896-1901

1

Introduction: The Context of Experiment

> The form, it seems to me, is to be appreciated after the fact: then the author's choice has been made, his standard has been indicated; then we can follow lines and directions and compare tones and resemblances. Then in a word we can enjoy one of the most charming of pleasures, we can estimate quality, we can apply the test of execution. The execution belongs to the author alone; it is what is most personal to him, and we measure him by that. The advantage, the luxury, as well as the torment and responsibility of the novelist, is that there is no limit to what he may attempt as an executant—no limit to his possible experiments, efforts, discoveries, successes. Here it is especially that he works, step by step, like his brother of the brush, of whom we may always say that he has painted his picture in a manner best known to himself.
>
> Henry James, "The Art of Fiction"

THE CAREER of Henry James has often and justly been divided into periods: the early novels, the long novels of the eighties, the final achievement of "the major phase" after 1900. Another period which has attracted less critical attention is the decade from 1890 to 1900. This curious phase in James's literary life is marked by his attempts to write plays in the first half of the decade and by a series of five novels in the last half. These novels are shorter than those of the eighties—*The Princess Casamassima, The Bostonians, The Tragic Muse*—and the long novels which come immediately after—*The Ambassadors, The Wings of the Dove, The Golden Bowl*. It is important to a critical understanding of these novels and of James's whole career that one look closely at these rather unusual works of fiction written between 1896 and 1901, for they point once again to James's continually changing and developing fictional techniques, his constant experimentation with style, subject matter, and form.

An examination of the five novels leads out of James's experiences in the theater, through the novels themselves, and looks ahead to "the major phase." But these five novels are not merely transitional; they are important works of fiction in themselves and one or two rank with the best of James's work or any other. Between 1896 and 1901, after the failure of his play *Guy Domville* early in 1895, Henry James published *The Other House* (1896), *The Spoils of Poynton* (1897), *What Maisie Knew* (1897), *The Awkward Age* (1899), and *The Sacred Fount* (1901). He also published a number of his finest short stories or tales and two important *nouvelles, The Turn of the Screw* and *In The Cage* in 1898. I shall concentrate on the novels, but James's other work during this period will fill in the background. For James himself these were the years of his prime, the years between age fifty-three and fifty-eight. A careful examination of the period and, especially, a detailed analysis of each of the novels will, I hope, show that James was at the height of his creative powers. It will also show something of the nature of fiction itself as James experiments with various forms.

THE CONTEXT OF EXPERIMENT

Except in studies which deal with James's whole achievement, such as those of F. W. Dupee and Oscar Cargill, this period has seldom been treated as an entity.[1] Studies of separate aspects of James's work by Marius Bewley, Dorothea Krook, Laurence Holland, J. A. Ward, and others have touched on or examined some of these novels; and there have been a number of valuable studies of individual novels within the period.[2] The attitude to the period as a whole, however, may be indicated by the descriptive phrases given to it by Professors Dupee and Cargill: "The Awkward Period" and "The Augean Stable." Although their work is valuable, I would choose a different term, that of experiment. Perhaps all the critical work can be brought into focus and the period characterized through a close examination of the individual novels in relation to this phase of James's career, as Richard Poirier has excellently done with the early novels and as F. O. Matthiessen first and most rewardingly did with "the major phase."[3]

Most critics have suggested that these years show no single achievement which can be ranked with James's best novels, but I feel their judgments are perhaps distorted by the experimental character of the whole period. The more radically experimental a novelist's work, the more difficulty we have in reaching some general agreement in our critical evaluations. This can change with time, as with Faulkner or Conrad, but it can still be seen in the disparate attitudes toward even Joyce and Woolf, or especially toward a more recent writer like Samuel Beckett, the present French *anti-roman*, or such American "anti-realists" as John Hawkes. James also presents an additional problem in that he is closely linked in many ways with traditional novelists like Balzac, Turgenev, or

George Eliot; and he is, of course, a charter member of F. R. Leavis's "great tradition." His followers, the novelists we tend to call Jamesian, like Edith Wharton, F. Scott Fitzgerald, or Elizabeth Bowen, are also essentially traditional. A radical exception, though also I think a Jamesian, might be Ivy Compton-Burnett, and her work perhaps points to the essential difference between tradition, which has often to do with subject matter and only to some extent with form, and experiment, which has more to do with form and technique.

Henry James during the late nineties was, as always, engaged in a concentrated search for an adequate form of artistic expression. As early as 1878 he had described his lasting concern in a letter to his brother William: "I think you are altogether right in returning always to the importance of subject. I hold to this, strongly; and if I don't as yet seem to proceed upon it more, it is because, being 'very artistic,' I have a constant impulse to try experiments of form."[4] His statement remains true of his work in 1896. James, like any other great artist, never found a form which was totally satisfactory, which would end his search; one has only to compare *The Golden Bowl* with *The Ivory Tower* or *The Sense of the Past* to discover this. Each new novel to some extent dictates a new form. But the late nineties, for James, more than other parts of his career, are marked by a thorough-going search for at least a basic form which can be adjusted to the demands of a particular subject. At this time, more than any other, he was subject to his "constant impulse to try experiments." And James, through experiment, did discover and refine several principal features of a basic form which make a kind of common denominator in *The Ambassadors, The Wings of the Dove*, and *The Golden Bowl*. I would sug-

THE CONTEXT OF EXPERIMENT

gest, then, that "experiment" is a more appropriate term for this period. Each of the novels during these years marks some new departure, the conscious development of some new technique which will often make possible the treatment of some new theme or subject.

For James this was above all a time of experiment in directions quite different from those he had traveled in the 1880's. One may speculate without ever being quite certain about the personal reasons for this change in strategy from the preceding decade. The close of the 1880's brought a crisis in James's career as a novelist. None of his last three long novels had sold well, and he seemed more and more to sense failure and, especially, the loss of an audience.[5] Several reactions are apparent in his letters at the time. Of these at least three are significant for what was to follow. He decided, first, as he told his brother, that *"The Tragic Muse* is to be my last long novel,"[6] and he described the same novel to Robert Louis Stevenson as "the longest and most careful novel I have ever written . . . and the last, in that form, I shall ever do."[7] It was his last Victorian novel, as we generally use the term, and the end of a decade of attempting to write novels which he thought would fit the popular, expansive form. James tells his brother in the same letter that he plans to write a number of "short things," to continue, as he always had, to turn out short stories.

James's second significant reaction at this time is to turn from the novel to the play. In his letters there are a number of allusions to his plans for writing plays, to his "campaign," as he seems to think of it, for conquering the English stage. This effort was brought on both by his fascination with the drama as a form, his early and continuing love for the theater, and (perhaps even more) by his desire to gain success and an audience, some kind of fame. The effort to do this in a medium new to him as a writer ended in failure, a failure which I propose to examine in more detail in the next chapter.

Thirdly, James had become aware in the late eighties of an increasing interest in England and of a concurrent loss of imaginative attachment to his native country. As he became more and more engrossed in England and the English social life and scene, he gradually became convinced that this was what he knew best and was therefore best fitted to portray in his writing. In a letter to William Dean Howells on May 17, 1890, James gives a clear description of his decision: "Henceforth I must do, or half do, England in fiction—as the place I see most today, and, in a sort of way, know best. I have at last more acquired notions of it, on the whole, than of any other world, and it will serve as well as any other."[8] *The Princess Casamassima* and *The Tragic Muse* had already been the first steps away from America and the "international theme." The plays of the early nineties continue in this same direction. All five of the novels of the late nineties, from *The Other House* to *The Sacred Fount*, have England and the English as their subject matter. Only in some of his short stories does James retain the American subject. Americans do not appear in his novels until his return to the international theme in *The Ambassadors* and *The Wings of the Dove*.

James himself was aware of some essential differences between the novels of the eighties and *The Other House*, *The Spoils of Poynton*, and their successors. The differences are basically those of form and technique. James comments in the preface to *The Golden Bowl*, the last and in a sense summary preface, that the novels written

THE CONTEXT OF EXPERIMENT

before 1895 were, when he reread them for the New York edition, not familiar to him, not in his later manner, his "present mode of motion" as he calls it in 1909.[9] Even later, writing the scenario for *The Ivory Tower*, he described *The Other House* as "a precedent, a support, a divine little light to walk by."[10] To discover that mode of motion and trace out the first steps toward it is the purpose of this study.

There is no violent break between the earlier novels and those of the nineties, but there are some basic differences which should be noted at the start. Before going into more detailed speculation about the thematic and formal nature of these experimental novels, we may note some of the more obvious changes. The long, "panoramic" novels of the 1880's, with fairly extensive variety in character and setting, are followed by novels that are much shorter, more compact, perhaps even more restricted in setting and numbers of characters. The experimental novels are much closer to what we generally consider "the short novel" (however we may define that elusive term). This is true even of the longer works of the period—*What Maisie Knew* and *The Awkward Age*. In scope they seem to resemble much earlier novels like *The Europeans* and *Washington Square* or the shorter novels of the eighties like *A London Life* and *The Aspern Papers*. The novels of the nineties often strike one at first as extended *nouvelles* (which may be accounted for in part, as we shall see later, by James's initial conception of most of them as short tales). There has been a drastic concentration in character, time, action, and scene, more concentrated even than in some of the earlier short works. Usually only a handful of characters are involved or even mentioned; the action is limited in duration (except in the first parts of

What Maisie Knew, a special case). The action and the situation are limited to apparently small crises in the personal relationships of a small group of people (a feature more common in the play than the novel). All of this tends to make the novel static. Quite often James's intention throughout these novels, as only occasionally in the earlier novels, is to explore or simply reveal a situation or a state of mind, rather than a sequence of events, an action. Most often the smallest act, or quite likely the failure to act, assumes the largest significance in representing a static condition.

There are also more extreme changes in specific novelistic techniques, which must be examined in detail in each novel, and which set this group of novels quite apart from anything James had previously written. Shortened and simplified as the novels are in some ways, they also exhibit a conscious elaboration of and concentration on technique, on the formal aspects of the novel, which move them away from novels like those of the eighties or ones which George Eliot and even James's much-admired Turgenev might have written, and closer to a novel that might have been the work of the somewhat distrusted Flaubert or Joseph Conrad. James draws fairly narrow limits around the subjects of these novels, but within these limits his technique produces a kind of structural complexity and virtuosity which is very different from and in some ways more challenging than anything he had done before.

In general, the techniques employed in these novels are now relatively familiar to us, but tracing their first development is worth some close study. In outline, James's experiments in technique can be divided into three kinds. A general concern with point of view, the Jamesian trade-

THE CONTEXT OF EXPERIMENT

mark, is characteristic of all the novels. In two of them—*The Spoils of Poynton* and *What Maisie Knew*—the basis of structure is the use of a third-person central consciousness, through whom all the experience of the novel comes to us and whose subjective response, growing, changing, and reaching for perception, is the center of interest in the novel. This third-person technique provides a certain objectivity through a perceptible separation between author and central consciousness, especially when that center is a very young girl like Maisie Farange. Related to this—in *The Sacred Fount*—is the use of a first-person narrator who describes the situation in the novel and his experience of it. The subjectivity of such a form is manifest in a kind of ambiguity and obscurity with the consequent difficulties of interpretation which have plagued the critics of this novel (like those of *The Turn of the Screw* where the technique is much the same). Here the author retreats and one half of the author-character relationship seems nonexistent. In one sense the author has become completely impersonal, we receive no help from him in our reading; but there is also a marked tendency in reading a novel like this to equate the author with the narrator in our desire to have him present, to have his authority to rely on. In the remaining two novels—*The Other House* and *The Awkward Age*—a third strategy becomes James's structural principle. Here James moves close to the drama, to the play in dialogue; and here the material is presented in the most objective form possible. *The Awkward Age* carries this experiment to its extreme. In these two novels, as in the first-person novel, the author has removed himself and his describing and commenting voice, but with the difference that here there is no one character in the novel whose responses replace the author's at the center.

The novels are conceived as plays, as extended dialogues, and the whole situation rather than the consciousness and perceptions of one character assumes central importance. *The Other House* and *The Awkward Age* show the most obvious part of James's debt to his experience in the theater, but that lesson also becomes manifest in a number of other ways.

In the two forms in which there is a central consciousness, either first or third person, James constructs his novel in a certain way which gives it a unique texture. This method can be tentatively described as a fairly regular alternation between a dramatic scene, derived from the play, and a meditation by the central character, often approaching an interior monologue. The experiments in these novels form the basis of that technique James often refers to in his prefaces, the balanced use of "picture" and "scene." The scene is of course also the basic structural feature of the novels conceived dramatically.

In all the novels the use of dramatic scenes focuses attention on the dialogue. Although James had his reservations about overdoing "the ostensible report of spoken words," what he called during these years "the abuse of the element of colloquy,"[11] in these novels he experimented with several techniques in dialogue which he was to involve directly with the theme and form of the novel. The dialogue, as we shall see, tends to become stylized and James often uses it as the vehicle for a certain kind of inquiry into the meaning of experience. The dialogue, often a question-and-answer passage between two or more characters, is part of a structural pattern which is implicit in all the novels and which can also be seen in the alternation of scene and meditation.

This basic mode of many of the technical features of

THE CONTEXT OF EXPERIMENT

these novels and of structure and theme in general is dialectic.[12] No matter how much the central situation in a novel is static, the structure is always to some extent dynamic and linear, moving from the first page to the last in what John Holloway has called the "trajectory" of the novel.[13] James's dialectical principles—conceiving dialogue, conflict between characters, themes, and structural patterns as a process equivalent to thesis, antithesis, synthesis—bring about a careful, balanced generation of the action and development of theme. "Balance" is the key word, for this is what finally gives the novels an artistic form as well as an organic sequence. Analyses of the overall structure and its chapter-by-chapter development in each of these experimental novels will, I hope, illustrate this dialectic pattern and will also bring out the various other recurrent structural patterns, some derived directly from the drama, such as a tendency for the action to fall into phases or "acts."

One must also note that James's experiments with dialogue and with meditation or subjective response, as well as with various short-story techniques and textures that are evident in *The Spoils of Poynton* and *What Maisie Knew*, determine his prose style in the novels. No generalization is sound without support from detailed examination of passages in all the novels, but it is undoubtedly true that James's so-called "late style," with its involutions and obscurities, has its immediate genesis in these novels. That style, however it may finally be characterized, is an essential part of the texture and even the form of the novels.

These technical, structural, and stylistic elements embody the themes of these experimental novels. The dialectical pattern discernible in the structure of the novels is present in the development of theme and meaning within that structure. In its finest form, in *What Maisie Knew* and *The Awkward Age*, the two developments are identical. James regularly sets up contrasting ideas, often embodied in characters or in a conflict within one character, out of which and through the action the meaning of the novel is synthesized. The conflict between art and life in *The Spoils of Poynton* and *The Sacred Fount*, between the "moral sense" and life in *The Spoils of Poynton* and *What Maisie Knew*, between innocence and experience in *What Maisie Knew* and *The Awkward Age*, the related epistemological question of knowing, of perceiving the difference between appearance and reality, in *What Maisie Knew* and *The Sacred Fount*—all these and many other thematic pairs provide the tensions that propel the action of the novel. The resolution of those tensions, as the action works through to an end, gives sharper definition and deeper understanding of the initial terms in the final dramatically rendered meaning or synthesis.

The main themes of these experimental novels, it is apparent from the brief description above, are essentially broad human ones, questions of life, morality, and consciousness. These are not novels of ideas for they are not concerned extensively at any overt level with political, economic, philosophic, or even artistic topics, in the way that *The Bostonians, The Princess Casamassima,* and *The Tragic Muse* to some extent are. James's interest, however, focuses on the social man in another tension which brings these novels as close as they can come to the social novel or the novel of ideas. For James the conflict between the ideally free individual and society with its conventions often results in alienation or estrangement for the individual in these novels. Social questions are insistently

THE CONTEXT OF EXPERIMENT

asked, if only implicitly, and concerned as the novels are with the English upper or upper middle class at the close of the nineteenth century (the *"fin-de-siècle,* Edwardian plutocratic prosperity" in the words of John Holloway), a picture of a society emerges from the novels.[14]

Some of James's fiction in the eighties had of course portrayed aspects of this society. *The Tragic Muse* and *The Princess Casamassima* had concentrated on English society, although the emphasis in the earlier novels is more on the relationships between classes or on politics and class, rather than on the social mores within a given class. The darker, more personal vision of the nineties, James's sense of the weakness of the individual in the conflict with society, is clearly present in the figure of Hyacinth Robinson; in fact there is little that is blacker later on. And the short *A London Life* (1888) concentrates on many of the explicit concerns of the later novels, especially sexual morality and its effects on the individual. But in both these cases the themes are treated without the experimental techniques used to sharpen the development of theme in the later novels.

James's "imagination of disaster," as J. A. Ward has shown, is present throughout his career. It is not new in the 1890's. James's vision is almost never a pleasant or smiling one, but in the nineties we begin to see much more clearly, as Graham Greene has pointed out, James's "passionate distrust in human nature, his sense of evil."[15] Thematically, the novels show a marked increase in the treatment of various social corruptions and evils: murder in *The Other House;* sexual promiscuity in *What Maisie Knew, The Awkward Age,* and *The Sacred Fount;* material greed in *The Spoils of Poynton;* a kind of social insanity or personal mental aberration in *The Sacred Fount;*

and of course the unspecified evil in *The Turn of the Screw,* which might stand symbolically for all the rest. In all this we can see James moving toward the extreme and unpleasant situations at the heart of the fiction of the next century. James's society has qualities not touched on by Howells and some of his other contemporaries, that are closer in a sense of evil and extreme forms of corruption to Zola, Conrad, or Hardy.

Many other themes and subjects not quite so grim—such as the search for love, the attempt to define the romantic imagination, the general social comedy—are also gathered into this description of a society and of the conflict between the best and the worst in it. The arid, articulate, intensely self-conscious society James portrays becomes almost a convention in itself, the only stage on which he can work out his themes and stories, the only world he knew, but one which he makes universal in showing forth clearly the difficult search for the free moral life. In the extreme contrast between the restrictive setting and the searching character the dialectic of the novels, especially in *What Maisie Knew* and *The Awkward Age,* becomes most intense and rewarding. His society gives James a world in which the problems of action which face all the central characters can be most clearly revealed in the two terms of fixity and freedom; within the stylized world freedom takes on greater meaning and value and also becomes much harder to attain. James's treatment, then, is both a criticism of society as it existed in his time and the use of an artificial arena in which his themes and individual human values are given meaning against a social background.

These novels present various sides of a search for understanding, the illumination of the human condition of

THE CONTEXT OF EXPERIMENT

a Fleda Vetch, Maisie Farange or Nanda Brookenham, or a general social situation. When this understanding seems most complete, when, in other words, all the implications of the themes are revealed and we feel genuinely enlightened, and when this is given aesthetic form by a structure that enhances the illumination, that unites at all points with the thematic development, then these novels are not only experiments but also great novels. And this, I think, happens in *What Maisie Knew* and *The Awkward Age*. Then with James the reader also can "delight in a deep-breathing economy and an organic form." Whatever the success, we can learn much from a group of the most varied and interesting experiments in the art of the novel.

Turning then from James's earlier fiction to this group of experimental novels at the very end of the century, the reader finds himself in a different region of the same country; the general terrain is familiar, it is recognizably James country, but many features of the land and the guideposts have changes. Many of James's themes are familiar from earlier works, but his approach to them has changed; in some cases it has become more sophisticated, in others it is simply different. At the same time there are new themes and new preoccupations which make up a somewhat different climate. Above all there is a different method, a different way of incorporating these themes in a novel, even at times an entirely different way of constructing a novel.

In a sense one can see in these years the beginning of a new kind of novel, as compared with the "Victorian" novels of the 1880's. One might call it, tentatively, the twentieth-century novel. It is in this half-decade that James begins to move toward that twentieth-century relevance that we do not find in most of his contemporaries, in George Eliot, George Meredith, or even perhaps Thomas Hardy. These novels represent much more truly the "new novel" than those Edwardian works to which James applied the phrase in 1914. Only Joseph Conrad can be paired with James in this claim he has on the contemporary imagination. Perhaps it is best then to think of this period as a transition from what we consider the nineteenth-century novel to what is typically recognizable as the twentieth. The disappearance of the author and his omniscient point of view, the concentration on points of view within the novel, increased dramatic representation of the action, and perhaps some troublesome obscurity as a result of all these—all now critical commonplaces—are characteristics of the modern novel. The movement from explicit social concerns to a kind of impressionism is a central development in the history of the novel. It is a movement in part from an emphasis on what is said to a greater concern with how it is said. But as James noted, we must always return to "the importance of subject," and Mark Schorer has pointed out clearly the changing but essential inter-relationship between subject and technique in the history of the novel: the novel "showed itself to be a work in which individual human relationships were dramatized through events within a social context, and the dynamics of the novel, the poles of its possible tensions, were thus established . . . If in recent times the novel has struggled more and more toward the condition of poetry, has become more and more concerned with internal states, has become more evocative and less documentary, that is because the gap between the individual human being and the social circumstances in which he exists has itself become hazardously wide. The novel documents this alteration."[16] One might justifiably say that the

THE CONTEXT OF EXPERIMENT

movement from *The Tragic Muse* to *The Sacred Fount* gives us exactly the documents we need to trace an essential part of the alteration. R. P. Blackmur has also described the "disappearance of the old establishment of culture" and the survival "in our new mass society" of "the pure individual—by himself, or herself, heir to all the ages" as the historical background against which we must view James's work.[17] These novels of the nineties show precisely this concern with the individual consciousness as it is left more and more alone, deprived of an established culture and alienated by the confused values of the new society. James's experiments are an attempt to find some underlying form, some embodying structure in the novel which can hold the individual in some desparate contact with life. The experiments show James moving toward if not altogether in the modern consciousness, toward poetry, evocation, a total concern with internal states. I think we can see the historical trend in miniature in these five years. James's methods and concerns have become our own.

2

The Early Nineties and the Drama

SOME SUMMARY of James's activities during the first years of the 1890's provides a necessary context in which to examine the later novels. In a sense, as noted above, one may characterize any of James's work by placing it either before or after these few years. They mark that great divide in his career which James mentions in his preface to *The Golden Bowl*, and they show on the surface a marked change of direction, a turning from the novel to the drama. Eventually the novelist profited greatly from his experience as a playwright, as well as from his continued production of short tales. I have already described the crisis at the end of the 1880's when James decided to give up the novel. At that time he turned his efforts to writing for the English stage and to an increasing number of short tales (written for money, he often claimed). We must examine more closely his attempts at writing plays, but one may note immediately that he completely failed to conquer the stage. Only an exceptionally ardent Jamesian can see much value in

THE EARLY NINETIES AND THE DRAMA

most of the plays he wrote. Even Graham Greene has called them "trash."[1] James's reaction to this failure, however, and to his whole experience in the theater is at first slightly misleading.

After the shock of the opening night of *Guy Domville*, January 5, 1895, when he was booed by his audience, James immediately abandoned his careful attempt to succeed as a dramatist and decided once again to dip his pen "into the *other* ink—the sacred fluid of fiction."[2] His sense of rejection and defeat is overcome by a feeling of renewal in the notebook entry which marks his return to the novel: "I take up my *own* old pen again—the pen of all my old unforgettable efforts and sacred struggles. To myself—today—I need say no more. Large and full and high the future still opens. It is now indeed that I may do the work of my life. And I will."[3] James, unlike his hero Dencombe in "The Middle Years," finds a second chance, and this is a justly famous passage. It makes an ideal epigraph for an analysis of the novels which follow this rededication. But James in his exhortation to himself overemphasizes his divorce from fiction and tends to discount the years in the theater almost entirely. While it is true that he did not write any novels during this period, the drama did not absorb his whole attention, and even while it did there were many seeds planted which would be harvested later.

One may turn first to his notebooks for an indication of the number and variety of subjects that constantly filled his imagination during these years and that he always jotted down, the fullest record of this sort in the whole of his career. Two thirds of the bulk of his notebooks (numbers III-VI in the published edition) cover the period from 1889 to 1901; and the years of the drama fill nearly a third of this. The ideas for almost all his later novels and many stories came to him when he was writing plays, and many of the "germs" of these later novels were, significantly, first conceived as subjects for plays. The notebooks, for example, provide us with dates of conception and brief initial sketches of the following novels: November 12, 1892—*What Maisie Knew;* November 28, 1892—*The Golden Bowl;* December 24, 1893—*The Spoils of Poynton;* December 26, 1893—*The Other House;* February 17, 1894—*The Sacred Fount;* November 3 and 7, 1894—*The Wings of the Dove;* January 12, 1895—*The Turn of the Screw.*[4] By the time James had given up the drama and recommitted himself to the novel, in January 1895, his notebooks were full of subjects for his later novels and in March and October of that year he sketched in the situations for *The Awkward Age* and *The Ambassadors.*[5] (Why James was most often inspired in the dead of winter might be left to a psychologist, unless one accepts the common-sense explanation that this was the time of year when he most often dined out and thus heard the most anecdotes.)

Nor did James entirely abandon the writing of fiction. There were always his "short things"; almost one fifth of his tales were written between 1890 and 1895. Some of his best short fiction was produced while his main efforts were apparently turned to the theater.[6] At least two kinds of story important to the later novels may be found in these years. First there are several stories in the early nineties, including "The Pupil" (1891), "The Chaperon" (1891), and "The Private Life" (1892), which foreshadow some of the themes and situations taken up in the novels which followed. And then there are nearly all the well-known stories of artists and writers, beginning with

THE EARLY NINETIES AND THE DRAMA

the slightly earlier "The Lesson of the Master" (1888) and increasing in number toward the middle nineties with "The Real Thing" (1892), "The Middle Years" (1893), "The Death of the Lion" (1894), "The Next Time" (1895), and culminating in "The Figure in the Carpet" (1896).[7]

James's preoccupation with such subjects as the relations between the artist and society or his public is at least in part a result, I believe, of the personal questions which disturbed him at the end of the 1880's and continued unresolved through his dramatic years and subsequent failure. The only piece of fiction which James published in the year following *Guy Domville* was "The Next Time," published in July 1895 in *The Yellow Book;* and it is, significantly enough, the story of a writer who tries for years to meet the popular taste, to be "vulgar" enough, as James repeatedly describes it. He of course fails, as James did; he can only write beautiful, artistic stories which no one will read. In his initial notebook entry on the story, on January 26, 1895, just three days after the passage quoted above in which he rededicates himself to fiction, James relates the conception directly to his own attempts "to take the measure of the huge, flat foot of the public."[8] The story is a parable of the futility of that desire and it marks the end for Henry James of any serious effort to gain popular success.

Questions about the nature and relationship of art and reality examined in some of these tales, like "The Real Thing," underlie the consciously artful novels of the nineties. Consciousness of himself as an artist is at the base of James's experiments. He had early noted that his "very artistic" nature made him want to experiment;[9] and near the end of his life he was to label himself "that queer monster, the artist, an obstinate finality, an inexhaustible sensibility."[10] It is this sense of himself as artist that reaches fulfillment in *The Awkward Age* and perhaps a point of no return in *The Sacred Fount* in this period. The conscious searching and questioning in the subject matter of the stories is transformed into the experiments with technique and form in the novels. It is also noteworthy that three of these stories—"The Death of the Lion," "The Coxon Fund," and "The Next Time"—mark James's closest association with the consciously aesthetic movement of the nineties; they were published in *The Yellow Book*. James's enthusiasm for this venture, however, seems to have been limited to the greater length he was allowed compared with his usual periodical markets. Nevertheless one of the features of *The Awkward Age* which has perhaps kept it from gaining adequate recognition is the suspicious aura of "art for art's sake" which has hung about it. *The Sacred Fount* has also seemed to many readers little more than a rather perverse aesthetic exercise. James's aestheticism, however, runs deeper than the slogans would indicate. His concern with form and technique is radically experimental at this time, but it is always directly related to, not separate from, the human subject it embodies. Perhaps one story, "The Figure in the Carpet," points most clearly to the reader's task with these novels. The figure and the carpet are inseparable, but each must be perceived clearly in its relationship to the other. The presentations of reality in highly complex structures and consciously aesthetic and experimental techniques is a difficult task for the novelist to accomplish (and for the reader to comprehend), but if successful it can be his greatest achievement. The stories of Dencombe and "the madness of art" and of Vereker and the

THE EARLY NINETIES AND THE DRAMA

hidden design give an indication of some of the concerns and difficulties in James's novels in the last half of the nineties and also remind one of some of his personal artistic goals.

One might trace the development of some of James's fictional techniques through these stories. They do provide one kind of transition from *The Tragic Muse* to *The Spoils of Poynton,* and many of them are greater artistic achievements than the plays James was writing at the same time. They are, however, seldom experimental; they seldom reveal the innovations in technique which are a main strand in the later novels. The stories generally follow a fairly set pattern; they are usually related in the first person by someone close to but often not at the center of the situation, and for the most part the action is described in retrospect by the narrator and only occasionally presented directly, either in dramatic scenes or integral pictures. The analysis of *The Spoils of Poynton* below will show, for example, that there is often a certain amount of conflict between James's short-story techniques and the novel techniques with which he was experimenting. Although it is important to remember that James often starts his novels thinking he will write a short story, a considerable transformation takes place as the work expands. The true relationship between James's achievement in the short story and in the novel brings up a complicated question of technique which can best be examined in individual works like *The Spoils of Poynton, What Maisie Knew,* and *The Sacred Fount* where both forms are directly involved. At present a different form and the other side of James's work in the early nineties must be considered.

II

During these years James's main activities were in the theater; he was continually engaged with managers, actors and actresses, all the usual business of stage production. We have no way now of knowing just how many plays James wrote during the period, for he seems to have destroyed the manuscripts and notebooks that must have contained some to which he refers in other places. Nevertheless the attempt was the result of a lifetime attraction to the stage which can best be followed in Leon Edel's excellent accounts and in James's own writings on the theater collected in *The Scenic Art*.[11] My concern here is partly with the kinds of drama which interested James and the kinds of plays he wrote, but especially with the ways in which this experience, so far from successful in the theater, was a preparation for and was valuable to James's subsequent experiments in the novel.

Perhaps the judgment of Francis Fergusson will prove the correct one, that James's "idea of dramatic form" is to be found mainly in his novels: "It was in the effort to 'dramatize' his subject [in the novel] that he made his greatest discoveries in dramatic form and technique."[12] The preparation for these discoveries, however, must to some extent have been in the writing of plays. James repeatedly refers to the lessons he learned in the theater, the greater understanding of dramatic form he gained in writing unsuccessful plays. In James's dramatic years one can see on the surface a desire for popular success and an effort to write his plays according to a formula he thought would bring him that success, a formula related to the central theatrical tradition he had watched throughout his life, that of the well-made play. Both the desire for

THE EARLY NINETIES AND THE DRAMA

success and the kind of play he tried to write eventually betrayed him, but the reasons for that betrayal and the technical lessons he claimed to have learned in spite of it are essential background to the analysis of the later novels. This is especially true in considering the two novels, *The Other House* and *The Awkward Age*, which James conceived in a form quite close to that of the play. But the effect of these years is also noticeable in an important way in the novels not so directly related to the play.

In spite of the five years given over to it, James's experience with the drama might at first appear to be slight. It resulted during these years in the stage production of only two plays, *The American* and *Guy Domville*, and in the two volumes of *Theatricals—Two Comedies* and *Theatricals: Second Series* which he published in 1894 and 1895 when he was unable to get the plays presented on the stage. As Professor Edel notes, however, James seems to have been writing plays or scenarios almost continually during the period, but only references to them remain. So we are left with the two produced plays and the four published ones: *Tenants, Disengaged, The Album,* and *The Reprobate*. We also know that he wrote a scenario with the provisional title *The Promise*, which seems not to have been completed as a play, but which he transformed into the novel *The Other House* in 1896.

These plays follow a certain form and try to appeal to a wide audience. From the problems of the "rightful heir" in *The Album* to the supposed wickedness of the hero in *The Reprobate*, James's plots are those of simple, comic intrigues. His plays are a series of light comedies in which superficial situations are followed mechanically to their logical conclusions, with thin and insubstantial character-types involved in conventional love-intrigues, and with hero winning heroine in the usual happy ending (with some exception to be made for *Guy Domville*).

In the prefatory note to *Theatricals: Second Series* James describes what he had hoped to achieve in the drama, reveals his sense of failure, and finally finds some slight hope of gain. The attitude James expresses is ambivalent and is the same one he expressed in a letter to his brother William before he started writing his plays: "The whole odiousness of the thing lies in the connection between the drama and the theatre. The one is admirable in its interest and difficulty, the other loathsome in its conditions."[13] On the one hand there is the love of drama, of mastering a technique, of selection and representation. On the other, however, is the note struck at the very beginning of the preface, that of the "disconcerted author," whose natural form is limited by the drama as well as the theater. It is a note of "frustrated effort," of "the theatrical straight-jacket." James calls himself a "perverted man of letters" following an unnatural calling. He points out the artistic inadequacies and failures of his plays and in doing so clarifies some of the ambivalence in his attitude. The atmosphere of the plays to begin with, he says, is that of "the uttermost regions of dramatic amiability, the bland air of the little domestic fairy-tale." Under the figure of the fairy-tale he goes on to describe the major motifs in his plays as the fairies Genial, Coincidence, and Sentiment in conflict with "the foul fiend Excision." "Then the mixture was to be stirred to the tune of perpetual motion and served, under the pain of being rejected with disgust, with the time-honoured bread-sauce of the happy ending." (James gave both *Daisy Miller* and *The American* happy endings when he rewrote them as plays.) He concludes his figure, "conformity to the tone of the particular variety had to be kept well in view," and he echoes this later: "If it forfeits its harmony with its type it forfeits everything."[14]

The rejection of course would be by the audience, and only success of this sort would be forfeited. The "type" was the social comedy that developed from the well-made play. Genial, Sentiment, and Coincidence are far removed from the vision of life in James's novels, but they are necessities in the type of play he was trying to write. The artistic failure of James's plays, recognized in his own preface, points the various morals of his experience in the theater. James was not experimenting in the true sense; he was following rules and he called his plays "exercises." As F. W. Dupee comments, "It was with his system, rather than his sensibility, that he wrote his plays."[15] Neither the audience, the medium, nor the type of play was adequate to James's vision as an artist.

Character, fine shadings, and complexity of development, all effects requiring expansion, were the main obsessions of James's art. They could not be satisfied before an audience that required "big, unmistakable, knockdown effects," for which one could not "spin things fine," as he put it in the dialogue "After the Play," written before he had set out on his theatrical ventures.[16] One wonders, of course, why he felt he must sacrifice so much to such an audience. The only answer seems to be his initial motive for writing plays—his dreams of success. He thought no other kind of play would be popular on the London stage in the nineties; and so he followed the rules of Sarcey, the principal French theorist of this kind of play, who insisted that the play be accommodated to the audience. The results, then, are simply another chapter in the tale of the artist's alienation from his audience.

The audience is not the only villain, though. The rules of the well-made play and the limits of the typical social or drawing-room comedy also played James false. Many critics, including Leon Edel, Francis Fergusson, and R. P. Blackmur, have commented on James's attraction to the well-made play; and Blackmur even finds it at the base of the form of the later novels.[17] But in James's plays the conventions, the artificiality, and the abstract inhuman quality of the form force him to give up any attempt to bring in true substance and life. William Archer's judgment at the time is a valid one and, while directed at the preface described above, is true of James's plays: "If he will only clear his mind of critical cant . . . and write solely for the ideal audience within his own breast, he will certainly produce works of art, and not improbably successful plays."[18]

The "critical cant" came mostly from the tradition James was following, that of the French well-made play. when James began to write plays he invoked the masters of that tradition in his notebook: "*A moi, Scribe, à moi, Sardou, à moi, Dennery.*" His ideal was the Theatre Francais of the seventies and eighties, and it is interesting to note that James invokes not the figures like Dumas *fils* and Augier who broke away from the tradition to some extent (and whom he also admired), but Scribe and Sardou, the purest adepts of the well-made play. The principal characteristic of their plays is that life is subordinated to technique—which might, at a stretch, be called art. The form of the play was all-important, a framework into which almost any human substance could be fitted with a certain amount of contrivance and an indifference to complexities, often necessities of character. The formalized development of the plot was the supreme rule. (The well-made play was so consistent in its reliance on formula that a recent critic is able to assert that every well-made play within the tradition will reveal seven structural principles.[19]) The main features of most of the plays are the subordination of character to the intrigue plot and its accompanying technical devices (the *raisonneur,* the *scene à faire,* the ficelle, and so on) and the moralistic though often trivial ending.

Some defenses of the well-made play will help point to some of what James may have gained from his practice, in spite of the restrictions which led to immediate failure, for as he noted in the preface to his second volume of plays, the drama will give him "more stores of technical experience than any other aesthetic errand." C. E. Montague in an early essay on the form focuses on the main problem: "There does appear in that period a remarkable coexistence of elaborate and precise technical theory and a poorness or shallowness of spirit."[20] Eric Bentley has pointed to the values that remain even in a play which is "all plot," which is "put together according to a *mechanical* scheme, not, like any really good work of art, according to an *organic* scheme."[21] For Bentley, "the practice of Scribe is a reminder that plot without much else makes better drama than much else without plot."[22] There is a certain value which resides in technique alone in a work, even without the informing human values which would make that work one of art.

For an aesthetic sensibility like James's this emphasis on technique was certainly attractive. One side of his artistic personality became more and more formulary, more interested in method and the technical aspects of his art, as is evident in his prefaces and in the experiments in the novel. James became, in fact, though not all of his own doing, the great rule-maker and law-giver for the art of the novel. His plays reflect mostly this side of the artist; they are worked out according to the formulas of the well-made play.

James's formal aestheticism, his critical as opposed to his creative imagination, affects the whole of his achievement after the drama and one must keep it in sight. But in the early nineties, as we have seen, it led him to try to master the well-made play. That tradition limited the development of complex characters and the exposition of a finely shaded moral situation just as much as the limited intelligence of the London audience did. This is exactly where the drama as he attempted it failed James, or where he proved inadequate to the needs of the genre. The complement of James's fascination with form is his interest in human character, in manners, motives, and morals. He could not find a way to bring this into the theater. The failure is probably not a great one, however, for it may suggest no more than that James's talent as an innovator, a creator of new forms, was in the novel and not the play. The "art" of the French theater attracted James, but there was no life in it when he tried to fit his talents to the rules.

One of James's contemporaries, Henrik Ibsen, was able to overcome many of these same problems, and his achievement in the drama is in many ways quite comparable to James's in the novel. As one of the great geniuses and innovators in the drama, Ibsen had been able to fashion out of the tradition of the well-made play a dramatic form which would accommodate, in fact center on, the portrayal with intensity and human perception of believable, complex characters. James saw and became interested in Ibsen's plays as they began to appear in London in the nineties. His mixed response, a sympathetic sense of Ibsen's strengths and limits, can be seen in the several essays James wrote on the plays both during and after his dramatic years. Because of the contrast with his own efforts in the drama and because Ibsen's example had some effect on the novels to follow, it is worth tracing out some of James's reactions.

James finds in Ibsen first of all the "perfect practice of a difficult and delicate art"; "he addresses himself so substantially to representation."[23] In another passage from the same essay on *Hedda Gabler* in 1891, James adds more praise for Ibsen's perfection in his art, his technical genius: "For those who care in general for the form that he has practiced he will always remain one of the talents that have understood it best and extracted the most from it, have effected most neatly the ticklish transfusion of life."[24] It was just this transfusion which James could not bring off in his own plays. The weakness in his plays he found clearly a major strength in Ibsen's: "The artist's exercise of a mind saturated with the vision of human infirmities; saturated, above all, with a sense of the infinitude, for all its mortal savour, of *character,* finding that an endless romance and a perpetual challenge."[25] There is life in character, and James's analysis of the character of Hedda Gabler shows the extent of his admiration and his sense of Ibsen's dramatic achievement, as will be noted below in the discussion of *The Other House* where James's comments have a special relevance.

One should certainly ask why James did not follow the example of Ibsen rather than the French. There are two apparent reasons for James's failure to relate what he saw in Ibsen's innovations to his own dramatic exercises. One of these is his stated antipathy to Ibsen's bitterness and lack of humor, what James saw as an atmosphere of bourgeois gloom. Related to this is his sense that Ibsen's plays would no more satisfy the English audience than his own, that Ibsen would in fact repel the English, as seemed apparent from the first reactions in the nineties (though James apparently failed to realize that fame could be had by capitalizing on this notoriety, a lesson he could have learned from Shaw). The two reactions are brought together in one comment: "He deals with a homely and unaesthetic society, he harps on the string of conduct, and he actually talks of stockings and legs, in addition to other improprieties. He is not pleasant enough or light enough; he is too far from Piccadilly and our glorious standards."[26] James's scorn for the English public is apparent here, although he catered to it in his plays, but more importantly it was the "unaesthetic society" that marked a great difference in temperament between James and Ibsen. James needed the fine consciousnesses of an at least partly "aesthetic" society to play out his drama in his novels. It provided him with a stronger contrast between intelligence and stupidity, between sensibility and unfeeling, and it was also essential to the surface comedy of James's novels that Richard Poirier has described. James's novels, however, especially *The Other House,* were to be far closer to Ibsen in spirit than to anything else in the drama of his time. The only other possible comparison, and probably even closer than with Ibsen, is to the poetic development of situation in Chekhov's plays.

The close parallel between what James saw Ibsen attempting on the stage and what he himself was to attempt in his subsequent novels can be seen in another passage from his essay on *Hedda Gabler:*

THE EARLY NINETIES AND THE DRAMA

Such a production as *The Pillars of Society,* with its large, dense complexity of moral cross-references and its admirable definiteness as a picture of motive and temperament (the whole canvas charged, as it were, with moral colour), such a production asks the average moral man to see too many things at once. It will probably never help Ibsen with the multitude that the multitude shall feel that the more they look the more intentions they shall see, for of such seeing of many intentions the multitude is but scantly desirous. It keeps indeed a positively alarmed and jealous watch in that direction; it smugly insists that intentions shall be rigidly limited.[27]

This would be an excellent description of almost any novel by Henry James, and of the more ordinary reactions to his novels. And it again makes clear his sense of separation between artist and audience. James could see a failure he feared in the complexity of Ibsen's art. His use of Ibsen, if it was "use" at all, was finally more indirect.[28]

Neither the tradition of the well-made play nor the novelty of Ibsen's new realism could give Henry James any success in the theater. His plays were even milder and less interesting than some of those of Pinero and Jones, who at least worked with some social questions and dared some conventions. And James's plays are far removed in spirit, subject matter, and artistic worth from George Bernard Shaw's plays in the nineties. In addition to *Hedda Gabler, Rosmersholm,* and all the other Ibsen plays that appeared in London at this time, these were the years in which *Mrs. Warren's Profession, Arms and the Man,* and *Candida* were written. Even a lesser play like *Widowers' Houses* retains more interest than any of James's. There are, however, as will be noted below, some connections between Shaw's dramatic technique, as he learned it from Ibsen and developed it himself, and the use James later made of his play-writing experience.

That later use came only after the experience of failure. James's strongest motive seems to have been the dual desire for success and communication with some kind of audience, and the drama is the medium which provides the closest personal contact an artist can have with an audience. But to make the contact James felt he had to change the aims of his art as he had developed them in his novels. The personal rejection he experienced on the opening night of *Guy Domville* sent him back to the novel. The rejection seems mainly to have given him the excuse he needed. Favorable reviews by Shaw and others had no effect on his immediate decision. It is almost as if James's sole interest had been personal acceptance and when that became impossible he returned to the art of the novel.

One still must look more closely at just what James gained from this encounter with the theater and from the writing of plays, that part of his experience he carried over from the circumstances of defeat into his next achievements. In a letter to William James on February 2, 1895, James in commenting on his failure reveals how he had conceived the whole effort: "The novelist has a fearful long row to hoe to get any practical relation to the grovelling stage, and his difficulty is precisely double: it bears, on one side, upon the question of method and, on the other, upon the question of subject . . . I have worked like a horse—far harder than anyone will ever know—over the whole stiff mystery of 'technique.' "[29] James's failure to solve the question of subject has been noted, but the achievements of the rest of his career testify to the value of his work in solving the mystery of technique. Eric Bentley, among others, has commented on the differences between the playwright and the novelist: "The novelist uses artifice, but in a setting of nature—natural scenery and natural characters. The playwright uses artifice in a setting of artifice—stage roles amid stage scenery. Such are the rules of the game, the controlling conditions of this art. While the novelist has the illusion of seeing actual characters in actual settings, the playwright has to learn to visualize the actor of the character and visualize him in that most unnatural of all settings: a theater."[30] The shift from one mode to another under these conditions is extremely difficult. For the novelist it generally means giving up a whole way of imagining an action or a character, sacrificing a good deal of freedom gained from the "natural" elements of his art. But the novelist has his own artifice to deal with in his own mode, and it is at this point that James effected a transfusion from the drama to the novel, making the novel much more representational, much more dramatic than it had been before. James's gains may be indicated briefly under a pair of closely related principles which he discovered could be translated from the dramatic to the fictional mode: the dual techniques of scenario and scene.

Scenario is a principle of planning; it is an "outline of the plot," as one dictionary tells us. For James this was to provide a technique for constructing a novel which was far more conscious and artful than any he had found before. It enabled him in theory to work out before the actual writing, as carefully and exactly as possible, details of character, action, and specific scenes. In effect the result would be a far more artistically conceived novel than a discursive one which merely let the plot develop gradually from the needs of character and situation as the writing progressed. The principle, as James indicates in his notebooks, came directly from his years of writing scenarios for possible plays. While speculating on the ideas for *The Wings of the Dove* and *The Golden Bowl* early in 1895, James asked himself if he should perhaps set down a scenario, and then he bursts out: "Compensations and solutions seem to stand there with open arms for me—and something of the 'meaning' to come to me of past bitterness, of recent bitterness that otherwise has seemed a mere sickening, unflavoured draught. Has a *part* of all this wasted passion and squandered time (of the last 5 years) been simply the precious lesson, taught me in that roundabout and devious, that cruelly expensive, way, *of the singular value for a narrative plan too* of the (I don't know *what* adequately to call it) divine principle of the Scenario?"[31] During the last half of the nineties James worked out this principle in two ways. On the one hand, there are complete scenarios like that for *The Ambassadors* and perhaps a lost one for the carefully balanced *The Awkward Age*. On the other, especially in the extensive notebook entries dealing with *The Spoils of Poynton* and *What Maisie Knew*, there are gradually developing and changing scenarios—fairly full initial plans which are gradually altered and adjusted by the force of the development of the novel. One can see in the novels examined below examples of the success of the principle and of the need for it when James fails to plan adequately and what he intends to be a short story grows into a novel. In almost all cases, however, the principal formal or structural features of the later novels, balance, elaboration of a central situation, the dialectic of themes, the careful alternation of narrative exposition of meditation and dramatic scene, are all the result of the careful preparation which the use of scenarios provided James.

The use of the second principle, that of "scene," is more

complex. What James called "scenic construction" is something more than, although it includes, the extensive use of dramatic scenes in dialogue for moments of crisis. In a sense it is the whole basis of representation in the novel, of rendering rather than telling. In the later novels, including the ones to be examined in detail, it developed beyond the techniques inherited from the play, although these formed the basis for development. James perhaps learned the same lesson from his own plays that Eric Bentley finds Shaw learning from Ibsen (although James may have learned it there as well). Shaw, following Ibsen, substituted discussion for the last term in the usual triad of exposition, complication, and denouement.[32] And this is just what James works with in many of the novels of the late nineties, especially in *What Maisie Knew* and *The Sacred Fount*, but also in *The Other House* and *The Awkward Age*. The drama, then, in this way at least, marks the break between James's earlier novels and his later ones. The scenic technique is not new to the later novels, or any novels, but James's experiments carry it beyond anything he had done before. James carries it through the pattern that Shaw used and develops it until it becomes a thorough-going and basic principle of conception and composition in all his novels. Scene becomes the key to character in action and in conflict with others, dialogue begins to assume specialized forms, and the "picture" elements become mainly "scene-setting," and are themselves very often "dramatized," made scenes without dialogue, quite often taking place in the mind of one of the characters. The balance between picture and scene is one key to the form of these novels; another is the realization that both scene and picture are dramatized, made immediate and living. Altogether, James's principle of scenic construction can best be seen in his comment on "an excellent *standard* scene" in the preface to *The Ambassadors;* it is, he says, "copious, comprehensive, and accordingly never short, but with its office as definite as that of the hammer on the gong of the clock, the office of expressing *all that is in the hour.*"[33]

This complex of uses of the dramatic technique is a major feature of James's experiments and his achievements in the novel between 1896 and 1901. One might best use James's own phrase from the preface to *The Awkward Age*—"projected form"—to describe this dramatic success. In these novels he worked out the techniques which would sustain him through the longer works of the next century. His first moves in solving the mystery of technique came perhaps in his plays. With the eventual solution worked out in the novels, James would be right in claiming an "acquired mastery of scenic presentation," and in saying "my infinite little loss is converted into an almost infinite little gain."[34]

At this point one is reminded of F. O. Matthiessen's description of James: "In every case he recognized the futility of loose generalizations about art. The only thing of value was the fresh and particular experiment."[35] And so I must turn directly to those experiments in the form of the novel which made James the master of his art.

3

The Other House

IN August 1895, about eight months after the failure of *Guy Domville* and the collapse of his theatrical ambitions, Henry James began work on *The Spoils of Poynton*. He finished it in March 1896 and, in what was to be a consistent pattern for some years, he immediately began work on another novel. Fully recommitted to his old profession, a more private and protected one than that of playwright, James contracted to publish this new novel in the *Illustrated London News*, a popular weekly. This was probably his last gesture toward an essentially mass-market. For this purpose James began to convert into a novel a play-scenario which he had first worked out in his notebooks on December 26, 1893, referred to as *The Promise* a month later, and finally completed in scenario form on December 21, 1895. This scenario became *The Other House*, a story, he commented, "which would greatly resemble a play."[1]

Because *The Other House* is both novel and play, first written as scenario and then as novel, it makes the connections between James's dramatic years and his succeeding period of experiment in the novel stand out much more clearly than they do in the earlier *The Spoils of Poynton.* I wish to examine *The Other House* first not only because it is a transitional novel, but also because it introduces in a much clearer and simpler way some of the main critical concerns which arise in the study of all the novels of the period. *The Other House* is a much less complex, much less ambiguous, performance than *The Spoils of Poynton,* and it is at the same time, although not necessarily for those reasons, a much slighter and less successful novel. As a result some of the elementary marks of the whole period, particularly in dramatic techniques and characterization, are more noticeable.

It is often easier to see the methods and specific concerns of a great novelist in a work which is not his best. His successes in other novels stand out much more clearly in relation to the attempts which do not succeed. The better novel resists our critical dissection; the various aspects of the novel—character, structure, and theme—cannot be separated so easily. By examining first the more loosely constructed novel, *The Other House,* we will eventually be able to penetrate further into the relatively flawless construction of *What Maisie Knew* and *The Awkward Age.*

One must also remember in dealing with *The Other House* that for James it had some special value. Even late in his career, in the plan for *The Ivory Tower,* James referred affectionately to his earlier novel: "Oh blest *Other House,* which gives me thus at every step a precedent, a support, a divine little light to walk by."[2] In examining the novel we may be able to determine just what James meant by this gnomic apostrophe.

THE OTHER HOUSE

The Other House resembles closely others of James's works, like *Covering End* and *The Outcry,* which are essentially plays printed as novels, with little added except additional stage directions and scene setting. *The Awkward Age,* of course, is the major piece in this group. But in much of its surface action *The Other House* is far more violent than almost anything else James wrote. The story is essentially that of a thriller, which has for its subject a strong obsessive passion, which finally becomes pathological. The superficial type of the action is melodrama, and the characters for the most part fit the stereotyped traditions of this form. What is finally of value in the novel lies in James's expansion and development of this limited form. In transforming the melodrama he had conceived for the stage into a dramatic novel, James achieves greater psychological depth and a more tragic vision and thus to some extent revitalizes the dramatic (or melodramatic) structure carried over from the play. The added space of the novel is necessary to James's vision; only with adequate room for detailed development, for "solidity of specification," can he fulfill his artistic intentions. Even as short a novel as *The Other House* gives him this space.

If one compares *The Other House* with an earlier novel like *The Portrait of a Lady,* several marked differences in technique are at once apparent. In the first place the portraits of characters are much fuller in the earlier novel; James shows a much greater concern for past history and provides what amount to small biographies for Isabel Archer, Ralph, and the Touchetts. In *The Other House* there is very little concern for any part of a character's past which is not immediately relevant to the present action. We learn, for example, almost nothing about Jean

Martle's parents, who live (and die during the course of the novel) in a very dimly seen Brighton. Even for the main character, Rose Armiger, James provides no history other than the briefest indications of relationship to Mrs. Bream and her step-mother. We know nothing of what she does when she is not present on the stage of the novel. While in *The Portrait of a Lady* James concealed past actions, such as Madame Merle's, for purposes of the plot, in order to reveal them at the relevant moment, in *The Other House* the characters and the action exist entirely in the dramatic present. There are no re-creations of past scenes, such as Isabel's interview with Mrs. Touchett. In fact, the whole description of Isabel's life in Albany, coming as it does in a backward shift in time, is a technique alien to *The Other House* and almost all the novels which follow it. We enter the action at a significant point and are only given that part of the past which is essential to our comprehension of the present action, and this comes to us primarily through generalized comment by the author or in brief allusions in conversations among the characters. The past only enters in within the conventions of the drama: Book First (the "Prologue" of the play into which James turned the novel in 1909) takes place four years before the day of the main action.

This concentration on the dramatic present brings to *The Other House* a dramatic unity which is only found in *The Sacred Fount* among the novels of this period. Several of the following novels, especially *The Spoils of Poynton* and *What Maisie Knew*, develop gradually from a rather generalized, semidramatic beginning to a completely dramatic ending. *The Other House*, perhaps because it was based on a previously worked-out scenario, is much more concentrated and in a dramatic sense more unified. If we look back to *The Portrait of a Lady* once more, the cause of this dramatic unity is apparent: the author has disappeared from *The Other House* and with him have gone most of the expository, summarizing, expansive passages of the earlier novel. We are left with characters in action in a small, carefully limited situation; and the situation is examined as fully as possible only through their actions. Expanding on Joseph Warren Beach's original definition of the "drama" in Henry James's novels as one of generating idea through opposed wills,[3] one may also say that in these later novels drama comes even closer to what is generally meant by drama in the theater. In *The Other House* there is a continuous illusion of present occurrence, which is never broken into by the author. In the novels that follow, this must be expanded to account for what goes on in a character's mind, but for *The Other House* this is not necessary. Here the mind intrudes only slightly and the significance is found in the present, continuous action, a continuously present scene. In James's development of a "scenic" method, his gradually worked-out use of the fully presented scene as a major aspect of a novel, *The Other House* represents one of his few attempts to do the totally scenic; *The Awkward Age* is another. What remained after this was to work out a form which would be totally dramatic, although not totally scenic. *The Other House* is an attempt at the immediacy of the form. It could be acted.

Within the limits of this dramatic form, James handles several themes which are to recur in his work during this period. Innocence and experience, freedom, moral action and guilt, and above all the nature and consequences of love—all these are elaborated in various symbolic actions, through a structure related to that of a play, and through several levels of plot, of which the main thrust is the transformation from love intrigue to thriller to tragedy. *The Other House* exhibits, far more than James's plays, an interest in the tragic implications of romantic love; and the greater complexity in character development in the novel allows James to portray fully an obsessed character whose predicament is finally tragic. In addition to these general areas, there are smaller features that are both noteworthy in this novel and important first steps toward the greater achievements in the later novels of this period and those of "the major phase."

II

The plot of *The Other House* is a fairly simple one. Two girls, Rose Armiger and Jean Martle, the one dark and the other light, the bad and good heroines, are in love with a young widower, Tony Bream, the charming, handsome young hero. Both their loves are obstructed, however, by Tony's vow to his dying wife that he will never marry during the lifetime of their daughter. Rose finally drowns the daughter, little Effie, and tries to blame Jean; but she is found out, the murder is concealed from the outside world, and Rose is sent away, exiled from society. Tony and Jean are then free to marry, but they are burdened by their consciousness of their own partial guilt in allowing the murder to happen. Obviously, the outline is fairly melodramatic. But although the novel is not finally successful, it does go below this melodramatic surface of romantic intrigue. Some examination of James's characterization, particularly that of Rose Armiger, and of the dramatic structure of the novel will give a better appreciation of the meaning of the action and of James's achievement in technique; and an evaluation of the novel must rest on a judgment both of the human values implicit in the character and action and of the novelistic, artistic values implicit in the developed form.

Since *The Other House* is an exclusively dramatic novel, two definitions relating to that form may be useful at the outset. Edwin Muir in *The Structure of the Novel* has described "the dramatic novel" as an identity of character and action—one defines the other; and one of the terms of Beach's definition of drama in James is that it is character in conflict.[4] These unities must be kept in sight in an analysis of character, for that procedure must to some extent work through the separation of character from action. An understanding of James's characterization and of the relationships between characters helps to clarify the central tensions of the action. James, in the development of his characters, also begins to break away from the weaknesses of his plays and get beyond the stereotypes, the purely mechanical counters of the well-made play. James begins with a set of characters basically related to these stock types, but almost all of them open out, go beyond the types, and become individuals with their own impulses to life. The combination of dramatic and novelistic techniques enabled James to approach one of his primary artistic goals: the representation, examination, and development of human character. Equally important, most of the characters are also Jamesian types; they reflect his central preoccupations and reappear in various mutations in later novels. It is enlightening to study the early forms of figures like Sir Claude in *What Maisie Knew*, Vanderbank in *The Awkward Age*, or even Merton Densher and Kate Croy.

In *The Other House* secondary characters like Doctor Ramage, the local physician, Mrs. Beever and her son

Paul, and Dennis Vidal, Rose's one-time fiancé, all act partly as spectators. Although they are drawn in by the violence of the action toward the end, and although they have their roles in the mechanics of the plot, they nevertheless stand apart from the central trio and provide a norm by which we can judge the action. Doctor Ramage and Mrs. Beever especially perform this function, a part of James's intention that they should "figure as the *public*, the judging, wondering, horrified world."[5] They represent the provincial village of Wilverley, as that world responds to the unnatural and violent emotion at the climax of the action, the drowning. Mrs. Beever's part is somewhat more complex than the doctor's; he is often merely a handy device in the plot, while she is the involved but somewhat detached spectator-commentator. While Doctor Ramage does occasionally fit the role of *raisonneur* in the tradition of the well-made play, Mrs. Beever assumes this part much more frequently.[6] She has the double role of arranger and representative of order; she is several times called "the Queen-Mother." She is also a theorizer about her fellow human beings, a spectator analyzing human action and schematizing her observations, a type that James was to take to its furthest extreme in *The Sacred Fount*. She feels herself "cold-blooded," "always seeing . . . the other party become the spectacle, while, sitting back in her stall, she remained the spectator and even the critic."[7] The spectator-theorizer is a common enough role in a James novel, but only a special kind, as will be shown in Fleda Vetch and Maisie Farange, can maintain a balanced vision in the face of the glare of life that customarily lights the last pages of these novels. Mrs. Beever's traditional, old-maidish arranging and her inept irony are too weak for the kind of analysis

James wants after the murder, and she disappears from the scene before the final chapters.

Only observers like Paul Beever and Dennis Vidal begin to be perceptive, sensitive, and strong enough to face the horror of Rose's act. Both Paul and Dennis are in love with Rose; all their actions are predicated on this. They are thus a more special kind of spectator, one who is constitutionally detached and observant, but is also directly involved emotionally so that while objective he is spared none of the direct feelings of the participants. Both stand somewhat apart from the central action of the book and, as rejected lovers, provide the reader with added perspectives into theme and action.

Dennis Vidal also represents a norm of intelligence and love against which the actions of the other characters can be measured. He is the only character who does not hide his emotions, who has no mask; each of his actions, except his final protection of Rose, is guileless. James's characterization of Dennis is partly grotesque, with an attention to small details—with his "small, smooth head, his seasoned sallowness and simple eyes," "his lean, fine brown hand," "his spare, clean brown chin," and the continual references to his just having returned from China—but this description of grotesque and outlandish appearance (heightened by excessive alliteration and repetition) is functional and sets him up in contrast to the perfect social manner and normal appearance of the hero, Tony Bream. The final effect of the descriptions points indirectly to James's meaning: the apparently odd and grotesque is real, while the socially perfect is all appearance. Dennis's role as observer is intimately related to but surpassed in importance by his representation of "the real thing," as Tony calls it. In this way his own fate, the loss of love, is tragic, and yet at the same time we can measure against him the divergence from the real and normal, the obsessional extent, of Rose's madness.

For the most part, Paul Beever is little more than a fat, inarticulate young man; James's descriptions of him almost always gain what substance they have from their humor. His role in the novel is almost entirely passive, a register of emotions and judgments where James finds him useful and a plot device to show, through Jean Martle's rejection of his marriage proposal, the strength of her love for Tony. At the end of the novel, however, Paul, for all his passivity, acts as judge and represents the stability to which all will return. The two main characters, Tony and Rose, are set off against Paul's norm in the final chapter. He tells Tony how to behave normally and gives the final Kurtz-like judgment of Rose: "'You're too horrible,' he breathed; 'You're too horrible.'" James uses Paul's blank surface and inarticulate emotions for contrast with the more violent actions and passions of the others, and he uses him finally as a point of view, even a norm, by which we can apprehend and judge the final morality of the book, and through which we can sense the return to normal order which marks the completion of the action.

Jean Martle, although she is on the scene little more than Vidal, Paul Beever, or Mrs. Beever, is more important because of her part in the love triangle. She is at first nothing more than the ingénue: beautiful, young, innocent, unformed, and somewhat imperceptive. She is also naturally good, has "perfect instincts," and, as Tony Bream believes, has the potentiality for development. His judgment is to some extent proved true; Jean does grow, does learn, becomes more than the stereotype. But not much more. In this novel she closely resembles a type that James was to develop more fully in later novels: the young girl growing and learning and trying against odds to live, like Fleda Vetch, Maisie Farange, Nanda Brookenham, and later Milly Theale and Maggie Verver. Jean Martle is also, however, a transitional figure between the earlier imperceptive innocents like Verena Tarrant in *The Bostonians* and Laura Wing in *A London Life* and the later heroines. She lacks the intelligence, the capacity for knowledge and understanding, which saves Nanda or Maisie. It is not simply that the innocent and ignorant, for James, will always fall before the threat of accomplished evil, that innocence is always the passive victim while evil is always active and finally victorious. All James's heroines fall or suffer some loss (except perhaps Maggie Verver), but in the process many of them, particularly in the later novels, have retained both their innocence and their ability to act and have understood their predicament. Jean, on the other hand, is forced constantly to plead ignorance and bewilderment to keep her innocence from being violated by the evil that exists in Rose. After the murder she turns on Rose screaming for revenge; almost no other Jamesian heroine has this lapse and with it Jean falls from virtue, becomes corrupted by Rose. Jean, however, in this may represent James's one recognition of the possible cruelty of the innocent, like that of Hilda in *The Marble Faun*. She does redeem herself slightly toward the end when she recognizes what Rose has done: "It's her triumph—that our freedom is horrible."

Jean Martle's flaws are to some extent weaknesses in James's characterization. Although he is true to the logic of the character, the spontaneous innocence of the ingénue is too unconscious to survive the test of Rose's evil.

Jean is too stupidly perfect to respond any way but the conventional one; she does not develop much, does not really learn. Her capacities for growth and change are merely asserted, not strongly demonstrated in action; she is an unresolved character made to carry the weight of too many undemonstrated qualities. As a result both innocence and love fail her.

James was to discover with his later heroines that the only way to preserve their innocence was to fuse it with knowledge; in other words, to develop an intelligent, perceptive innocent, one who could exhibit full consciousness of herself and her situation. Jean's last perception, quoted above, is a step toward this, but James had some distance to go in his analysis of the innocent; it was to occupy this half-decade and more. Isabel Archer is perhaps the best-known heroine of an earlier novel who combines innocence and intelligence, but there is a considerable difference in emphasis. With Isabel, James focuses on her growing knowledge, and her innocence is simply a given quality; in the later novels the focus is equally on knowledge and innocence and the dialectic between the two.

One further reason for the weaknesses noted in the character of Jean Martle is James's primary interest in the two main figures in the novel, Tony Bream and Rose Armiger. In a triad resembling that in *The Wings of the Dove* (Kate–Rose, Merton–Tony, Milly–Jean), the innocent receives much slighter treatment, even though the elements James notes in her character were to become more complex than anything in Tony and perhaps even Rose.

Tony Bream's character develops from four central qualities: the importance that he gives to social appearance over human reality, his passivity, his excessiveness,

THE OTHER HOUSE

and his natural virtues. All four of these are worked out fairly carefully by James, and out of the combination comes the catastrophe at the end of the novel and Tony's final awareness, his recognition of his responsibility and his flaws. And as a typical example of James's "weak hero," one can find in Tony elements which go into such diverse portraits as those of Owen Gereth, Sir Claude, Gustavus Vanderbank, Chad Newsome, and Merton Densher.

Tony Bream is from the start an example of the socially brilliant highly mannered gentleman. For much of the novel he seems little more than the charming, overly good-humored host at a country weekend; his conscience almost always centers on social appearance and duty. As Dennis Vidal notes early in the novel: "To look at him was to recognize the value of appearances and that he couldn't have dropped upon any scene, however disordered, without by the simple fact, re-establishing a superficial harmony" (51). His mask is his social manner, and in the final "disordered" scenes that breaks and something more meaningful appears in his character.

A direct consequence of the emphasis on social appearance is Tony's passivity; he recoils from any direct contact with serious emotion. His whole attitude toward Jean Martle's potentiality and beauty is a passive one. He enjoys her precisely because she can ask nothing of him; he is free to lie back on his sofa and watch her develop, as he literally does at one point. He also accepts rather too easily his wife's demand for the vow because it means he will not have to act. His passivity of course sets off the violent consequences of the entire action. The blindness and stupidity which are the result of this passive confrontation of life lead to his downfall and his recognition of his faults.

Curiously mixed with Tony's passivity is a quality of excess, of having naturally a little too much of everything, except control. James's description of Tony's "passive excess" is a good example of his occasional use of stage directions, set-pieces of characterization, to introduce and complement the dramatic representation of character:

> To look at him was immediately to see that he was a collection of gifts, which presented themselves as such precisely by having in each case slightly overflowed the measure. He could do things—this was all he knew about them; he was ready-made, as it were—he had not had to put himself together. His dress was just too fine, his colour just too high, his moustache just too long, his voice just too loud, his smile just too gay. His movement, his manner, his tone were respectively too free, too easy, and too familiar; his being a very handsome, happy, clever, active, ambitiously local young man was in short just too obvious. (20)

This is the central flaw in his character. He is almost an automaton, a "ready-made" man. When emotions do force themselves on him, his excessiveness takes over, he loses control and gets into what Mrs. Beever calls "one of his states." In all this excess there is no fixed center, no base to his character. He is "fifty things at once."

In the midst of this basic disorder, Tony's instinct is for harmony: "His native impulse [was to] accommodate and harmonise." It is this that Dennis Vidal recognizes in the "value of appearances," but the impulse is finally an impotent one, based as it is on a superficial social desire for order and good feelings. His blind attempts to avoid problems and tensions are the basis of the desire for harmony, the desire to marry Paul to Jean and Rose to either Dennis or Paul. He almost always overlooks the human needs and passions of the other characters.

THE OTHER HOUSE

And this leads directly to his fall. Tony discovers at the end only the hollowness in himself, "all abysses." Between all the accidents which form his character and the substance of the man, there is truly a shadow. In the catastrophe he becomes "passive and tragic." All the excesses are damned up and he is left in "an attitude in which the whole man had already petrified" (210). At the same time the shock of the murder leads to one of recognition. Tony's perception at the instant he hears of his daughter's death leads him to confess the murder himself, and his assumption of guilt marks his recognition of responsibility in having allowed Rose to love him. The final comment of the novel, however, the repeated judgment that "they like you too much," is an indictment of both Tony's excessive gifts and his passive attitude. He is finally rather stupid, rather nice, well-meaning and ineffectual, but still ironically noble in his recognition of guilt. His well-meaning sterility and weak nobility, while typically Jamesian, are something like those of the heroes of Ibsen's *Hedda Gabler* or *Rosmersholm*. His faults are essentially those of the Ibsen hero, and he is not as strong as his women. Hedda Gabler would have rejected him as she does Tesman.

The difference between Tony Bream and Tesman, however, is simply the addition of Tony's physical attractiveness and social brilliance (and James's humor in treating these), and this determines the different reactions of the heroines of the two authors. The example of Ibsen is especially relevant at this point, for a comparison of Rose Armiger and Hedda Gabler reveals some of the dramatic bases of James's creation. Both Leon Edel and Oscar Cargill have commented on the relationship, but the striking similarities need to be examined more closely.[8]

Hedda Gabler and several other Ibsen heroines were played in London by James's close friend, Elizabeth Robins, and *The Other House* was initially planned as a play for her.[9] In his essay on a production of Hedda Gabler in which Miss Robins had the lead, written some two years before the conception of *The Other House*, James described Hedda as "infinitely perverse . . . a perfectly ill-regulated person," and he comments on Ibsen's use of her in the play:

> What "use" . . . is to be made of a wicked, diseased, disagreeable woman? . . . The "use" of Hedda Gabler is that she acts on others and that even her most disagreeable qualities have the privilege, thoroughly undeserved, doubtless, but equally irresistible, of becoming a part of the history of others. And then one isn't so sure she is wicked, and by no means sure (especially when represented by an actress who makes the point ambiguous) that she is disagreeable. She is various and sinuous and graceful, complicated and natural; she suffers, she struggles, she is human, and by that fact exposed to a dozen interpretations.[10]

This could serve as a description of Rose Armiger, who acts on others in a way similar to Hedda. James makes certain, by having Rose murder little Effie, that the reader sees she is "wicked," but the other ambiguities imposed by the disagreeable, suffering, and human aspects he strongly emphasizes in Rose Armiger.

Since Rose Armiger has traits which are found again in later novels, in the varied figures of Mrs. Beale, Mrs. Brookenham, Kate Croy, and Charlotte Stant, James's methods here have an added significance. James starts with the characteristics of the stock melodramatic figure, the dark heroine, often the villainess. Rose is dark-haired, and often her face is chalky-white. She is sensual, full-lipped, and she is "handsome" rather than beautiful. Her name, Rose, is also a conventional symbol for passion. To this base, however, James adds elements of ambiguity. The impression that Jean Martle has of Rose in their first meeting establishes the pattern; Jean cannot decide "whether she was awfully plain or strikingly handsome," but Rose's smile produces the second impression, that she is handsome while plain, "an ambiguity worth all the prettiness in the world." The capacity to produce the second impression works in another way. Rose always responds in a calculated fashion, as the momentary hesitation before her smile and her "peculiar way of looking at a person before speaking . . . this detachment," indicates. She masks her own initial reactions behind the smile of sociability.

The social appearance, however, does not quite mask her peculiarities. She is for Jean "strange," with a kind of "foreign charm." And her unnaturalness is emphasized by her dislike for children (even before Effie is an obstacle to her love for Tony). Her ambiguity and strangeness are reflected in her social situation; she is disinherited, has no home, no parents—one of the essential contrasts between Rose and Tony and his society. Cast off as she is, her strangeness, ambiguity, and rootlessness are in part cause of the inability of the others to penetrate beyond her surface while they are at the same time aware that there is something beyond.

Ambiguity of appearance and her disinherited state are also evident in the struggle between intellect and emotion within her. Rose is almost never natural; each of her actions and expressions is calculated. In her free but limited situation she is forced to "live by her wits." When her emotions overcome her wits, she collapses, as when she rejects Dennis Vidal in Book First and again at the end of the novel. Similarly, she is always described as clever, her speech is full of "conscious irony," but when alone or when backs are turned, her features repeatedly convulse into anguish and extraordinary passion, revealing the enormous tension that retaining her social mask involves. Tracing the development of the psychopathic tendency that comes to life under her tension and her repression of emotion is the story of the novel. Her final collapse is the snapping of her mind, the loss of all mental and emotional control. For the murder is accomplished with all the effort of her great ability to calculate and with all the strength of her passion for Tony, and she is left empty.

The combination of intelligence, emotional power, and her dignity as an isolated human is what gives Rose and her final fall a tragic cast. She is from the start a figure of frustration and gloom, fighting herself and her fate. When Jean first sees her with her head buried in her arms, she is "a figure of woe," and she carries this quality through to the end. While her actions repel the reader, her struggle gains his sympathy. The element that James noted in Hedda Gabler, her suffering, struggling humanity, is what raises the novel of which her counterpart is the heroine somewhat above the level of a simple melodrama of passion and violence, of conventional love and hate.

Rose is also a considerable achievement as a dramatic character. We see her only from the outside, never from within. Nothing is ever shown from her point of view; there is no "going behind" into the mind of the character. We realize the strength of her emotions by seeing her collapse, and we recognize the quality of her mind through her actions and the careful purpose and intention revealed in them. Most of all we see her in her speeches, and in these she is a character for the stage as none of the others is. James goes beyond the stereotyped figure and is able to do in the novel what he had been unable to do in a play, develop a purely dramatic character, revealed through speech and action.

III

More parallels to the drama and several weaknesses in *The Other House* are apparent on turning from an analysis of character to an examination of the structure of the novel. As noted above, Edwin Muir has found an identity of character and action to be a distinguishing feature of the dramatic novel, but closer analysis of the novel at hand will point up various other aspects of this kind of novel. One must avoid, of course, a too arbitrary separation of character from action, as James warns in "The Art of Fiction," but the critic must at some point try to see the structural features of the novel as clearly as he can in and for themselves. Character is an integral part, but only a part.

A starting point for the examination of the structure of *The Other House* lies in a brief look at the play into which James eventually, in 1909, converted the novel. The act divisions are important to a preliminary outline of the structure of the novel and point to one of the main flaws in it. Where the novel is divided into three books, the play is composed of a prologue and three acts: the prologue corresponds to Book First; Act One to Book Second through Chapter 22; Act Two to the last half of Book Second; and Act Three to Book Third. The novel and the play both follow the standard pattern of action in a well-made play: exposition, complication, climax and denouement. The prologue and Book First are the exposition, Acts One and

Two and Book Second are the complication, and Act Three and Book Third are the denouement. Both depart from convention, however, with the addition of what James called the "prologue" and with the unusual length of the complication. The three-book structure of the novel is slightly closer to the standard three-act structure, except for an unusually long second act (the weakest section of the novel), because the break between Acts One and Two in the play is an unnatural one—there is no break in the action.

Within this fairly standard form and of immediate consequence to James's dramatic conception of the novel is the division of acts into carefully marked scenes. Each chapter of the novel, except the first, is a separate, dramatically rendered scene, composed of action and dialogue, and usually set off in the action by the entrance or exit of one or more characters. There is very little narrative, almost no authorial comment of any sort; the novel is really a series of conversations in which James follows throughout his often-repeated injunction: "Dramatise! Dramatise!" James violates this scenic principle, however, with an experimental method that becomes increasingly important in his later novels. Almost every chapter-scene is presented from the point of view of one of the participating characters, what James called "going behind" into the unspoken reactions of one of the characters. For example, in the two scenes involving Rose and Jean alone, James always gives, in very brief notations, Jean's reactions, her unexpressed thoughts, bewilderments, and emotions. James uses this device again in Book Third to present several chapters of the denouement from Dennis Vidal's point of view as an outsider, slightly involved but not as emotional as the others, thus gaining an objectivity

THE OTHER HOUSE

not possible from any other point of view. James's use of this technique in *The Other House* is often quite slight, almost unnoticeable; it merely gives a slant to each scene, a position from which to see the action. Often this point of view is of no real consequence to the action, and of no particular gain in psychological depth; and in two cases, in the chapter in which the murder is revealed, and with Rose Armiger, James presents his materials entirely dramatically. We never see through Rose's eyes and are never given entrance to her thoughts. Nevertheless, the ability to present an almost entirely dramatic scene and still retain the advantages of a point-of-view character becomes one of the central principles of James's novelistic technique, and he continued to experiment with it in novels like *What Maisie Knew*.

Within the scene, however, the most important technique is James's handling of dialogue. Given the effort to present the action of the novel dramatically, dialogue takes on a major responsibility, even more than in an acted play. Although James later comments quite severely on what he called "abuse of the elements of colloquy" or excessive reliance on dialogue (see for example his remarks on Gissing in *Notes on Novelists*), his method in *The Other House* and *The Awkward Age* shows that he was willing at times to indulge himself with novels almost entirely conversational. Dialogue, of course, is also noteworthy from the standpoint of the common reader as the most peculiar, arcane, and Jamesian feature of many of the late novels.

Two operative principles stand out in the dialogue of *The Other House*.[11] The first of these is a question-and-answer technique. In this two characters, usually, attempt to analyze or simply to understand the details of the action and to comprehend each other's motives or the motives of some absent character. This generally involves what might be called an interrogation scene, a device that becomes quite important after the murder as the characters try to understand what has happened, but which is equally useful in presenting ordinary conversation. For example, the scene between Rose and Dennis in Book First is built around a series of questions which each asks the other in an effort to understand the present situation—from the author's point of view, to present that situation to the reader. An example of the continual attempt on the part of the characters to get at each other's motives and the meaning of actions can be found in the scene of Paul Beever's proposal to Jean Martle in Chapter 20. Not only does he ask indirectly for her answer to his suit; he also asks for an interpretation of nearly every remark she makes. The effect of this technique throughout the novel is to increase the element of mystery and, more importantly, to emphasize repeatedly the failures in communication between individuals, the absolute impossibility that there can be any articulate understanding among these people. In a later novel like *The Awkward Age* the technique can develop into a rapid, effective sort of communication, almost a shorthand dialogue when two characters understand each other intuitively, but discussion of this will be reserved until a later chapter. Finally, in *The Other House* and more generally, the impetus provided by question-and-answer when developing new material establishes a rapid movement in the novel.

Parallel to this technique is that of the debate. The most significant example is in Chapter 25. Here Rose and Jean meet in the obligatory scene, a convention of the well-made play, between the two principals whose wills are most violently opposed.[12] This direct confrontation is presented in a series of movements resembling a legal argument or a debate. The immediate prize is little Effie, who is present throughout the chapter and who represents the ultimate object, Tony Bream. The actual result of this clash of thesis and antithesis, of the conflict between Jean and Rose, is the murder of little Effie. The movement of the contest is significant. Rose first tells Jean of her engagement, a lie. Jean congratulates her and is drawn into a discussion of her own refusal of Paul's proposal. This allows Rose to accuse Jean of turning Paul down to get at Tony. Jean is shocked by the accusation, "caught up in a current of fast-moving depths—a cold, full tide that set straight out to sea" (161). Her antagonist is then described in the following terms: "Rose was silent for a moment, but without prejudice, clearly, to her firm possession of the ground she stood on—a power to be effectively cool in exact proportion as her interlocutress was troubled" (162). Her "possession of the ground" of her argument and Jean's position as "interlocutress" reveal the conception of the scene. Rose then denies that she is engaged and asserts that she has only said so in order to catch Jean in a moment of pleasure at seeing her rival removed. She goes on to say that Dennis really has proposed, but that she has not yet accepted him, another lie. Rose has throughout been holding onto Tony's daughter, and Jean tries to gain possession of the little girl and to end the conflict by saying that she will never marry. The maneuver fails. Rose refuses to relinquish the girl and then accuses Jean of wanting to kill Effie in order to be free to marry Tony, thereby revealing indirectly her own motives. The statement shocks Jean even more and forces her to plead for the little girl. Rose announces her conditions for giving up the child: Jean must renounce her love for Tony. She refuses and Rose carries off the child, the literal and symbolic prize in all this claim and counterclaim, and a few minutes later drowns her.

The tension generated by this argument is considerable, particularly when we recognize what it has precipitated. Much of the power comes from the repeated pattern of challenge and response, of accusation, rebuttal, and statement of conditions. Rose has the prosecutor's role in the scene; she sets up the questions and forces the answers from Jean, whose attempts at rebuttal, because they are truthful and she has been shocked, are weak and defensive. Rose's technique and the language of debate can be seen in one of several long speeches she makes. Jean has just said that although "it's very good" of Rose to take an interest in her engagement, she does not feel that it concerns her. Rose's answer is:

"But however good it may be, it's none of my business: is that what you mean? . . . Such an answer is doubtless natural enough. My having hoped you would accept Paul Beever, and above all my having rather publicly expressed that hope, is an apparent stretch of discretion that you're perfectly free to take up. But you must allow me to say that the stretch is more apparent than real. There's discretion and discretion and it's all a matter of motive. Perhaps you can guess mine for having found a reassurance in the idea of your definitely bestowing your hand. It's a very small hand and a very pretty hand, but its possible action is out of proportion to its size and even to its beauty. It was not a question of meddling in your affairs—your affairs were only one side of the matter. My interest was wholly in the effect of your marriage on the affairs of others."(161)

The whole speech sounds like a reasoned argument for

THE OTHER HOUSE

some human right, while it is actually a calculated attack intended to hurt and shock. The diction gives it its character of reason and argument; several passages make use of the abstract and debate terminology in which Rose characteristically disguises her emotional attack. The peculiar use of these techniques and diction in emotional scenes generates in this novel a strong dialectical force which propels both action and emotion. The whole chapter is a fine example of what Austin Warren has called the dialectical mode as it operates in James's scenes. As Warren notes, the mode is social, analytical, and intellectual.[13] The social aspect is clear in the sarcastic respect for compliments and niceties, for the proprieties of conversation between two young ladies in the 1890's. The analytical qualities are immediately present here and in the question-and-answer technique; the whole scene is an analysis of motive in which Rose's intellectual powers are unquestionable. The only weakness in the scene is perhaps the length of the speeches. The passage quoted above is about half the speech, and there are many of equal length in the novel—an inevitable slowing of the pace. What one must look for in later novels is a combination of the intellectual power of the long speech and the rapidity of movement of the short (for example, in *The Awkward Age*). One experiment, as will be seen in *The Spoils of Poynton,* is to move the intellectual, analytic aspects of such a speech into the mind of the perceiving character.

Analysis of dialogue leads to a more general consideration of the structure and patterns of movement in the novel. The quality of suspense or mystery, noted in relation to the question-and-answer technique, is one of the basic structural principles of the novel. In *The Other House* James uses the standard features of the love-intrigue plot to motivate the story; in this case the operative question is: who will get the man? After the introduction of the vow in the first book, the whole of Book Second is an analysis and development of all the various love relationships; each of the girls is in love with Tony Bream, each has another suitor and a proposal to decline, and each is encouraged by Tony to accept the other lover. Book Second does little more than develop these relationships, and James uses the slight suspense developed in these machinations while he builds Rose's obsession to the point of murder, for the whole novel really hangs on the fate of little Effie. After the murder the intrigue changes from love-game to murder story, even detective story in the first chapters of Book Third, and the plot is kept moving by the attempts to solve the mystery and punish the criminal. James exploits the techniques and concerns of the mystery writer, plots carefully so that Tony, Jean, and Rose will all be suspect, and arranges Dennis Vidal's whereabouts to give Jean an alibi.

Below the level of the love-game and mystery story which provides the surface movement and design of the novel, James is working with far more profound material. The imminent crisis in Rose's obsessive love gradually requires much more of the reader's attention and emotional response until by the first chapter of Book Third the nature of that crisis commands the whole form of the novel. The major weakness of the novel is that this interest is delayed so long, a feature I shall examine more closely below, but at this point we realize that there are two plots operating in the novel—thriller and tragedy.[14] The quality of the melodramatic love story is paramount throughout the first two books of the novel and provides the motives for the action in those books. This action climaxes with the murder. All the questions of love-intrigue are in a sense erased or recast by the murder, and more serious ones are eventually posed. The thriller plot needs only the solution of the mystery—the discovery by the others that Rose is guilty—and the punishment of the murderess to complete it. But with Tony's admission of guilt at the end of Book Second, his recognition of responsibility at the moment of shock, the tragic plot assumes control of the structure, and the novel attains a level of seriousness common in James's fiction but not wholly apparent earlier in this novel. The tragic plot involves a deeper examination of the moral issues of the action than the thriller or love-intrigue could have elicited. Instead of the simple actional suspenses of the first two books, Book Third is informed by questions of guilt, responsibility, and punishment, of the nature and varieties of love.

One explanation for this double plot can be found in the disparity between James's initial conception of the story and the novel he actually wrote. In the first entry concerning *The Other House* in his notebook James conceived the action centering on Tony Bream, and this is reflected in the love-intrigue plot.[15] In this entry James is interested in what Tony would do after taking the vow, and how the two women would try to win him. In the tragedy, however, Rose becomes the center; she gains the reader's greatest interest and feeling. The conflict between concept and actuality represented by the double plot, while it is a mark of the failure of the novel in an over-all sense, indicates the strength of James's insight into the story he conceived. Rose is much the stronger and more interesting character, and given the power of her obsession, James was forced to a more profound statement than the first two books of the novel would suggest and than he had originally planned. This disparity between notebook conception and the subsequent novel is one that comes up several times in this period, as will be seen, and points to the need for careful comparison between the two.

As I have mentioned, the love-intrigue plot almost destroys the structure of the novel, for it results in what James called a "misplaced middle." Book Second is overextended simply by the needs of the love story, with its development of cross-relationships, and by the needs of the thriller, with its placement of characters and the imputation of motive. Details of plot are added without any consequent deepening of meaning. By contrast, the meaningful weight of Book Third is far out of proportion to its shortness; it overbalances the social chatter and courtship of Book Second. The impossibility of any organic form in *The Other House* is apparent when the middle book is compared either with the careful introduction of themes, characters, and motive in Book First (the prologue or "overture") or with the resolution of the more significant tragic themes in the last book.

One feature of the denouement of the novel is a complex set of recognition scenes. The most important of these are the confrontation of Dennis and Rose in Chapter 29, the union of Tony and Jean in Chapter 32, and the final short-lived union of Paul Beever and Rose in the last chapter of the novel. In the second of these Tony and Jean realize the consequences of future conditions of their love, the burden of guilt and freedom which Rose has by her action placed on them. They recognize the full horror of their situation.

The pattern of recognition is even more intricate in Rose's scenes. In the first of these, Dennis Vidal recognizes his commitment to his passion and submits to Rose when she claims him. Rose, however, is still prideful and egotistic, and she defends her actions evasively and reminds Dennis of her earlier self-abasement before him in a remarkable speech: "Did I only stoop, in my deep contrition, to make it easier for you to knock me down? I gave you your chance to refuse me, and what you've come back for then will have been only, most handsomely, to take it. In that case you did injustice there to the question of your revenge. What fault have you to find with anything so splendid?" (196). Rose, even after the murder, is still the logician, forcing Dennis to accept his love for her. The whole passage is colored by her need for love, for safety, and by her pride. Her pride is so strong that even Dennis's confession that he knows Jean did not commit the murder, that he saw Rose with little Effie, only brings Rose to accuse Tony of the murder, in an attempt to keep her ego intact. Only her face reveals the suffering: "She has so altered as to be ugly . . . ravaged and disfigured, wrecked in the gust that had come and gone" (194). She has at this point lost only her mask, none of her strength.

The final recognition scene completes the structure of the novel. After her capture of Dennis, Rose begins to doubt whether she has him secured, and her doubt forces her to try to explain to Paul her conception of what she has done. By this time she has lost her emotional power and is indifferent. She recognizes the hideousness of her features; she thinks of herself as "the horror and the shame." But she cannot admit the full meaning of her crime, cannot make the confession aloud, and so she can only conceive it in terms of failure and mistake. Out of love, she says, she acted to make Tony hate Jean: "You'll say my calculation was grotesque—my stupidity as ignoble as my crime. All I can answer is that I might none the less have succeeded. People *have*—in worse conditions. But I don't defend myself—I'm face to face with my mistake . . . It's a storm that's past, it's a debt that's paid. I may literally be better" (225). Her confession is implicit, but she seems to have little sense of guilt. Only when she later says, Iago-like, "I shall never speak again," does the impact of her guilt become clear. Her mind can rationalize the murder in terms of abstract, inhuman motive and intention, but her emotional recognition is clear, and her final act reinforces this moral perception. Paul, when she insists that Dennis will not return, offers to take her away. Within his love, in spite of his horror, lies her salvation, her ease; he becomes "my safety, my safety." But Dennis does return for her, and she responds "with a low, deep moan." She goes with him, "and they passed quickly into the night." She has chosen, in her recognition of her guilt, punishment over safety; for Dennis will not stay with her—as Tony says, he will "put the globe between them. Think of her torture." This last recognition scene completes the novel; the whole movement of motive and motion is resolved in a final act of perception. Rose is not purged of her disease, but she has accepted her punishment; and although it may not be the conventional, lawabiding one, it is a classical form of banishment which points to the kind of tragedy enacted in this last book. All that remains is the conventional restoration of order in the remaining short scene between Tony Bream and Paul Beever. With that the action is complete and the movement of the tragedy returns to stasis.

IV

Underlying the structure of the novel are symbolic motifs which point to the various themes of the novel and the meaning implicit in the structure. Complexes of imagery and symbol give a clearer conception of the form of the novel, the way it is built, and at the same time directly convey the meaning. The religious imagery which surrounds little Effie's role in the novel is a minor note of this type. Julia Bream demands "mystic rites and spells" for Tony's vow; he must "swear by all the gods" a vow "on his sacred honour." The baby itself is initially described as "a large white sacrifice, a muslin muffled offering which seemed to lead up to a ceremony." The "ceremony" is the public announcement of Tony's vow that he will never marry during the lifetime of his daughter—a thrice-repeated oath—and little Effie symbolizes this vow throughout the novel. Religious images in relation to her are repeated several times in the novel, notably on pages 102 and 103 where Rose is described as "priestess of a threatened altar" and Effie as "a poor little lamb of sacrifice." Finally, in the scene immediately preceding the murder, Rose gives the child a "kiss that was like a long consecration" and leads her off to the slaughter of the innocents.

The use of little Effie as symbol of the vow points beyond the naturalistic level, for she also represents the physical presence of her mother and the misguided love that led Tony's wife to impose the vow. The mother in turn leads back to the evil which underlies everything in the novel—Julia's stepmother. All the mystic rites and vows that surround little Effie at the beginning of the novel are totemic attempts to ward off the evil influence of the stepmother. The tie between Julia Bream and Rose Armiger is also the stepmother, who was Rose's aunt. The two girls were brought up by her; Julia was only rescued by marriage, while Rose "could take care of myself. I could fight." In Book First the stepmother has recently made a visit to Julia, and Rose blames Julia's death on her: "She only stirred up the wretched past and reopened old wounds," "the force of that horror possesses [Julia's] whole being." The evil embodied in the stepmother, unnamed and unspecified like the evil in *The Turn of the Screw*, finally finds its outlet in Rose, but it is also kept present through the whole action as the evil which threatens little Effie. The myth of the evil stepmother is as old as the story of Cinderella, but James gains force from it by leaving it quietly in the background until Rose destroys the symbol of the magic vow and releases the tragedy.

James at several points in the novel tries to establish a conflict between old and new, but Mrs. Beever's healthy, though unconscious traditionalism is offset by the evil influences of the past represented by the stepmother; and Tony's modernism, all electric bells and new clocks, is too slightly developed to be of much significance. In the same way, the attempt to reveal some of the causes of Tony's weakness by pointing out that his house, Bounds, is nearer town, civilization, and society, while Mrs. Beever's Eastmead is closer to nature and the countryside, fails to go very far in indicating the failure of moral restraint in a traditionless society. All this is swamped under the far greater impact of the evil influence of the past on the present which is central to the structure of the novel. The plea for tradition and the attack on contemporary social behavior, the whole question of the old morality versus the new, must wait for fulfillment in *The Awkward Age*. What James accomplishes in *The Other House* is to introduce through the device of the vow something like Maule's curse in *The House of the Seven Gables* in the form of a little girl who remarkably resembles Hawthorne's little Pearl in her structural role.

THE OTHER HOUSE

The thematic role of past and present, however, gives a clue to one of James's customary modes of thought. One of the patterns nearly always discernible in a novel by Henry James is the establishment of opposites in character or theme out of which some solution is reached through a combination or synthesis. This dialectical pattern is of considerable significance in later novels, and the examination of several examples of it here will show the kind of operation I have in mind and will help to point to the meaning of the novel.

I have noted several instances of the disparity between appearance and reality in the analysis of characterization, especially in regard to Tony Bream and Rose Armiger. Rose invariably tries to give an impression contrary to her immediate feelings. And Tony, although his feelings are usually natural enough, instinctively values social appearance over personal feeling. Even Jean, next to Dennis Vidal the most natural of the characters, attempts to disguise her love for Tony. Questions of what is natural and unnatural in human behavior are brought out by the masks Rose assumes. Rose's masks hide her feelings and make them unnatural, forcing them toward the act of murder. Rose always meets someone with a particular "face": she presents a "white, uneasy face" and she has a "wonderful, white, mobile mask." This mask behind which she hides her true emotions and her calculations later becomes symbolic. Directly after the revelation of the murder, when she tries to blame Jean, "Rose's mask was the mask of Medusa." James follows up this mention of the myth and establishes the Medusa as a symbol for Rose in the final chapters. Tony is later described as literally "petrified" by Rose's actions. Finally both Dennis and Paul look at Rose and are trapped by her. Her conquest of Dennis is sealed with a "stony kiss," and he too is petrified in a way, "a creature trapped in steel."

The contrast or conflict between appearance and reality, however, is something more than a representation of characters who act naturally and openly and those who furnish themselves with masks and thereby make their actions unnatural. In Rose's part-triumph over the natural, one can see an additional dialectic of innocence versus experience or knowledge, and this will be even more fruitful in later novels. The innocent, even ignorant natural character, like Jean and even perhaps Tony, is forced for full awareness to acquire a knowledge that includes both good and evil. This becomes the true reality, as it is also the synthesis of the conflict between appearance and reality and between innocence and knowledge. It is expressed most clearly in Book Third. There all the characters have been introduced to reality in the form of the murder, the true revelation of Rose's character; and the reality that comes through knowledge is horrible, "a monstrous reality" in the relation between Rose and Dennis, and "the agony of the actual," "the red real" for Tony and Dennis as they come to mutual understanding. Dennis, the character who is presented as closest to the real, is forced to recognize that the whole event was more real than a "black, bloody nightmare." Apprehending the real, then, as opposed to the partial reality of natural instincts and social behavior, includes a knowledge of evil and of the role of appearance, which has masked unnatural, but powerful and evil instincts.

The fruit of this knowledge in *The Other House* is an understanding of love, the chief subject of the novel. The perverse form which Julia Bream's love for her child takes initiates the action, and the whole study of love in the novel overrides the intrigues of the middle section and leads to tragedy. Nothing good comes of love, although the possibility of a tainted fulfillment is left open to Tony and Jean. Effie has died because of her parents' love. Jean's love has come closest to the natural and beautiful, yet its strength and impossibility, and her refusal to renounce it, have led directly to the murder. Dennis's love has been transformed to suffering and has its basis in Rose's effect on "God knows what baser, obscurer part of me." Tony has acquiesced so passively in his enjoyment of being loved that he has allowed the action to run its course. Each of his actions arises out of his passivity and is directed toward some kind of weak self-gain. All this is an intimate part of his recurrent fear of emotion. What he desires is something half-way, a love that is confined "to the breezy, sunny forecourt of the temple of friendship, forbidding it any access to the obscure and comparatively stuffy interior" (118).

The horror and destruction of love to which the action leads is, of course, traceable to Rose's passion more than to the inadequacies of the others. Without Rose, the shallowness of the love-intrigue would rule. Her love is generally allowed to express itself indirectly, either in act or by imputation, but the few times James does describe it directly he chooses his imagery carefully. It is a "measureless white ray of light" which "covers [Tony] with a great cold lustre that made everything for the moment look hard and ugly" (107). It "chills" Tony as it later chills Jean in "the cold current." The intensity of Rose's love, however, transforms her from a figure of pure evil into one of pathos. And this intensity also gives a tragic character to the climax and resolution of the novel. Rose's flaw is her passion which enables her to commit murder.

Her love draws pity while at the same time her madness, the excess in the love, inspires fear. The repeated cry, "It's horrible. It's horrible," runs through the last chapters. The truly tragic fate represented here is to endure without love, without speaking, exiled from all human contact.

Rose is doomed because of her love, but she is also helpless from the start because of her background, symbolized by the evil stepmother (her aunt) and by her rootlessness, her lack of a safe "anchorage." She has nothing outside herself, and her love for Tony is primarily an attempt to give herself a place, to establish contact with the social world of wealth, position, and life. Rose's background gives her a kind of freedom, but no fulfillment; and she tries to escape that lonely freedom through love for Tony Bream, the social figure, rather than for Dennis Vidal, "the real thing." But she fails even in this, and, as Doctor Ramage comments, it was "the temptation of solitude" that partly led to the crime. Rose is always alone in her freedom, as James skillfully insists by letting the reader see her only from outside.

Rose's punishment is her exile; she is driven back into isolation. And total isolation, without speech, is a far greater punishment, far more profound moral judgment, than Jean's desire to kill Rose, which is the standard, social, lawful reaction. As Tony says, "Her doom will be to live," to be forced to live a dead life without communication. A comment by Eric Bentley in an essay on Chekhov is quite relevant: "Life knows no endings, happy or tragic. (Shaw once congratulated Chekhov on the discovery that the tragedy of the Hedda Gablers is, in real life, precisely that they do not shoot themselves.)"[16] Shaw might well have congratulated Henry James, for his transformation of the usual ending, the punishment by death of the guilty one, reveals a common insight with Chekhov, as perhaps the social scene and the failures in communication are reminiscent of *The Cherry Orchard*.

James's moral insight thus goes beyond the conventions of tragedy and the late nineteenth-century stage. In addition to the unconventional ending, his moral vision has shown that the guilt for any action goes beyond any one individual: Rose is merely the active member of a group of failures in love. Consequently Jean and Tony both suffer punishment. Tony confesses the crime in recognition of his own guilt, while Jean begins in Chapter 32 to recognize that her love for Tony has been the immediate cause of the murder. In her torment she ironically points the direction of their perceptions: "We seem beautifully eager for the guilt" (217).

The moral division of guilt among the various characters is part of James's judgment. The meaning of the novel lies in the final conception of love and freedom. Rose's love has denied her life, Jean's innocence is destroyed through her love, and Tony has only provoked the desire to possess him. Effie is sacrificed to love, the self-love and possessive love of her elders, backed by the misguided protective love of her mother. Love dooms each of the characters; it denies life to each of them. But James's final judgment goes farther and is based more on his idea of freedom. Freedom has been restricted for Tony, Jean, and Rose by Tony's vow. Once the obstacle, little Effie, is removed, the other characters, except Rose, achieve their freedom. Rose, as agent of relief, is driven back into the freedom of isolation, where freedom means nothing. Tony and Jean are now free to marry, and Tony comments that this is a part of Rose's punishment, that she has only set them free. But Jean realizes that their freedom will always be stained by their guilt; the opposites are always mixed. And so her final comment sums up the paradox, the dialectical resolution, essential to the meaning of the novel: "It's her triumph—that our freedom is horrible" (220).

The complexity of moral action in the last book of *The Other House* overcomes to some extent the faults in characterization and construction which mar the novel. I have felt it important to examine at some length this novel which is not too well known and certainly of less stature than many of James's because of the techniques and concerns in later novels for which it prepares the way. But even though it is not a first-rate novel, James constructs out of the materials of a fairly melodramatic stage play a novel that proceeds through the dramatic use of scene, dialogue, and character to a tragedy close in temper both to Ibsen and Chekhov, but impressive principally in James's own form—the novel. With unusually violent and emotional material, James goes beyond the superficialities of his plays and of the long second book and, with the help of techniques learned in the theater, constructs a thoroughly dramatic novel. In *The Other House* Henry James has not completely developed the structural techniques and themes which are to dominate the rest of this experimental period, but these matters are there in embryo and in spite of its weaknesses the novel is an impressive trial that foreshadows later achievements. This early experiment in working his way out of the theater was necessary for the future.

4

The Spoils of Poynton

"THE OTHER HOUSE" is technically quite close to James's theatrical experiments in the early 1890's. *The Spoils of Poynton,* however, seems initially more closely related in technique to some of the longer stories James was writing during those same years—stories like "The Lesson of the Master," "The Coxon Fund," "The Altar of the Dead," and "The Figure in the Carpet." James seems to be aiming in the first part of the novel at the typical "single effect" of the short story, in this case the quarrel over and disposition of some furniture and art objects. The novel is at first also not noticeably scenic; James's technique is a condensed narrative of events much like that in the stories. As the story gradually gains added complexity, however, long, dramatic scenes are introduced and there are complications of motive and effect. This shift from short-story techniques to those of the dramatic novel is intimately connected with James's principal experiment in the novel, the use of a central consciousness or point-of-view character, the heroine Fleda Vetch. The gradual involvement of point-of-view character with dramatic scenes and techniques provides an interesting story of construction which we can follow in the novel and in James's notebook comments on his work in progress. As one does so, it becomes clear that *The Spoils of Poynton* is a transitional novel, one in which James was trying to integrate dramatic strategies and novelistic techniques, together with certain themes and character types, all of which would be valuable in his later novels. It is a way, for James, of working back into the novel form.

Closer connections with short story rather than drama may also be inferred from the earlier composition of *The Spoils of Poynton*. *The Spoils of Poynton* was written before *The Other House;* James began the novel in the summer of 1895, a few months after his failure in the theater, and finished it in March 1896, when he immediately began *The Other House*. The two novels were published concurrently in periodicals in 1896, although *The Spoils of Poynton* was not presented in book form until February 1897, after the later novel had been put out in October 1896. After working through *The Spoils of Poynton,* a process which led to certain discoveries about the use of the drama in the novel, recorded in the notebooks, James returned to the almost totally dramatic conception of *The Other House* to experiment with those insights. That process, however, begins in the early, nondramatic chapters of the first novel.

The whole development can be followed in James's comments on the construction of *The Spoils of Poynton* in his notebooks and in his later reflections in his preface to the novel. These tools are especially valuable here, although they must always remain secondary to the reading of the novel itself. The critic is fortunate in that, of the novels of this period, this is one of three which are discussed in James's prefaces to the New York edition, and it is one of two which are given a fairly complete record of composition in the notebooks.[1] James's comments can be of great critical value at each stage of the analysis of technique, structure, and meaning.

Some consideration of the surface similarities and contrasts between *The Other House* and *The Spoils of Poynton* will point up the somewhat different experimental features of the latter. Although the two short novels are almost identical in length (approximately 65,000 words in *The Spoils of Poynton* and 70,000 in *The Other House*), they are essentially different. In *The Other House,* the emphasis is on plot, while in *The Spoils of Poynton* it is turned toward character.[2] There are only three characters central to the latter, while two others, Mona Brigstock and her mother, have important nondramatic or minor roles; in *The Other House* there are six, perhaps seven, characters who are essential to the action. The limitation to three characters, through one of whom we see all the action, should provide simplicity and concentration. In fact, however, the action itself is less simple than that of *The Other House.* It is split between the question of the fate of "the spoils" and the resolution of the love affair between Fleda Vetch and Owen Gereth. These two actions are of course interrelated, primarily through the character of Fleda, and it is this unity through character rather than action which constitutes the essential difference between the two novels. In general, then, *The Other House* appears to be almost all surface, all presented drama, with what depth there is achieved through the dynamics of the drama, the various forms the action takes.

In *The Spoils of Poynton,* on the other hand, depth is achieved through psychological penetration, through insight into the single character of the heroine, the central consciousness; this penetration is related more to a situation than to an action and is essentially static rather than dynamic. James, then, is experimenting at almost the same time with two quite different solutions to the problems of the novel—with the drama and with the use of a single point of view, involving techniques traditionally more novelistic than dramatic.[3]

The principal of these novelistic techniques is James's "going behind" the dramatic surface of the action into the consciousness, the impressions, motivations, feelings, and reasonings of the central character. This gives the reader far greater understanding of the single character than any dramatic representation could. James's technique is, of course, both traditional and experimental; it looks toward both the nineteenth- and twentieth-century novel. Many novelists have gone behind the dramatic surface, but James accomplishes it without any, or at least with negligible, comment of his own as author. Every feeling, impression, thought, is presented directly as the character's, even as the character experiences them. James's experiments in this direction are not properly "stream of consciousness," nor even interior monologue, but rather a more rational and ordered form of representing mental and emotional activity. With Fleda Vetch this often takes the form of a meditation over the experience presented to her. In this novel, in contrast to *The Other House* where James used point of view only as a focusing effect without halting the action, Fleda's meditations almost always interrupt the action. They are pauses in the action while Fleda considers the implications of the action up to that

THE SPOILS OF POYNTON

point and works out the possibilities for acting in the future; the meditations function almost as summaries at certain points in the novel. They do, however, like Isabel Archer's all-night meditation in *The Portrait of a Lady,* operate dramatically as they show the process of Fleda's thought in a dramatic context. For the reader they provide a character's subjective response to the action of the novel about which James, as author, is being as objective as possible. This, the main nondramatic or novelistic feature in *The Spoils of Poynton,* delineates it most clearly from *The Other House* and points to the importance of character in it. In these two novels, which can be considered as existing almost simultaneously at the beginning of this experimental period, James utilizes two distinctive modes, which he tried out and developed through half a decade. And toward the end of *The Spoils of Poynton* he is partly successful in bringing the two modes together in one novel.

II

In *The Spoils of Poynton* our attention is focused on character, on the central consciousness, or free spirit, and the "fools" with whom she must contend. In his preface James emphasizes character in relation to drama:

Character, the question of what my agitated friends should individually, and all intimately and at the core, show themselves, would unmistakeably be the key to my modest drama, and would indeed alone make a drama of any sort possible. Yes, it is a story of cabinets and chairs and tables; they formed the bone of contention, but what would "become" of them, magnificently passive, seemed to represent a comparatively vulgar issue. The passions, the faculties, the forces their beauty would, like that of antique Helen of Troy, set in motion, was what, as a painter, one had really wanted of them, was the power in them one had from the first appreciated. Emphatically, by that truth, there would have to be moral developments—dreadful as such a prospect might loom for a poor interpreter committed to brevity. Character is interesting as it comes out, and by the process and duration of that emergence . . ."[4]

A great weight of meaning in this novel rests on character and characterization, and a brief analysis of James's techniques in this and the results will introduce the elements of the action and point to structure and meaning. It is more revealing to examine these techniques under James's own categories of "free spirit" and "fool," for the types are more his own than the stage types found in *The Other House*. "The fixed constituents," James comments in his preface, "of almost any reproducible action are the fools who minister, at a particular crisis, to the intensity of the free spirit engaged with them. The fools are interesting by contrast, by the salience they acquire, and by a hundred other of their advantages."[5] All the characters in *The Spoils of Poynton*, except Fleda Vetch, are fools. They are "fixed" in their attitudes and behavior, with little or no possibility for development or change. They are the characters whom R. P. Blackmur describes as "the very agents of the action. They represent the stupid force of life and are the cause of trouble to the intelligent consciousness."[6] They are the representatives of the will in its conflict with intelligence, and in this conflict only they can act, can be agents.

Certain qualities of this "stupid force of life" are indicated in James's portrait of Mona Brigstock, who is, as James says, "*all* will." James's description of Mona is almost entirely comic and tends to dehumanize her. Mona is repeatedly seen as a blank; she hasn't "the ghost of an expression to her countenance. Tall, straight and fair, long-limbed and strangely festooned, she stood there without a look in her eye or any perceptible intention of any sort in any other feature. She belonged to the type in which speech is an unaided emission of sound, in which the secret of being is impenetrably and incorruptibly kept."[7] She is lifeless, a "Waterbath Brigstock"—the harshness of the consonants emphasizes Mona's machine-like awkwardness. She has a "motionless mask," a "voice like the squeeze of a doll's stomach," and "eyes that might have been blue beads." She is obstinate, willful, "the massive maiden at Waterbath," "a magnificent deadweight" with big feet who is always "romping" in a surfeit of ponderous energy and activity. Mona is treated throughout much of the novel as a grotesque, and her mother, who represents her late in the novel, is even more comic: "She was really somehow no sort of person at all . . . She had a face of which it was impossible to say anything but that it was pink, and a mind it would be possible to describe only had one been able to mark it in a similar fashion. As nature had made this organ neither green nor blue nor yellow there was nothing to know it by: it strayed and bleated like an unbranded sheep . . . Mrs. Brigstock had brought it with her . . . Fleda was quite prepared to assist its use might she only divine what it wanted to do" (172-173). Ridicule of Mrs. Brigstock's mind places it, like Mona, in some neutral zone between animal and machine. But that zone is life, where will and action overpower intelligence. This comic dehumanization of the human being who is "all will," who represents life at its strongest and dumbest, shows James balancing the opposing forces by using satirical characterization to undercut the power of the unexamined life.

Owen Gereth, with whom Fleda falls in love, is another of the fools. He is more human than the Brigstocks, but his foolishness and fixedness are unquestionable and he finally becomes one of them. He acts only at Mona's bidding or the whim of his own emotions. He is "handsome and heavy," natural, even innocent; but he is also stupid, weak, and impressionable—"he was hollow, perfunctory, pathetic" (95). As with Tony Bream, Sir Claude, or Vanderbank and many other Jamesian "heroes" the combination of artlessness and weakness, together with a handsome social figure, attracts the heroine. Fleda's love is for both the best and worst in him, and she sums him up in this way: he is "pointlessly active and pleasantly dull," and "absolutely beautiful and delightfully dense." He is a type, the young English gentleman, completely competent for his social role but totally helpless in any private life that goes beyond the forms. The social appearance has its sexual appeal, and this is one half of Fleda's love:

In the country, heated with the chase and splashed with the mire, he had always much reminded her of a picturesque peasant in national costume. This costume, as Owen wore it, varied from day to day; it was as copious as the wardrobe of an actor; but it never failed of suggestions of the earth and the weather, the hedges and ditches, the beasts and birds. There had been days when he struck her as all potent nature in one pair of boots. It didn't make him now another person that he was delicately dressed, shining and splendid, that he had a higher hat and light gloves with black seams and an umbrella as fine as a lance; but it made him, she soon decided, really handsomer, and this in turn gave him . . . a tremendous pull. (150)

Owen, however, is totally absorbed in himself and too weak to have any will of his own. Although this weakness also attracts Fleda, it means that Owen on his own must succumb to the active figure, Mona Brigstock. Owen is, in an almost literal sense, one of the "spoils" of Poynton and the whole system of English social life James is portraying. He is a fixed object, like "the things" themselves, over which the others struggle.

Owen's mother, Mrs. Gereth, is another of James's "fools," and one whom he calls "the very reverse of the free spirit."[8] In the words of the preface, she is a "figure" rather than a "character"; in other words, a vivid and living portrait of a person in whom there is no chance for growth or change. Mrs. Gereth's fixedness is caused by her "disproportionate passion" for "the things," the art objects of Poynton. Each act is motivated by this ruling passion, and the result is somewhat similar, though not treated as comically, to what we have seen in Mona Brigstock: "All Mrs. Gereth's scruples were on one side . . . and her ruling passion has in a manner despoiled her of her humanity" (37).

This effect shows itself in two aspects of her character. Mrs. Gereth is devoted to an ideal of aesthetic beauty which is qualified by her possessive greed, no matter how much she and Fleda may try to discount this. Her devotion blinds her to any human feelings that Fleda in particular may have. For Mrs. Gereth serves a strong faith which focuses all her actions on one object and fixes her in one attitude. She worships "the things," and the language James uses to describe this worship is appropriately religious. "When I know I'm right I go to the stake. Oh, he may burn me alive," she says in describing her removal of "the things" from Poynton to Ricks. But the religious attitude is offset by repeated reference to "the things." Mrs. Gereth's devotion, her religion, is purely materialistic. Her passion remains that of the collector, the creatively sterile —only one stage above the Philistines like Owen and Mona. The art itself is devalued by the repeated appellation "the things," and by the nature of the objects themselves: "chairs and tables, cabinets and presses, the material odds and ends of the more labouring ages"[9]—there are no paintings. " 'Things' were of course the sum of the world; only, for Mrs. Gereth, the sum of the world was rare French furniture and oriental china" (24). This combination of materialism and aestheticism forms the basis of Mrs. Gereth's character.[10]

Mrs. Gereth's materialism is responsible for her limited morality. For her the only morality is that of "the things," of material goods. In the service of her ideal she is, as Fleda notes, "nothing if not practical." In this pure practicality, every act is considered for the good it will do "the things." This also fixes her response to Fleda. Mrs. Gereth always thinks of Fleda and her secrets, passions, and abilities in terms of what use they can be to her ideal. She "uses" Fleda continuously from the time she first offers her to Owen at the end of Chapter III until she finally forces her back to London to attract Owen. Then "the things" are lost, Fleda is of no more use, and Mrs. Gereth's revulsion, though temporary, is violent. She acts each time under a ruling passion, out of materialism, and with a pragmatic conception of value.

Mrs. Gereth is, however, a much more sympathetic character than this analysis would indicate. She is at times (most of this is through Fleda's eyes) "a reigning queen," "a proud usurper," "Don Quixote tilting at windmills," a "wizard" and a "conjurer." She is almost always a martyr, as she claims, in relation to the spoils. Her martyrdom is the direct result of the circumstance that most excuses her passion. For she is disinherited by law, an English tradition that excluded the widowed mother from any inheritance in the father's estate. The injury and Owen's apparent lack of any family feeling (we must remember that she shows very little herself) almost justify her actions, but the complex of traits that make up the figure of Mrs. Gereth keeps the reader from judging until the end of the novel. In spite of James's assertion that Mrs. Gereth "was not intelligent, was only clever," we need the clarity and intelligence of her attack on Fleda in Chapter XVIII to provide us with a clearer conception of the meaning of both their characters. Mrs. Gereth does from time to time arouse our compassion, and she balances Fleda's freedom with her own fixity—half the fault of her personality and half the results of her social situation. Mrs. Gereth is not free, but she has a certain amount of will and a strength of passion which causes her to act. Were Fleda not ultimately the victim of her actions, we would have only compassion for her. As it is we can only realize that she acts partly from a good motive and partly from a tremendous selfishness.

In connection with this discussion of Mrs. Gereth's character, Richard Poirier's excellent analysis of the comic sense and characterization in the early novels must be adjusted slightly to apply to James's later fiction. In discussing James's comic handling of the "fixed" character or fool, Poirier says:

> His comedy in these instances is invariably used in defence of the human capacities which he sees being thwarted not *within* the fools but by them, in their dealings with his favorites . . . He satirizes all those who are not capable of rev-

erence for impractical aspiration. Encouraged by James himself, we have been calling these characters "fixed," and we are not allowed to find extenuations for their inadequacies. They may amuse and even please, but they are wholly incapable of those evidences of feeling and intelligence which would direct us to probe beyond their loudly apparent grotesqueness.[11]

Mrs. Gereth transcends just those limitations which Poirier finds imposed on the early characters. Part of her attractiveness, as I have pointed out, is in her own thwarted capacities. And she is immensely reverent toward her own aspirations, which are in the given situation impractical (though not so much so as Fleda's), but which she follows with a thoroughgoing practicality. The strength of Mrs. Gereth's passion leads us far beyond her grotesqueness to her place beside Fleda after the storm of tragic loss has passed and calm has returned. The quality of her feelings, at once diminished and heightened by the quality of their objects, attracts us to her. In the figure of Mrs. Gereth James is able to establish a complex fool who escapes the early limitations of her type and any comic grotesqueness to become a suffering human being in the novel. She points the way out of fixity to the free spirit.

The many qualities which make up the free spirit, Fleda Vetch, are intimately related to, in fact are necessary to her structural role as central consciousness, one of the main achievements of *The Spoils of Poynton*. Many of the same traits will also reappear in the central female figures of succeeding novels, like Maisie Farange, Nanda Brookenham, and Milly Theale. Fleda is a "character" rather than a "figure," and she undergoes change and moral development; but it is the conception of the free spirit that makes Fleda special and also makes it possible for her to serve as the point of view for the novel. She is the free spirit and "the free spirit, always much tormented, and by no means always triumphant, is heroic, ironic, pathetic or whatever, and, as exemplified in the record of Fleda Vetch, for instance, 'successful' only through having remained free."[12] James also asserts that Fleda has "acuteness and intensity, reflexion and passion, has above all a contributive and participant view of her situation."[13] Perhaps there is too much. Fleda seems to be almost everything a human being can be, everything we would wish for in a heroine. In the context of the novel, however, certain traits gather strength and become determinant, others prove weaknesses, and some remain no more than possibilities.

One might first examine the implications of the label, "free spirit." Setting aside freedom for the moment, Fleda's "spiritual" qualities rest in her nonphysical attributes. She exists in idea and ideal, in feeling and imagination. She is intensely sensitive in her feelings, but has the added capacity to interpret and criticize, to "appreciate" (one of James's favorite verbs for this) the quality of her experience. She has a "finer consciousness" than the others, and two qualities, her intelligence and her imagination, enable her to approach life.

Intelligence is necessary to the central consciousness, and James is careful to insist upon Fleda's, even to the point of asserting it as narrator: "No one in the world was less superficial than Fleda"; "she was a person who could think ten thoughts at once" (92, 170). At the very opening of the novel, however, James sets about establishing Fleda's intelligence without having to assert it himself. When she first appears Fleda is "dressed with an idea," which we see revealed in her conversation with Mrs. Gereth and which sets her apart from Owen's "frank dread of people's minds" and Mona's basic mindlessness. After Fleda's role has been immensely complicated by her realization of Owen's attraction to her in Chapter VIII, we see all her powers of reflection at work in the intense meditation scene in the next chapter, a scene in which her conceptions determine the course of the action for much of the rest of the novel. Fleda's awareness is necessary to the reader's. Her conceptions grow toward a final understanding. Without this intelligent appreciation the reader would be lost, as would much of the novel. She is by no means all intellect, however. The other half of Fleda's "appreciation" is her imaginative or intuitive response to the other characters and to the situation. She "both sees and feels," as James notes. Her response to the "things" of Poynton is imaginative and intuitive, as is her ability to make something out of the lesser things of Ricks. At the end of the novel, she is able to salvage something out of the disaster; she can possess the spoils imaginatively. These qualities set her apart from the others and, as we shall see, prepare for her loss at the end of the novel.

A third feature of Fleda's spirit is the overriding motive which informs all her "appreciation." Her primary response to the living reality she tries to understand or appreciate is a moral one. As her mind attempts to understand her experience, she tries to convert understanding into action. In this, she operates within the limits of a moral aspiration which she hopes will give meaning to each act—limits of honor, loyalty, "keeping faith." The meditation in Chapter IX is a perfect example of her effort to understand the particulars of experience and her own feelings and then work out a scheme of moral action based on her own perception, a scheme which will provide for the rights of all the characters and insure honor in each act.

THE SPOILS OF POYNTON

If Fleda's "spirit" is made up of intelligence, imagination, and moral response, her "freedom" is defined by the kind of existence these qualities make necessary. Freedom is a significant theme in most of the novels of the nineties, and Fleda's capacity as a *free* spirit is central to her situation in the novel. She is free first of all in the sense of being cut off, unconnected. Her intelligence isolates her from the average person. She is often misunderstood by both Owen and his mother, who accuse her of using "the strangest words" and who claim not to understand her motives. Fleda is characteristically in "deep and lonely meditation" when Mrs. Gereth first comes upon her in Chapter I, and she seldom moves far from this condition. We see her in the familiar role of the outsider, the observer, at first essentially uninvolved in the struggle between Mrs. Gereth and her son. When she is finally drawn into this struggle through love, she is made even more lonely, for she cuts herself off from Mrs. Gereth and is left either to her father's empty flat in West Kensington or to solitary possession of her sister's provincial drawing room. Her isolation is somewhat like Rose Armiger's, and her family situation is reminiscent of Kate Croy's and just as unrewarding.

Immediate consequences of her intellectual isolation can be found in Fleda's imaginative life. Although the isolation of intelligence gives her only a limited sort of freedom, it does allow her imagination to expand upon the materials of life with which her contact is so tenuous, and in this expansion Fleda's imagination is often naively romantic. Her first response to Ricks, for example, is to construct an "indulgent fancy" about the maiden aunt who had lived there and undoubtedly suffered. James also uses the cliché of the effects of novel-reading. Fleda several times pictures Owen as the hero of a novel, and he even becomes for her a ruddy medieval peasant. Part of her growth in the novel lies in overcoming this habit of constructing a "fairy tale" in which "she dodged and dreamed and fabled and trifled the time" (44).[14] Her romanticizing is the direct result of her sensitivity forced back on itself in her isolated freedom.

The limits imposed by her freedom also affect the nature of her moral response. For Fleda this means a kind of selflessness, an altruism which finds expression primarily in self-denial; in direct contrast to Rose Armiger, the isolated Fleda finds her morality to a great extent in social virtues, in loyalty and contractual bonds which personal relationships impose. This tension between isolated freedom and social obligation results in Fleda's self-denial. And in her isolation, half-consciously knowing herself better than the others, Fleda conceives morality as a kind of romantic heroism. She sees her heroism as self-denial, but also as "some high and delicate deed" which must be performed with a "kind of pride." Pride, heroism, high deeds are all a part of Fleda's freedom, her otherness. Her imagination and even her intellect give her only these romantic possibilities, and she sees herself for much of the novel as the noble heroine of a high-minded romance, a figure much like Conrad's Lord Jim.

Such is her freedom. Fleda is free to be a martyr, to surrender herself for high principles. The "free spirit" in *The Spoils of Poynton* is an intelligent, imaginative, isolated, and romantic moral idealist—"heroic, ironic, pathetic" as James said. Fleda is intelligent, sympathetic, and freer than the others, but at the same time she is hampered by the conditions of these traits. Her actuality imposes limits on her ideality. With the free spirit, who is the ideal in all James's novels, the condition of idealism

THE SPOILS OF POYNTON

must be merged with the conditions of life. One way in which James accomplished this is to limit the meaning of freedom, to give the heroine a mental and ideal freedom while restricting actual living freedom by isolation. Thus the free spirit is also "fixed" by her conditions. "Free" and "fixed" are not, then, necessarily applicable to different characters; there is no arbitrary system. The terms best describe a point in the action or an over-all tendency. Fleda's significance in this sense rests in her freedom and what she is able to perceive as a result of that freedom, in spite of romancing, naive, isolated, and inexperienced girlhood. The disparity between her heroism and her pathos is ironic, and it is also deeply meaningful. The way to that meaning is through the structure of an action of which Fleda is the central recording consciousness. James's experiment in character is bound in with experiments in form.

III

Fleda's structural role, which has been touched on above, is that of the central consciousness, "that member of the party in whose intenser consciousness we shall most profitably seek a reflexion of the little drama with which we are concerned" (10). The drama of *The Spoils of Poynton* is Fleda's growing awareness: "The progress and march of my tale became and remained that of her understanding."[15] From the middle of Chapter I we have no other viewpoint. In his initial notebook idea, or "germ," James had concentrated on the struggle between mother and son, but he soon added the third party, the observer who herself is drawn into the action and finally becomes the significance and subject: "The whole idea of my thing is that Fleda becomes rather fine, DOES something, distinguishes herself (to the reader), and that this is really all that has made the little anecdote worth telling at all."[16] The unity of the novel resides in Fleda, and one of the prime virtues of the central consciousness technique is that the novel has a residual center regardless of the vagaries of conception and form in its various parts. As it is in *The Sacred Fount* or *The Turn of the Screw*, the reader's attention is drawn to the mind through which he experiences. That mind is in no case a transparent medium; James is always concerned with the effects of experience on sensitive observers like Fleda Vetch, Lambert Strether, Merton Densher, or Maggie Verver.

Every novel, however, is an action, and (Samuel Beckett notwithstanding) only so much of that action can be mental, totally within the mind of the central character. Internal and external movements, mind and act, are combined in the structure. Structure itself, the way the author handles these movements, is revealed in technique and texture. In *The Spoils of Poynton* there is a considerable difference in these latter between the early and later chapters. Texture and technique in *The Other House* were consistently dramatic, and this suggests what is unusual about the first section of *The Spoils of Poynton*. There are no scenes, no extended dramatic passages; a few lines of dialogue now and then, and a few long speeches by Mrs. Gereth are all that break into the picture of Waterbath and Poynton in the first hundred pages. The first third of the novel, then, is nondramatic; it is simply a description and summary of Fleda's gathering perceptions of places and people. There is little narrative impetus to the section; events are subordinate in the impressionistic novel, which is what James started writing.

There are perhaps two explanations for this opening.

THE SPOILS OF POYNTON

First, we learn from the notebooks that James was, as usual, convinced at the start that he was writing a short story. His initial idea centered on the mother and son, the observing girl, and the resolution of the conflict over the things. All this was to be worked out in "three acts"; the story would run to about 15–20,000 words.[17] Even with this initial conception, which leaves out the love story and its complications of motive, James was forced to "summarize," to attempt to condense and foreshorten the action of his story. By the time he had written seventy pages of manuscript, however, he began to complain of lack of space, that there was "no room at all for my people to talk."[18] And this is quite apparent in the final version up through the meeting of Owen and Fleda in London (in Chapter VI). Conversations are merely reported, or described at second hand as they register in Fleda's mind, with only the essential remarks given verbatim. There is little dramatic immediacy in the whole section; we are inside Fleda's mind continually, with no relief through rendered action. The material, however, expands, and James is forced to accommodate additional and more complicated motives. He gives up the plan for three acts even before conceiving the love story: "My only issue, here . . . is in multiplying my divisions."[19]

In the same entry in which he complains of lack of room for talk, James hits upon what he feels will solve his problem:

What I feel more and more that I must arrive at, with these things, is the adequate and regular practice of some such economy of clear summarization as will *give* me from point to point, each of my steps, stages, tints, shades, every main joint and hinge, in its place, of my subject—give me, in a word, my clear order and expressed sequence . . . When I ask myself what there may have been to show for my long tribulation, my wasted years and patiences and pangs, of theatrical experiment, the answer, as I have already noted here, comes up as just possibly *this:* what I have gathered from it will perhaps have been exactly some such mastery of fundamental statement—of the art and secret of it, of expression, of the sacred mystery of structure.[20]

The solution is the principle of scenario, which will enable him to arrange and clarify the outlines and complexities, the structure of his story before he begins to write. This was to prove valuable for *The Ambassadors,* certainly, and perhaps for *The Awkward Age;* but *The Spoils of Poynton* was too far along for that principle to help what was already done, and, too, James was writing for immediate serial publication and so had no time for any extensive revision.

Two months later the notebooks reveal that the novel was still growing; James now estimates the length at 30,000 words—less than half the eventual total. He has yet to work his way into the second mode of the story, which, from the initial words of Chapter VIII, is "scenic": dialogue and dramatic scenes broken only by Fleda's meditations. In his notebook, although he keeps coming back in his "little theatrical trials," James is thinking primarily of scenario rather than scene. Finally, he begins to press for something "dramatic," "an absolute and unmitigated action."[21] After the completion of Chapters VIII and IX, which are totally scenic, there must have been little doubt in James's mind about the governing technique under which he was to proceed. For although he continues to try to hold down the length, in the last notebook entries on the novel, before composing the scene with Owen and Fleda at her father's flat, James

THE SPOILS OF POYNTON

recurs often to his dramatic conception. He speaks of "the SCENIC intensity, brevity, beauty—make it as straight as a pure little dramatic action."[22] And again, the novel must be "unarrested drama . . . a close little march of cause and effect"; it must be "as straight as a play."[23]

The notebooks thus reveal that James was still trying to work out his dramatic techniques, which adds to the initial handicap of the short-story conception. The use of scene, so consistent in *The Other House,* arrives late in *The Spoils of Poynton,* but it gives the novel considerable momentum when it comes. Dramatic intensity is achieved by the scenic method, first used at length in Chapter VIII; and although the first chapters are excellent in their manner, that manner was not suitable to a whole novel. The change in mode is also related directly to a change in idea; Owen's tacit declaration of love in Chapter VIII draws Fleda into the center of the conflict. With the central consciousness now the central actor instead of merely observer, directly involved in every action, James is free to cast his fiction in dramatic scenes and thus recover some of the "waste" of the dramatic years. This effort in *The Spoils of Poynton* at bringing together the central consciousness and the scenic method becomes, after further experiment in novels like *What Maisie Knew,* the characteristic Jamesian fictional technique, familiar in *The Ambassadors, The Wings of the Dove,* and *The Golden Bowl.*

The lessons of the notebooks point toward the replacement of the short story by the drama as a source for technique and help to explain the differences in texture in the novel. But the dramatic method introduces further structural questions. James first conceived *The Spoils of Poynton* (or *The House Beautiful,* as he called it) "in three chapters, like 3 little acts,"[24] and at least one critic has based his analysis on that form.[25] This, I think, tends to disregard both James's comments in his notebooks on the difficulties he was having with the complexity and length of the novel and the actual structure of the novel as we read it. James was unable to keep his action within three acts, and the divisions that do become apparent in reading reflect equally separate phases of the action and changes of place. Place is extremely important in the novel,[26] and an outline of the progressive phases of the action and a notation of movement from place to place will point up that significance and clarify the actual structure.

The first phase of the action more or less corresponds to the opening short-story-like chapters discussed above. Opening at Waterbath, the setting moves through London to Poynton, with a short visit to Ricks at the end of Chapter V. This phase of the action ends in Chapter VI, which provides a transition from Poynton back through London to the long stay at Ricks. These first five chapters correspond to the exposition in a play. The oppositions among the characters are established (Owen and Mona versus Mrs. Gereth, Fleda, and "the things"). Mrs. Gereth's fear of Owen's marriage, her disinheritance, and Fleda's "appreciation" are all introduced. In this first movement the main emphasis is on Mrs. Gereth, her fears, and her quarrel with her son. Fleda's infatuation with Owen and her determination to protect him are only touched on and are secondary to her role as companion and sympathizer to Mrs. Gereth. Finally with Owen's engagement and the preliminary visit to Ricks, the complication of the action is almost prepared for. Chapter VI is, as noted, transitional. In London for her sister's marriage,

Fleda encounters Owen alone and his attraction to her is made evident. The exposition is now complete and the material for the complication established, in much the same way that James uses the first chapters of *The Other House* as a prologue. The generalized, nondramatic summary of Mrs. Gereth's misfortune has also reached a limit, for without some dramatic action it would lapse into mere squabble and stalemate.

Chapter VII opens the complication of the action, the second phase, which extends through Chapter XII. The entire section is set at Ricks, and the action is far more dramatic, leading to an extended scene in Chapter VIII. In Chapter VII Fleda arrives at Ricks to find that Mrs. Gereth has carried off all the treasures of Poynton. This complicates both the question of the fate of the spoils and Fleda's own personal feelings of commitment to both Owen and his mother. It forces her toward a choice, although she cannot at the moment make one. This section builds through dramatic scenes to two climaxes which further implicate Fleda in the action. Although the thread that controls the movement of the characters is still the fate of the spoils, Owen's attraction to Fleda and her own gathering emotions begin to replace Mrs. Gereth's motives at the center of the story. In this section the novel actually becomes Fleda's story, with her conflict partly the conventional one of love (for Owen) versus duty (to Mrs. Gereth and the things). Her sense of duty, however, is complicated by her feeling that rightfully the spoils belong at Poynton, that Mrs. Gereth is in the wrong. The problem of duty is introduced in Chapter VII, as Fleda reacts to Mrs. Gereth's transfer of the spoils. The initial climax immediately follows; the interview with Owen in Chapter VIII introduces the love theme. There is then a pause in the action, a meditation scene (Chapter IX) in which Fleda decides that there are three secrets she must keep: her own feelings, Owen's feelings, and her knowledge that Mona will not marry unless the spoils are restored. Fleda's moral role is further complicated when Mrs. Gereth guesses two of the secrets: Fleda's love for Owen and the cause of Mona's behavior. The second climax of the section is this recognition scene between Fleda and Mrs. Gereth (Chapter XI). Love now rules Fleda's emotions, and her moral determination to keep the secret of Owen's love controls her actions. The second phase ends with what is to become a characteristic period of Fleda waiting for something to happen. Mrs. Gereth urges her to act, but her only act is to flee Mrs. Gereth, to get away from the overriding will of another (Chapter XII).

The first two phases of the action comprise only a little over half the novel. The double movement of the action focuses first on the fate of the spoils and then on Fleda and her relationship with Owen. The second phase complicates both questions, interweaving them intricately so that any decision Fleda makes will affect equally either the fate of the spoils or her love for Owen. In technique James has moved from impressionistic narration to dramatic scenes. Each chapter in the second section is a separate scene in which Fleda is present with either Mrs. Gereth or Owen, or a meditation in which Fleda is alone. The result is a division of the action into the love question when Owen is present and the material question when Mrs. Gereth is the antagonist. Fleda, of course, provides the unity, tying both themes together in her involvement and in her intervening meditations.

It is tempting to see the rest of the novel as a third act, the resolution of the action. It is this, in a sense, but as such it would be disproportionately long, as long as the first two acts combined, and it does tend to divide into smaller units approximately equal in length to each of the first two sections. Thus, it seems to me that Chapters XIII-XVI form a unit and Chapters XVII-XX another, with the final two chapters (XXI-XXII) an epilogue, a restoration of order and final, ironic completion of the action. Each of these units follows the same pattern: three chapters in London followed by a visit to Maggie at her provincial home. The principal difference between the two is that in the third section Owen is Fleda's antagonist and in the fourth Mrs. Gereth is.

The development of the love relationship is central to the third section. Owen and Fleda meet in London, at her father's West Kensington flat, and pretend to discuss the recovery of the spoils. Here most of the dialogue concerns Owen's engagement to Mona, but after fleeing to her sister Maggie's, Fleda finally reveals her love to Owen. She enforces his pledge to Mona, however, insists that Mona herself must break it, and sends Owen back. This combination of climax—the discovery and revelation of love—and anti-climax—the self-imposed separation of the lovers—propels the action into the fourth section. The love motif has assumed complete control of Fleda's actions, and is the central concern in the novel.

This control is emphasized by the initial action of the fourth movement. After Owen has left Fleda waiting for ten days (a clear indication of her fate), Mrs. Gereth resumes her place by Fleda and reveals that what before was central to the reader's expectations, the return of the spoils, has already been accomplished off-stage. Anticlimatically, Mrs. Gereth has returned the spoils in anticipation of Owen's giving up Mona and marrying Fleda.

She has ironically accomplished just the opposite, removing the only obstacle that was holding Mona back. Mona then takes advantage of Owen's weakness and Fleda's moral scruples and gets all the "spoils," the "things" and Owen. The movement of this phase is toward a partial resolution, and the gradual revelation of the catastrophe in the first two chapters of this section is heightened by the pathetic search for Owen in the third (XIX). The last chapter of this fourth section, again at Maggie's, shows both Fleda and Mrs. Gereth in pathetic collapse after the failure of the chance for love and the chance for the things.

The climax of the action in this fourth section is the fine obligatory scene between Fleda and Mrs. Gereth at the hotel in London. James brilliantly matches the materialistic, worldly vitality of Mrs. Gereth against the idealistic, naive sensitivity of Fleda. The scene, entirely in dialogue, is an argument or debate (similar to that between Rose Armiger and Jean Martle in *The Other House*) in which each proclaims her view of the world as she tries to understand her failure. We shall have to come back to these two views, but the scene is superb in itself, and equally impressive as a resolution, a climax to the action of the novel. After this there can only be collapse.

The final two chapters can only be seen as an epilogue, a method of relieving the tensions and feelings that have been exposed in the fourth section of the novel. Chapter XXI, the return of Fleda and Mrs. Gereth to Ricks, provides this relief. Explicit in the chapter is Fleda's recognition of what has happened, the restoration of order through self-knowledge. The last chapter of the novel continues the epilogue, but the final destruction of the spoils in the fire at Poynton is an incident that must be examined more fully below in direct relation to the total meaning of the novel. It is neither an afterthought nor an ironic twist; the fire fully rounds out the action. Without it the reader would be left with a sense of incompleteness, with some of his expectations unsatisfied.

This four-part movement, five if we include the epilogue, gives us an understanding of the structure of the action. It is a movement from material questions to emotional and moral ones, from duty into love and, finally, the combination of the two. And the structure after the initial section, is dramatic, a series of confrontation scenes building to a climax in Chapter XVIII. Fleda is increasingly drawn into the current of the action until she is swept off her feet by love and attempts to pull herself out with a moral act. The meaning implicit in this structure is the meaning of Fleda's actions; and an additional element in that meaning is the role of place in the structure of the novel.

Alan H. Roper has pointed out the significance of place in the battle imagery of the novel, and he has noted the use of a flight metaphor.[27] Fleda, for example, characteristically flees from Owen at the end of each interview (she twice scrambles up the stairs in an effort to get above the action). But looked at with structure in mind, place and flight combined reveal an additional pattern. We must remember that Fleda really has no "place," "no home of her own." Poynton represents the good and beautiful to her both aesthetically and materially (in a way similar to Rose Armiger's attachment to Bounds and Wilverley). The entire movement of the novel is an enforced retreat, a withdrawal on Fleda's part from the initial vision of Poynton. From Poynton she goes to Ricks, a surrogate

Poynton, filled during her visit with the spoils of the more magnificent house. From Ricks she descends even further to London and her father's tawdry flat, with its pathetic collections and "smutty maid," and thence to Maggie's unpleasant provincial town. She returns to London once more, but to a hotel and to an uncertain wandering through the streets (no fixed "place" at all). The final collapse is again at Maggie's, far removed from the splendors of Poynton. This downward spiral into no-place reflects the pattern of Fleda's action—a flight, withdrawal, sacrifice, a retreat into the wasteland where she learns the meaning of her actions and of life. This somewhat mythic pattern is recapitulated in the last two chapters with the return to Ricks (less the spoils), the final journey through the wasteland of London, and the pilgrimage to Poynton only to see it also wasted, by fire—despoiled for all possession. This whole symbolic movement reflects the progress of Fleda Vetch in mind and body through the novel.

IV

One important link between the structural patterns we have been tracing and the themes and meaning of the novel is the pattern of Fleda's thoughts. The movement of Fleda's mind reflects both the structure and the arrangement of themes in the novel. Fleda's thought patterns, when she is consciously intellectualizing, are almost always logical. Her essential impulse is toward hypothesis and plans of action, careful analysis of cause and effect and a consequent determination, with the aid of her moral sensibilities, of the proper act. She is seen often "inventing a remedy or a compromise . . . preparing a plan" (44). An example will illustrate the general character of Fleda's meditations. Mrs. Gereth has told Fleda that she would send the spoils back from Ricks to Poynton for her:

> To send the things back "for her" meant of course to send them back if there were even a dim chance that she might become mistress of them. Fleda's palpitation was not allayed as she asked herself what portent Mrs. Gereth had suddenly descried of such a chance: the light could be there but by a sudden suspicion of her secret. This suspicion in turn was a tolerably straight consequence of that implied view of the propriety of surrender from which she was well aware she could say nothing to dissociate herself. What she first felt was that if she wished to rescue the spoils she wished also to rescue her secret. So she looked as innocent as she could and said as quickly as she might: "For me? Why in the world for me?" (115)

And she proceeds to act out the consequences of her thought. The language of the passage is abstract, a careful probing of cause and possible effect, of the motives and behavior of others. Fleda's emotions are implicated in her thoughts, but the language remains that of reasoning and logic. This is James's characteristic mode of portraying the consciousness of his central consciousness; it can be seen again in almost all the novels to follow. And the logical movement of thought through cause and effect into action is the same mental activity that one discovers in James's notebooks, for his scenarios and notes are at bottom little more than an elaboration on the logical consequences of the given, with little room left for chance or absurdity. Fleda's intellectual patterns are revealed in passages of reflection like the above, in her innumerable plans always under continuous revision, and in her almost Socratic dialogues with Owen as she tries to teach him the right way to act.

The dialectic of moral analysis that goes on in Fleda's mind is a reflection of the thematic development of the whole novel; the following analysis by Fleda is typical of the manner:

> Fleda at this, felt her heroism meet its real test—felt that in telling [Owen] the truth [that with Mona out of the way his mother will return the spoils] she should effectively raise a hand to push his impediment out of the way. Was the knowledge that such a motion would probably dispose for ever of Mona capable of yielding to the conception of still giving her every chance she was entitled to? That conception was heroic, but at the same moment it reminded our young woman of the place it had held in her plan she was also reminded of the not less urgent claim of the truth. Ah the truth—there was a limit to the impunity with which one could juggle with that value, which in itself never shifted. (159)

The dialectic between truth and heroism, conceived both abstractly and as moral action, typifies the whole process of the novel. Fleda is the juggler here, but no greater one than James in his handling of the themes of the novel. Our search for meaning, therefore, must be in the abstract, and at the same time dramatic, conflict of opposites, antithetical modes of action and of principles.

In the "moral drama" of *The Spoils of Poynton,* the major themes of love, morality, and action are inseparable from their antitheses: possession, practicality, and inaction or sterility. And the major themes themselves are often in conflict; love and morality are at odds in the last half of the novel, and the problem of action implicitly underlies the development of Fleda's understanding throughout the novel. Knowledge and innocence, will and sterility, freedom and fixity, are all correlates of the question of action and involve the other major questions of the novel. Parallel to these themes is the separate but important one of art, with the aid of which Fleda arrives at moral understanding. In such a schematization of abstractions one must not overlook the dynamic nature of the dramatic novel itself. Just as one of the structural patterns is movement from place to no-place, so within Fleda's experience there is movement—from innocence to knowledge, from her early romantic conceptions to her final, more stoical ones. There is perhaps even movement from action to inaction, to an uninvolved state of mind. Meaning is given us in dramatic terms of movement, experience, growth; the philosophical drama is strongly based in the physical one.

The nature of Fleda's love is at the heart of the action. James makes clear the early, naive character of Fleda's infatuation. She conceives of marriage as a union of complementary characters: "She herself was prepared, if she should ever marry, to contribute all the cleverness, and she liked to figure it out that her husband would be a force grateful for direction" (10-11). One strong feature of her love through the first part of the novel is that it is mostly maternal: Owen has "a child's eyes" in a "man's face," and this appeals to Fleda. She desires through much of the novel "to cover him, to protect him." Even her final act, sending him back to Mona, has a good deal of the mother instructing her son in the proper way to behave. This is, of course, only one side of her love. There is also passion, and Fleda, as we have seen, is attracted by Owen's masculinity, his looks and his physical qualities. But there is often a disparity between what Fleda sees in Owen and what James shows us of him; where for Fleda he is simple and natural, for us he is stupid and uncontrolled. Both Fleda's infatuation and her passion are often colored by her romanticizing, by her seeing Owen as the "young gentleman," the hero of a novel, or as country squire. Fleda loves him, but Owen in the end fails her precisely because these social appearances are valueless and his personal qualities lack any nobility or self-control. Once Mona has him again, he cannot resist. Fleda's initial infatuation deepens to love and a desire to make something of Owen, but he responds only to mothering. Perhaps Mrs. Gereth's greatest failure is revealed by the character of her son. Fleda's love is strong and complex, but the taint of romanticizing makes it difficult for her to see Owen clearly, and she loses him.

The nature and complexity of this love are pointed up by the way Fleda acts and does not act in the novel. One of Fleda's primary reactions in her role as the innocent center of consciousness is bewilderment in the face of the "tangle of life." Fleda has great intelligence and imagination, but until the end of the novel she has little understanding. Her difficulty lies in not knowing how to act on what she perceives and feels, or not understanding why other people act the way they do. This gap between perception and act results in Fleda's inaction, or in her typically negative maneuvers. She keeps secrets, keeps quiet, tries not to show her response at all; note, for example, her responses to finding the spoils at Ricks and to Owen's various revelations of love. She does not act to keep Mrs. Gereth from carrying everything off, just as she does not leave Ricks after she has decided she must. There are various other representations of the same impulse; she typically runs away from Owen and does not let him know where she is, and she spends a good deal of the time simply waiting for something to happen, for someone else to act.

This passivity is reflected in the love relationship. Owen weakly tries to get Fleda to act for him, and she in turn tries to get him to act for himself and in effect relies on Mona for action. She continually finds her "safety in silence." Of course she has for the most part quite serious moral reasons for her behavior, but her passivity and unwillingness to act are thrown up against her as the novel comes to a climax. In the confrontation with Mrs. Gereth in Chapter XVIII Fleda's first recognition is of "how little she had done." Later she realizes that almost all she has done has been negative: "I . . . sent him back to her. I made him go, I pushed him out of the house. I declined to have anything to say to him" (219). Mrs. Gereth's final judgment, as the two of them are left at Ricks, is that Fleda is the only one who "comfortably understands" but that "for action you're no good at all" (245).

That Fleda is essentially passive and her actions generally negative is related to her moral responses to her situation. We have already seen that Fleda's morality is selfless, altruistic, and founded partly on a conception of romantic heroism. That morality also adds to and conflicts with the impulses to love and action. In much of the novel James describes Fleda's moral responses in a curious mixture of religious imagery and the language of a business contract, which leads to an uncertain mixture of manners and morals in determining Fleda's behavior. Fleda wishes to act with honor and without vulgarity, and at the same time she conceives the whole moral problem as Owen's keeping his word to Mona; his promise to marry is for Fleda his "sacred pledge" or, on the other hand, "keeping faith on an important clause of his contract." She early refers to the "kind of punctilio for a man known to be engaged" (65), and when he begins to show interest in her, "she asked herself what he had done . . . with his loyalty or at least with his 'form'" (64). Later, Fleda's conceptions are more clearly related to morality: "You mustn't break faith. Anything would be better than that . . . She must love you—how can she help it? *I* wouldn't give you up! . . . The great thing is to keep faith. Where's a man if he doesn't? If he doesn't he may be so cruel. So cruel, so cruel, so cruel!" (196-197). Even here, however, the nature of her moral response is complicated, first by the nature of Fleda's reaction to Owen's admission just preceding this moral outcry that he is not quite free of Mona: "'Ah you see it's not true that you're free!' She seemed *almost to exult.* 'It's not true, it's not true!'" (196, italics mine). Her exultation points to the negative and passive impulse, in the same way that her morality is restrictive, an imposition on her freedom, as well as Owen's. Mrs. Gereth's plea to Fleda to "let herself go" is countered by Fleda's acceptance of "full responsibility," an admirable morality, but one which points to the loss at the end of the novel. Fleda has the "courage to suffer," and her vow of silence to keep Owen's secret conflicts with "her little gagged and blinded desire." Fleda has not the courage to act, and her morality imposes restrictions on her freedom of emotion and action, and on that of others. At the end she gives up action with stoicism and "the vow of a nun."

Throughout the novel Fleda's scruples, which lead to inaction and renunciation, have been contrasted with Mrs. Gereth's practicality, her pragmatic use of Fleda to gain the ends she desires—a morality dictated by devotion to the spoils. This contrast, which has been pointed out by Eliseo Vivas,[28] is central to the moral scheme of the novel; for, in conflict as they are, as responses to life, as attempts to meet the demands life makes, they both fail of any great measure of success. Fleda is left more satisfied in her serenity in defeat than Mrs. Gereth in her bitter resignation, but both altruistic idealism and pragmatism have been found wanting when they conflict with the claims of life itself in its blindness and strength, its amorality.

This conflict is intensely dramatized in Chapter XVIII, in which Fleda and Mrs. Gereth each proclaim their own principles. Underlying the drama is the fact that Owen and the spoils are already lost. The woman and the girl, however, refuse to admit the finality of this, although their arguments are attempts to assign the guilt for the loss. Characteristically, Mrs. Gereth blames Owen and then Fleda, while Fleda insists on her own guilt. Typically Fleda, while perceiving what has happened and what her share in it is, is still bewildered, still feels ignorant: "I don't know what girls may do." Mrs. Gereth attacks Fleda's complexity of motive, her elaborate set of moral decisions which have kept her from acting: "your systematic . . . your idiotic perversity . . . such wonderful exactions . . . sweet little scruples" (219). Fleda recognizes this for what it is, "a showy side of the truth" but nonetheless part of the truth. Ironically she has in the midst of the diatribe "a blinding glimpse of lost alternatives," presumably all those that would have led to action and possible conquest rather than sacrifice and surrender. Mrs. Gereth's attack continues, and Fleda surrenders her last moral scruple; she consents to look for Owen. In her anger, Mrs. Gereth sets Fleda irreconcilably apart from the normal: "One doesn't know what one has hold of in touching you." Fleda eventually recovers enough of her self-possession to make one last plea for her way of seeing life: " 'You simplify far too much. You always did and you always will. The tangle of life is much more intricate than you've ever, I think, felt it to be. You slash into it,' cried Fleda finely, 'with a great pair of shears; you nip at it as if you were one of the Fates! If Owen's at Waterbath he's there to wind everything up' " (224). James is right in his choice of adverb. The speech is fine, the finest defence in the novel of Fleda's way of seeing. But the complexities and ironies in the speech reveal the weakness of Fleda's viewpoint. Most obviously, even if she doesn't really believe it, she draws the wrong conclusion from her fine generalizations; Owen is at Waterbath winding things up, but ironically in just the opposite way from Fleda's assertion. One can only say that the statement as a whole is both true and false. Life is both intricate and simple, complex and fine, and at the same time stupid, powerful, and crude. The result is of course chaos, a chaos of complexity and crudity. Fleda, in pleading for her own way of seeing, refuses to recognize the force of the simplest forms of life, the pure will of the Mona Brigstocks. The final irony of her judgment reveals that. And Mrs. Gereth's reply to the speech, violent as it is, is as true as Fleda's creed: "I do simplify, doubtless, if to simplify is to fail to comprehend the inanity of a passion that bewilders a young blockhead with bugaboo barriers, with hideous and monstrous sacrifices" (225). James indicates the exaggeration of the position in the alliteration as he indicated the weakness of the other in the false conclusion Fleda draws. Both visions are true, one "the showy side," the other the delicate and shaded side. Without the room to accommodate both, the reader will mistakenly side with one or the other. The reader must understand with the author that Fleda is at once "heroic, ironic, pathetic"; heroic from her own point of view, pathetic from Mrs. Gereth's, and ironic for the reader who must reconcile the two.

Questions of love, morality, and action are resolved in the synthesis toward which Fleda moves; and this movement is toward self-sacrifice and renunciation. Fleda's principal impulse is to sacrifice herself in love or for an altruistic morality, and her inaction is merely a reflection of this. Fleda's intellectual maneuvering can be seen in the dialectical form of establishing a position, testing it against life (the situation or one of the other characters), and then being forced to retreat, regroup, and establish a new, less secure position. At each move she learns something, but she also gives up some of her carefully guarded secrets or defenses. In Chapter XVI, for example, in her last interview with Owen, Fleda's plans have been reduced one by one to "the plan of separation" from Owen, and when she finally surrenders her last secret (her love for Owen) and herself, "it was as if a whirlwind had come and gone, laying low the great false front she had built up stone by stone. The strangest thing of all was the momentary sense of desolation" (189). Desolation is her fate in the total movement of the book, and the action is completed only when she surrenders her last resource, her dignity and moral sense, and goes searching for Owen with Mrs. Gereth. All her negations and inactions point to this, as does her slow retreat from place into no-place, from the splendors of Poynton to the mean provincial town. She has been used by Mrs. Gereth, but at the same time her own motives and ignorance have led to her being used; and she has in a sense accomplished her goals—

gotten the spoils away from Mrs. Gereth and kept Owen faithful to Mona—but this has meant her own martyrdom, has meant sacrifice to the point of desolation.

The spoils are ultimately involved in this desolation, and the development of the theme of art parallels this movement in the novel. Art, for Fleda, means knowledge; twice her experience with the spoils is referred to as "a taste of knowledge," an initiation. There is, on the other hand, a dichotomy, already noted between art and "the things"; and the spoils of Poynton stand for both. Throughout the novel the meaning of art is interwoven with the terms of its possession; the artist and the collector are combined and recombined. Mrs. Gereth is in a sense both, while Fleda's father represents the collector without a sense of beauty. At one time even the spoils are considered sterile: "No art more active than a Buddhistic contemplation could lift its head there" (148). Fleda, of course, is more than a collector. She paints, has taken lessons in Paris. After the loss of Owen, Fleda comes to a tentative understanding of the nature of art, an understanding completed only by the final chapter of the novel; thinking of the spoils, she reflects that she equally "was of the religion, and like any other of the passionately pious she could worship now even in the desert. Yes, it was all for *her;* far round as she had gone she had been strong enough: her love had gathered them in" (235). She holds the spoils in her imagination and visualizes them as immortal, outside of human concerns, existing only in her mind which no desire for possession can violate: "They were nobody's at all—too proud, unlike base animals and humans, to be reducible to anything so narrow" (235). Fleda finally understands art as something that can only be held in the mind with a strong, almost religious devotion and can best be held in that desolate desert to which she has been reduced and has reduced herself, giving up all the acquisitive hopes of base animals and humans. Art is thus something separate from the crudities of life, and the ambiguities about the spoils—art or thing—are removed only when Fleda has a vision of them beyond their physical embodiments. Here again, the impulse is toward separation from life, toward renunciation of the physical; although here of course there is something left to fill the desolate spaces.

The last two chapters are more in the main movement of the novel, although still concerned directly with the question of the spoils. The last two chapters resolve the action, provide an ending beyond the total despair at the end of Chapter XX. Fleda goes past her bewilderment to understanding and acceptance of her position. She becomes the philosopher, satisfied "in showing how serenely and lucidly she could talk," and after her "vow of a nun" at the end of Chapter XX she is "the one who knew most." Her knowledge derives from her renunciation; the experience of loss, failure, forces her to realize that she cannot judge others, or judge life, in terms of her own sensibility. She had acted that way with Mona and lost Owen as a result. Finally, in "her great command of her subject," she understands Mona: "She's a person who's upset by failure and who blooms and expands with success." This charitable judgment implies just the reverse in herself, a person devoted to failure and unable to accommodate success. She sounds a note true to her own sense of life when in Chapter XXI she describes the quality of life at Ricks after the failure as "the impression somehow of something dreamed and missed, something reduced, relinquished, resigned: the poetry, as it were, of something sensibly *gone*" (249). Embodied in this is Fleda's whole experience in the novel and the whole poetry of her character.

One can only understand the last chapter, which concludes with the burning of Poynton,[29] in the light of these central themes. The burning is more than just the final result of the storm of passion.[30] The chapter is in a sense outside the movement of the book; the action is complete, and order has been restored in the preceding chapter. One must see this chapter, then, as a coda, a symbolic recapitulation of the themes and movements of the novel. In it Fleda learns her lesson over again with finality. Once again she goes to Poynton "as a pilgrim might go to a shrine." She moves through the wasteland of London and out into the storm. Her motive is to recover physically something of the spoils of Poynton and of her love, symbolized by the Maltese Cross, which combines again the motifs of art and religion. And she goes at the behest of Owen, of love. Her journey and the fire, then, symbolize the entire pattern of loss in the novel. It is the one final sacrifice which burns understanding into Fleda's mind. The "cruel, cruel night" in which Poynton burns leaves her with a mature tragic knowledge which goes beyond the easy stoical acceptance of the scene at Ricks. "She felt herself give everything up," and she feels "the raw bitterness of a hope that she might never again in life have to give up so much at such short notice" (266). She experiences once again her sacrifices and all the pain with them. The lesson of love and possession, of isolation and the attempt to grasp life, is retold here. Theme and form come together in the symbolic, destructive action of the fire, and we are left with the final irony in the ambiguity of the station-master's reply to Fleda's disbelief in the loss: "What can you call it, miss, if it ain't really saved?" The fire is the final physical denial, but it may also be the final spiritual gain.

The basic form of the novel thus becomes clearer. It is essentially a form of sacrifice, a "tragedy of renunciation." And yet James claims that Fleda is successful in remaining free. Actually, the novel shows us that freedom is desolate and tragic, a freedom of the spirit without the freedom to engage life. One aspect of Fleda's character tells more about this. There is something in her of the old-fashioned, stereotyped Victorian girl, who wants in her passivity to be taken, who denies her own possibility of action, in contrast to the modern girl who could act for herself (the same contrast can perhaps be drawn between Milly Theale and the Maggie Verver of the last half of *The Golden Bowl*). The old morality, the strong "moral sense," that Maisie confronts, is represented in Fleda; and under the old morality the young girl does not reveal her love. We can see this psychology operating when Fleda in her revulsion from failure (Chapter XVIII) characterizes her love as "idiotic" and "strange"—"from the first there was a bitterness and a dread" (217). Fleda is drawn far down into a situation which finally destroys the old morality, makes her go out looking for Owen. She is forced to sacrifice everything she has thought she was.

What we are left with, and what Fleda is left with, is an irreconcilable split between the self and life. The fear of life which forces James to place art on a level of pseudo-religious mystique, which forces him to find his story in the "germ" and to hate the expansion life gives to it, is the same fear that he has dramatized in Fleda, in her constant struggle with and retreat from the blind forces of life. James characteristically writes a drama of the consciousness, and in *The Spoils of Poynton* all his values are finally in that consciousness, the spiritual freedom that is left to Fleda. But in this novel, the consciousness is so pure that it cannot be reconciled with, or joined to, life as it is lived. James admits in his preface that Fleda is "sterile," that she can only appreciate, not act. Biographically, the retreat from life may reflect James's reaction to his failures on the stage. But the subject has taken hold, and the subsequent novels deal with the conflict between consciousness and life in a variety of ways. Fleda has recognized the lesson of the conflict and she recognizes it most strongly at the moment when her final gesture fails, when she is forced to give up everything. The movement of the novel, in Fleda's mental development and in the action, is a continuous stripping of all Fleda's mental defenses; and life is left in triumph. The spirit is left free but the connection with life is broken. The structure of the novel points toward that separation. Life goes on, and the spirit goes on, to the infinite loss of both.

Many aspects of *The Spoils of Poynton* can be found in the novels that follow. Fleda is as innocent and unworldly as all the later young girls we meet, even Maisie in her childhood. But, although this innocence is central to Fleda's failure, it is not the central theme it becomes in *What Maisie Knew* or *The Awkward Age*. The experiment with the central consciousness becomes more and more an analysis of consciousness itself, an examination of its relationship with life and with the meaning of reality. The understanding of moral action merges with discovering what is real (something Fleda never questions). There are also further experiments with structure and technique, with dramatic scenes and dialectic patterns, in an effort to achieve what James called "organic form."

James comes close to his goal in the last phases of *The Spoils of Poynton*, and as he focuses more closely on Fleda and the themes immediately related to her role in the novel, he discovers a structure that will hold drama, central consciousness, and theme tightly together. The experiment of *The Spoils of Poynton* is successful in itself, for we cannot fail to be moved and to sense the importance of the experience, and that experiment is immensely fruitful for the novels to follow.

5

What Maisie Knew

NOW fully recommitted to the novel, James began a third immediately upon finishing *The Other House* in August 1896. This third novel, *What Maisie Knew,* took him almost a year to write and is more complex and ultimately more profound than either of the two preceding novels, which together were completed in just over a year. Although character, technique, and theme in *What Maisie Knew* occasionally echo *The Other House* and *The Spoils of Poynton,* James gave himself a much more difficult artistic problem to solve in his new novel. For by selecting a young child as the central consciousness, James is led to examine the process of education and the ability to distinguish between reality and appearance, truth and falsity—epistemological problems hardly touched on in the previous two novels. At the same time, using a child as register of all the action and perception in the novel requires a careful distinction between what she sees and what she understands or "knows." In *What Maisie Knew,* as in Twain's

Huckleberry Finn or Joyce's *A Portrait of the Artist as a Young Man,* this is primarily a matter of style, the development of a linguistic method of showing the reader what Maisie sees which will simultaneously indicate the meaning to him, even though the child herself may not, probably will not, be fully aware of that meaning. James notes this difficulty in his preface:

> Design . . . would be to make and to keep her so limited consciousness the very field of my picture while at the same time guarding with care the integrity of the objects represented . . . The one presented register of the whole complexity would be the play of the child's confused and obscure notation of it, and yet the whole, as I say, should be unmistakeably, should be honourably there, seen through the faint intelligence, or at the least attested by the imponderable presence, and still advertising its sense.[1]

This double-vision demands great artistic skill, much more than that required by the character of Fleda Vetch, and James's careful tracing of Maisie's perceptions as the distance gradually narrows between sensations and understanding is a major achievement in the form of the novel.

What Maisie Knew grows out of one of Henry James's characteristic "germs": an anecdote heard at dinner in November 1892. James jotted down the story in his notebook and returned to it in August 1893, in the middle of his dramatic years, with the notion of writing a short story of some 10,000 words.[2] He evidently dropped the story for two more years and picked it up around December 22, 1895, while writing *The Spoils of Poynton,* again conceiving it as a short story which he hoped to publish in *The Yellow Book.* On that date James worked out the story at some length, planning ten chapters but still estimating the length at 10,000 words.[3] He again took it no further, perhaps realizing that it was too complex to be so easily accomplished, for there are no further entries until September 1896, after *The Other House* had been completed. At that time James indicated that he had written the first four sections, and the next notebook entry on the novel a month later shows him fully involved with his subject. Characteristically, in his last entry on the novel in December 1896, James estimated that another 10,000 words would finish it.[4] The novel expanded considerably as he worked on it and he did not complete it for another seven or eight months after he had reached about 90,000 words. *What Maisie Knew* was finally published serially over the spring and summer of 1897 and in book form in the fall of the year.[5]

What Maisie Knew shows James in his full power as a novelist. It reflects his major preoccupations during this period, which had begun to form in the two preceding novels and were to mark his work past the end of the century. A concern with tawdriness in London high life, reminiscent of the unpleasant affairs in *A London Life* (1889), and its effect on an innocent character becomes central in this novel and in the two following novels. Characters in *What Maisie Knew* reflect the special types that James was attracted to, types familiar to the reader of *The Other House* and *The Spoils of Poynton* and even earlier novels, but there is further development here. The themes of morality, freedom, knowledge, and perception (all but the last of which are important in the two previous novels) receive even fuller treatment in *What Maisie Knew*. Finally, in structure and technique, James continued to experiment with a central consciousness and a dramatic form, but in *What Maisie Knew* both these techniques, and many other structural procedures, are so fused as to reflect almost perfectly the meaning of the novel.

II

One could examine the characters in *What Maisie Knew* under the terms that James affixed to those in *The Spoils of Poynton*—free spirits and fools. That distinction will again be useful, but the characters in the present novel go beyond those categories in various ways; Maisie in particular, as the free spirit, and Sir Claude, as the fool or fixed character, expand the meaning of these respective labels. Freedom itself becomes a major theme and the implications of it are clearer in the conclusion of the story, in which character and theme merge. We must approach these themes first through James's characterization.

In remaining true to the lessons learned in the theater, James focuses his story on a handful of characters who themselves revolve about the center of consciousness, Maisie Farange. The half-dozen characters in *What Maisie Knew* fall into three pairs, more or less balanced, but subject to changes under the dramatic tensions of the novel. Beale and Ida Farange, Maisie's actual mother and father, form one pair; her eventual step-parents, Mrs. Beale (formerly Miss Overmore) and Sir Claude, form a second; and Maisie and her last governess, Mrs. Wix, form a third (although this last is not truly accomplished until the end of the novel). Around these central pairs, who provide the dramatic action of the novel, there are a number of minor characters who increase the richness of the novel (and keep the reader amused as James would insist) but who contribute little to the dramatic action—robust cockney nurses and maids, like Moddle and Susan Ash, and the at once sympathetic and repellent lovers of Maisie's parents, ironically named the Captain and the Countess.

The two who fit most closely the category of fixed character or fool are Maisie's divorced parents, Beale and Ida Farange. Neither changes in the course of the novel; both are there primarily to "minister . . . to the intensity of the free spirit engaged with them."[6] Both are vile, unfeeling, self-centered, and grotesque figures, who are in direct contrast to Maisie and who gain our interest only in their relation to Maisie, since we see them through her. James dwells on this quality of interest in his preface; his comments are valuable to an understanding of the role Maisie's parents have in the novel:

> Ida Farange alone, so to speak, or Beale alone, that is either of them otherwise connected—what intensity, what "objectivity" (the most developed degree of being anyhow thinkable for them) would they have? How would they repay at all the favour of our attention?
>
> Maisie makes them portentous all by the play of her good faith, makes her mother above all . . . concrete, immense and awful; so that we get, for our profit, and get by an economy of process interesting in itself, the thoroughly pictured creature, the striking figured symbol.[7]

The "economy of process" renders them perfectly; in contrast to their daughter they are most often pictured not dramatized, and the exaggerations which are part of the process turn them into symbolic figures, something slightly different from operative characters.

Beale Farange, the simpler and less potent of the two (the less frightening for Maisie), is portrayed in the first part of the novel only by his appearance, vulgarity, and loud sociability. James sets the tone and establishes the pertinent details in his initial description, in the short five-page overture to the novel which introduces the situation and the Faranges. That tone and those details never change in quality:

> Beale Farange had natural decorations, a kind of costume in his vast fair beard, burnished like a gold breastplate, and in the eternal glitter of the teeth that his long moustache had been trained not to hide and that gave him, in every possible situation, the look of the joy of life. He had been destined in his youth for diplomacy and momentarily attached, without a salary, to a legation which enabled him often to say, "In *my* time in the East": but contemporary history had somehow no use for him, had hurried past him and left him in perpetual Piccadilly.[8]

"Perpetual Piccadilly" is definitely part of the contemporary scene in this novel, and one characteristic that James returns to again and again is a concern for personal appearance. In the one scene in which Beale Farange is directly, dramatically present for any extended period, James repeatedly notes in an ironic tone those "natural" details of appearance: Beale continually looks at his clothes and stands "with his nose at the glass . . . while he brushed specks of ash out of his beard" (184). The burnished breastplate of a beard and the glittering teeth are his marks; he is more a suit of armor than a human being. The metallic cast to the man is part of James's comic surface and serves to fix the character in the same dehumanizing way in which James had treated the Brigstocks in *The Spoils of Poynton*.

James dwells even longer and more acidly on the figure of Ida Farange. He concentrates on her appearance and indicates an essential unreality or inhumanity of character and a pervading quality of exaggeration or grotesqueness which becomes bitterly comic. Ida "carried clothes, carried them as a train carries passengers" (8). She is a "picturesque parent" (69) whose "visits [to Maisie] were as good as an outfit; her manner . . . as good as a pair of curtains" (86). The note of sexual promiscuity is also introduced through Ida's appearance: her neckline is cut "remarkably low" and "the lower the bosom was cut the more it was to be gathered she was wanted elsewhere [than in the nursery]" (86). When she appears to Maisie for the last time in the garden at Folkestone, she is again a suit of clothes, "a high fair drapery . . . which had glided toward [Maisie] over the grass" (208). More than merely garments, however, Ida is also an actress—perhaps like Rose Armiger, only Ida has nothing to hide behind her false appearance. She, like Beale, poses before the mirror, if only figuratively: "[She] postured to her utmost before the last little triangle of cracked glass to which so many fractures had reduced the polished plate of filial superstition" (218). James invests all this appearance and posturing with a grotesqueness which becomes both comic and horrifying. She is like "some gorgeous idol" with "huge painted eyes—they were like Japanese lanterns swung under festal arches" (143). When she looks at one of her lovers it is with a "face that was like an illuminated garden, turnstile and all, for the frequentation of which he had his season ticket" (144). All the unnatural images converge in one which places Ida alongside Beale as more an inanimate object than a human being; when she embraces her daughter, Maisie can only feel "as if she had suddenly been thrust, with a smash of glass, into a jeweller's shop-front" (145). Ida's principal characteristic, both "natural" and comic, is of course her proficiency at billiards, a result of "the sole flaw in Ida's beauty . . . a length and reach of arm" which is evidently exceptional (7). "Billiards was her great accomplishment and the distinction her name always first produced mention of" (7). References to this talent (an example of James's frugal but extremely effective use of detail) occur throughout the novel and in contrast to her failure as a mother can only heighten our impression of Ida's abject and comic grotesqueness.

Ida and Beale are both figures who amuse and repel; James's scorn and exaggeration reinforce our understanding of Maisie's fear of her parents, her instinctive withdrawal from contact with them. For to her, in addition to being outlandish, they are huge ("they made up together, for instance, some twelve feet three of stature" [7]) and vicious, perfectly willing to sacrifice Maisie to their pleasures or to ignore her entirely. The two of them represent their society at its worst. They are symbols of triviality and decadence and have no other dramatic role than the fixed one of representing a broader society and setting off Maisie's innocence.

The second pair of characters, Sir Claude and Mrs. Beale, are Maisie's step-parents, married to Ida and Beale and eventually involved in an affair with each other. Mrs. Beale is Maisie's governess at first, as Miss Overmore, and although her name is significant of her character, she is much the simpler of the two. Mrs. Beale is at first, like Rose Armiger, another of James's disinherited characters, poor and in search of wealth and security. She likes Maisie enough to give her some of the affection her parents do not, and Maisie is attracted both by the affection and by her beauty, but the governess is attracted by the gaiety of Beale's social life and his attractive, man-of-the-world appearance.[9] Her excessive susceptibility to men (note again her maiden name) also turns her away from Maisie after she has replaced Beale with Sir Claude; James ironically hints that consultations with Sir Claude over Maisie's studies provide the excuse for "the obscure intercourse she enjoyed with Sir Claude" (163). Mrs. Beale remains much the same throughout the novel, until she becomes violent in the conclusion when trying to hold her gains. Although she provides one of Maisie's various alternatives and a further example of the sexual promiscuity of the adult society, she seems until the final scenes little more than a figure set in to balance the number of characters (two parents, two remarriages, two step-parents, and so forth).

Sir Claude first appears in a picture that Mrs. Wix shows Maisie, and she is entranced by his "general glossiness and smartness" (48), just as she is initially by Mrs. Beale's beauty. Again, when she first meets him, his appearance wins her: "He was by far the most shining presence that had ever made her gape" (57). Maisie rapidly converts this presence into a figure of romance: "He looked . . . quite as Mrs. Wix, in the long stories she told her pupil, always described the lovers of her distressed beauties—'the perfect gentleman and strikingly handsome'" (61). It is later significant that these clichés come first from Mrs. Wix; but it is also important that both Maisie and Mrs. Wix eventually come to think of him as a kind of romantic prince. This romantic figure is flawed, however, by his weakness for women, his ready submission to them, which accounts for his marriage to Ida. He is, like a great many "perfect gentlemen" in James's novels, essentially decent, honorable, well-mannered, and foolishly weak. Like Tony Bream and Owen Gereth he is attractive to women but really helpless before them. He is the same unconscious, hearty gentleman they are; but this is only a part of his character.

Sir Claude has another dimension lacking in many of James's gentlemen; he, alone with Mrs. Wix in the novel, senses the horror in Maisie's position. He can escape the limits of his ego and see the results of actions for other people, as, for example, in his recognition of what Ida has actually done by abandoning her daughter. Sir Claude sees that Ida's

> "action is just a hideous crime. It happens to satisfy our sympathies in a way that's quite delicious; but that doesn't in the least alter the fact that it's the most abominable thing ever done. She has chucked our friend here [Maisie] overboard not a bit less than if she had shoved her, shrieking and pleading, out of that window and down two floors to the paving-stones." (244-245)

This kind of moral perception, reinforced emotionally by the concluding image, and Sir Claude's general intelligence set him somewhat above his predecessors Tony Bream and Owen Gereth. These attributes mark Sir Claude as a step toward later heroes, ineffectual men who have some recognition of their own responsibility and weakness, like Vanderbank and Mitchett in *The Awkward Age* and especially Merton Densher in *The Wings of the Dove*. For Sir Claude, although fixed by his weaknesses and unable to change, is the only one who can grasp the final meaning of the action, who can understand what Maisie knows and has become. Perception and decency balance weakness; intelligence makes him something between fool and free spirit.

Mrs. Wix, Maisie's governess, is also something of a

fool and something of a saint. She is old and dowdy, a "frump" James calls her in his notebook entries. Her physical appearance is grotesque, although not as frightening or outlandish as Ida's, and the details of it are significant of her plainness even of mental attitude and her role in the novel:

> She wore glasses which, in humble reference to a divergent obliquity of vision, she called her straighteners, and a little ugly snuff-coloured dress trimmed with satin bands in the form of scallops and glazed with antiquity. The straighteners, she explained to Maisie, were put on for the sake of others, whom, as she believed, they helped to recognise the bearing, otherwise doubtful, of her regard; the rest of the melancholy garb could only have been put on for herself. With the added suggestion of her goggles it reminded her pupil of the polished shell or corslet of a horrid beetle. (25)

The straighteners symbolize both Mrs. Wix's faulty vision and her way of looking at the world; and her dress distinguishes her from the rest of Maisie's society. Maisie, however, is closer to her than any other person in the novel.

Mrs. Wix, in spite of her grotesquenesses, is the one character with whom Maisie immediately feels secure; Maisie feels "the charm in Mrs. Wix's conveying that somehow, in her ugliness and her poverty, she was peculiarly and soothingly safe" (26). She is trite, speaks repeatedly in clichés ("He's a slave to his passions," "You've nipped it in the bud"), and yet she shares with Maisie the pleasures of childhood: "Her conversation was practically an endless narrative, a great garden of romance" (27). She thus functions in the novel as Maisie's companion, her only friend, in a way the familiar Jamesian confidante (especially near the end in Chapters XXV and XXVI). She can share Maisie's experience because she is something of an undeveloped child herself, who only makes a fool of herself when she ventures into the adult world and exhibits her fascination with Sir Claude.

She shares Maisie's infatuation and romantically adores Sir Claude in a way that is both pathetic and comic. Her imaginary romance begins with her first sight of his portrait and develops through the early chapters of the novel in various dreams of an establishment just for Maisie, Sir Claude, and herself. Eventually her jealousy of Sir Claude's lover, Mrs. Beale, colors all her judgments and she is blinded even to Maisie. James develops the passion to an almost ridiculous girlishness when, in response to Sir Claude's asking why his ostensible freedom from his spouse is any different from that of Mrs. Beale which she has just attacked, Maisie watches Mrs. Wix respond: "Maisie could scarcely believe her eyes as she saw the good lady, with whom she had associated no faintest shade of any art of provocation, actually, after an upward grimace, give Sir Claude a great giggling insinuating naughty slap" (256). Her naughty insinuation, of course, is that his freedom allows him to be with Mrs. Wix. James adds a few lines later an ironic comparison between Cleopatra and Mrs. Wix in her "infinite variety" —"Age cannot wither . . ." Finally she offers herself to Sir Claude in desperation and in a way that is almost sexual: " 'We'll go off together and we'll live together without a cloud. Take me, Take me,' she went on and on"—as James comments, "an exhibition that, combined with her intensity and her decorations, appeared to suggest her for strange offices and devotions, for ridiculous replacements and substitution" (262-63).[10] The excess and grotesqueness of her feelings contrasts with Maisie's own adoration of Sir Claude, but it also tends to color many of her other characteristics.

Mrs. Wix combines with her appearance and pathetic passion a strict, prudish morality, a narrow vision of what constitutes proper behavior (which perhaps accounts for her "upward grimace" before slapping Sir Claude). Her morality is based on the Bible, the Ten Commandments, on unchanging moral laws. The inadequacy of this moral law is clearly revealed in the conclusion of the novel when she tries to inculcate Maisie with a "moral sense" like her own. We will return to this later; it is enough at present to say that its inadequacy is balanced somewhat by the dignity that Mrs. Wix almost always attains when she stands up for her narrow morality. After all, most of the other characters are immoral by any standards. Mrs. Wix's "moral sense" in a way gives her the role of the child's mother, her moral teacher, who attempts to shield her from and prepare her for the world. Maisie finally goes beyond this outdated, narrow morality, but when she is without Mrs. Wix, she is truly alone.

Mrs. Wix is definitely a fixed character in the novel, but she is charmingly, comically fixed; even when we grow impatient with her, as in her obsessive search for Maisie's "moral sense," we realize the values of safety and loyalty she represents. James's unusual allusion to another fictional character perhaps epitomizes her role as James conceived it: she is like Mrs. Micawber—"she will never, never, never desert Miss Farange" (126). She also has something in her of Mr. Longdon in *The Awkward Age* and Susan Shepherd Stringham in *The Wings of the Dove;* she is the proper companion for the young innocent. Although it may be inadequate, there is safety in the old morality.

Characterization, then, in *What Maisie Knew* is somewhat more complex than in the novels which immediately preceded it. There are stereotypes—the handsome hero, the dowdy governess—but James attains considerable individuality within the type. The principal techniques he uses are fairly simple: caricature through exaggerated comic description; a careful attention to appearance—clothes, looks; and generalized psychological attributes—weakness for the opposite sex, egocentricity. Except for Maisie, to whom we shall come shortly, there is very little examination of motive beyond the obvious, very little "going behind." Yet with the more important characters, like Sir Claude and Mrs. Wix, and even occasionally with the lesser, like Beale, Ida, and Mrs. Beale, speech, gesture, and action, particularly in dramatic scenes, provide individuality within the type. Sir Claude reveals an unexpected intelligence, Mrs. Wix an admirable loyalty, and Mrs. Beale finally a violent selfishness. Motives emerge as the characters act, as they try to force Maisie's response in one way or another. The variety which eventually is achieved is much greater than James had yet been able to encompass in the tight dramatic form in which he was beginning to work. It points the way to even greater variety in character in *The Awkward Age*.

III

Simplicity in outline, the exaggeration and concern with appearance, reflect the mind through which the reader observes these characters, the mind of a child. As Maisie's perceptions become more complex, so also do the people she observes. And this brings us to the final character in the novel, Maisie Farange, one of James's greatest achievements. Maisie is so much the center of the novel, her character is so much an integral part of the structure and themes, that to examine her attributes draws us into the whole meaning of the book. Since the construction of Maisie is the construction of the entire novel, we will do better to examine them together.

Maisie's structural role is that of the center of consciousness, the point-of-view character. James employed this same technique, of course, with Fleda Vetch in *The Spoils of Poynton,* but in *What Maisie Knew* he sets himself the added difficulty of working within the more limited consciousness of a small child; the problem is that Maisie sees more than she understands of her experience. This presents a problem of clarity, and James describes his solution in his preface:

> The infant mind would at the best leave great gaps and voids; so that with a systematic surface possibly beyond reproach we should nevertheless fail of clearness of sense. I should have to stretch the matter to what my wondering witness materially and inevitably *saw;* a great deal of which quantity she either wouldn't understand at all or would quite misunderstand—and on those lines, only on those, my task would be prettily cut out. To that, then, I settled—to the question of giving it *all,* the whole situation surrounding her, but of giving it only through the occasions and connections of her proximity and her attention; only as it might touch her and affect her, for better or worse, for perceptive gain or perceptive loss: so that we fellow-witnesses, we not more invited but only more expert critics, should feel in strong possession of it.[11]

The reader's attention is led beyond Maisie's limited comprehension to a more sophisticated one of his own, based entirely on what Maisie sees.

One structural result of this is that James of necessity gave up the balanced alternation of scene and meditation he had used in *The Spoils of Poynton*. The little girl, Maisie, simply does not have the conceptual powers for any extended logical meditation. James, however, does not completely ignore Maisie's conceptualizing. The development of her mind is important in the novel and there are meditations, carefully worked-out representations of her understanding, at particular stages in the action. These, however, are few and fairly brief, irregularly presented, and our attention is constantly directed beyond Maisie's understanding. The first pages of Chapter XX are an excellent example of the way James augments Maisie's meditations with the obvious implications of Sir Claude's behavior (200-207). A shorter, more excerptable passage in Chapter XVII indicates his method:

The wretched truth, Mrs. Beale had to confess, was that she had hoped against hope and that in the Regent's Park it was impossible Sir Claude should really be in and out. Hadn't they at last to look the fact in the face?—it was too disgustingly evident that no one after all had been squared. Well, if no one had been squared it was because everyone had been vile. No one and everyone were of course Beale and Ida, the extent of whose power to be nasty was a thing that, to a little girl, Mrs. Beale simply couldn't give chapter and verse for. Therefore it was that to keep going at all, as she said, that lady had to make, as she also said, another arrangement—the arrangement in which Maisie was included only to the point of knowing it existed and wondering wistfully what it was. Conspicuously at any rate it had a side that was responsible for Mrs. Beale's sudden emotion and sudden confidence—a demonstration this, however, of which the tearfulness was far from deterrent to our heroine's thought of how happy she should be if she could only make an arrangement for herself. (159-60).

The careful combination of indirect discourse with Maisie's reflection on what she hears allows James to present fully what she understands and what she does not about the "arrangement" between Mrs. Beale and Sir Claude. The progression of the passage down to Maisie's innocent desire for an arrangement of her own makes the reader aware through irony of the gap between Maisie's knowledge and what is actually going on. In just this way the "more expert critic" is able to follow the liaisons that Maisie in her innocence sees but misinterprets. In passages such as the one just quoted James involves the drama in meditation, or nondramatic pause for reflection, by using indirect discourse; the passage is actually a suppressed scene. The method achieved here is less artificial and accomplishes more than the alternations between drama and meditation in *The Spoils of Poynton*.

In this modified dramatic use of the central consciousness, the point of view is also the reader's. He, equally with Maisie, must experience the events and make his judgments of the action. He also sees the appearances of the various characters in the simple outlines that Maisie gives, but he must fill in those outlines. James's technique in this necessitates a further distinction—among the central consciousness, reader, and a third person, the narrator.[12] The narrator directs our understanding through style, particularly through the irony implicit in Maisie's innocent reactions to uninnocent events, a relationship formalized and made ironic in James's language. This procedure makes the over-all tone of *What Maisie Knew* far more ironic than that of either of the immediately preceding novels. James indicates his intentions in his preface, explaining why he decided not to limit himself to the child's vocabulary—a decision that takes the novel in a different direction from *Huckleberry Finn:*

WHAT MAISIE KNEW

> Small children have many more perceptions than they have terms to translate them; their vision is at any moment richer, their apprehensions even constantly stronger, than their prompt, their at all producible, vocabulary . . . It is [Maisie's] relation, her activity of spirit, that determines all our own concern—we simply take advantage of these things better than she herself. Only, even though it is her interest that mainly makes matters interesting for us, we inevitably note this in figures that are not yet at her command and that are nevertheless required whenever those aspects about her and those parts of her experience that she understands darken off into others that she rather tormentedly misses.[13]

The "we" in the final sentence of the passage refers both to James's selection of language as narrator and to the use that the reader makes of the language. As James notes of his heroine, we are "courting her noiseless mental footsteps," and these are articulated by the narrator. Complexity and irony are added through language to the simplicity of Maisie's vision.

The strict limitation of point of view occasionally forces James to back off from Maisie's reactions to stress an effect, and the irony then becomes blatant. Two passages are clear examples of this: Maisie's last meetings with her father and mother, especially Chapter XIX and pp. 217-21. As Beale Farange attempts to make Maisie give him up so that he can retain "all the appearance of virtue and sacrifice on his side" (187), James's revulsion and anger become evident and turn his irony into a sarcasm that goes beyond any perception that Maisie could have had. James describes Beale's appeal in an imaginary, though direct speech. Although Maisie undoubtedly senses some of its violence, James makes it almost too explicit: "I say, you little booby, help me to be irreproachable, to be noble, and yet have none of the beastly bore of it. There's only impropriety enough for one of us; so *you* must take it all. *Repudiate* your dear old daddy—in the face, mind you, of his tender supplications . . ." (187). Later James calls the whole affair "the most wonderful appeal any gentleman had ever addressed to his daughter" (191), and he follows with a sarcastic reference to Beale's "completing the prodigy of his attitude and the pride of his loyalty by a supreme formulation of the general inducement" (191): Beale implies that Maisie wants to give him up for Sir Claude's money. In the meeting with her mother, James again abandons Maisie's point of view to try to give the full horror of Ida's similar attempt to abandon her child. In following Maisie's "noiseless mental footsteps," the violence of some of his material occasionally compels James to make a bit of noise himself.

In addition to these technical effects, limiting the point of view also affects the themes of the novel. The child is naturally a spectator, a passive figure who observes the adult life around her. Not until she matures can there be much question of acting or not acting, of will, as there was in *The Spoils of Poynton*. In addition to the structural role of Maisie, then, James is forced to concentrate on more "passive" moral and epistemological themes. Maisie is characteristically, as both center of consciousness and small child, the passive center of all the action:

> The sharpened sense of spectatorship was the child's main support, the long habit, from the first, of seeing herself in discussion and finding in the fury of it—she had had a glimpse of the game of football—a sort of compensation for the doom of a peculiar passivity. It gave her often an odd air of being present at her history in as separate a manner as if she could only get at experience by flattening her nose against a pane of glass. (107)

WHAT MAISIE KNEW

The direction of events in the novel, of Maisie's growing up, is to place her on the other side of that pane of glass and involve her directly in action. But until the last act, Maisie remains the football, the passive observer, and can only look and guess while she is passed or kicked from one parent or step-parent to another. James, as narrator, tries to give aid to his inarticulate, passive central figure. Abandoning the attempt made at strict objectivity with Fleda Vetch, James becomes directly involved in the presentation of Maisie's thoughts and the world around her. His complex and ironic style in this novel is the direct result of the choice of an innocent child as reflector.

IV

The style of *What Maisie Knew* has additional complexities beyond the operative irony discussed above. The active participation of the narrator in the novel, through the style, adds a great deal to its richness and to the completeness with which we see both the action and the heroine. Surface humor and more extensive use of figurative language, in addition to irony, increase the stylistic complexity and are central to *What Maisie Knew*.

The comic tone of the novel is most obvious in James's description of the characters, as in the comic exaggerations in the figures of Ida Farange and Mrs. Wix noted above. The minor characters are usually Dickensian caricatures, described in terms of some simple exaggerated, eccentric characteristic. Beale's mistress, the Countess, is always referred to as "the brown lady" after Maisie sees her coming out of "The Forest of Flowers," a side-show which is "a large presentment of bright brown ladies" (171). "She had a nose that was far too big and eyes that were far too small and a moustache that was, well, not so happy a feature as Sir Claude's" (193). The perceptions are Maisie's, but the comic turns are James's. The description of one of Ida's lovers, Mr. Perriam, is equally comic: "He seemed . . . to have moustaches over his eyes, which, however, by no means prevented these polished little globes from rolling round the room as if they had been billiard-balls impelled by Ida's celebrated stroke" (91). The comedy broadens to the moral in one of Maisie's initial conceptions: "The positive certitude . . . that the natural way for a child to have her parents was separate and successive like her mutton and her pudding or her bath and her nap" (17). The comic tone of much of the novel helps to keep Maisie's experience from being too pathetic, keeps the squalor of her environment at a distance; and the decrease in comic touches of this sort toward the end of the novel heightens and solemnizes Maisie's triumph.[14]

The added richness in James's style is also apparent in his imagery and in his use of figurative language. A good deal of this is used in describing Maisie's education and is directed to pointing up the theme of education that runs through the novel; we see her "flattening her nose upon the hard window-pane of the sweetshop of knowledge" (137), and there are references to "the temple of her studies" (113) and to a year that "rounded itself as a receptacle of retarded knowledge—a cup brimming over with the sense that now at least she was learning" (66). Most of the figurative language is directed to providing equivalents for Maisie's perceptions and the manner of her perceiving. The image of Maisie with her nose pressed to the pane corresponds, as we have seen above, to her structural role as observer, just as the series of metaphors James uses in the first paragraph of Chapter I captures that same quality of experience:

WHAT MAISIE KNEW

> Only a drummer-boy in a ballad or a story could have been so in the thick of the fight. She was taken into the confidence of passions on which she fixed just the stare she might have had for images bounding across the wall in the slide of a magic-lantern. Her little world was phantasmagoric—strange shadows dancing on a sheet. It was as if the whole performance had been given for her—a mite of a half-scared infant in a great dim theatre. (9)

Maisie's magic-lantern show is not quite like that of the young Marcel in *Swann's Way;* for her the unreality is that of the world with all the violence and passion she is forced to see. Maisie is in the midst of the fury, but also outside it in not being able to "know" what it is about. In this early passage the main direction of the novel is obliquely suggested—the change from spectator to participant, from infancy and unreality to maturity and reality. Another image early in the novel adds to our sense of the felt reality of Maisie's experience: "Everything had something behind it: life was like a long, long corridor with rows of closed doors. She had learned that at these doors it was wise not to knock—this seemed to produce from within such sounds of derision" (33-34). When Maisie finds a few open doors in the final movement of the novel, this imagery is further heightened and symbolizes an important theme, to which we will return. At present it is enough to say that James uses imagery and metaphor to heighten our understanding of and our response to Maisie's experience. The gain is equally in the translation of her emotions and in the intensification of the reader's.

The complexity of language in *What Maisie Knew* is also related to the abstract diction of logic examined in the two previous novels. But here there are fewer extended arguments or debates, fewer tracings of the logic of thought. Maisie is in a sense too young for logic, and the pattern of her thoughts most often reflects emotion or sensation. James, however, as the novel progresses does attempt to convey her more intellectual conceptions, and his language accordingly becomes more abstract as, for example, in this passage describing Maisie's conception of Sir Claude's motives:

> Maisie was able to piece together the beauty of the special influence through which, for such stretches of time, he had refined upon propriety by keeping, so far as possible, his sentimental interests distinct. She had ever of course in her mind fewer names than conceptions, but it was only with this drawback that she now made out her companion's absences to have had for their ground that he was the lover of her stepmother and that the lover of her stepmother could scarce logically pretend to a superior right to look after her. Maisie had by this time embraced the implication of a kind of natural divergence between lovers and little girls. (204)

The language of abstraction and conception is beyond Maisie's conception, but James needs it to follow the complexities of her growing understanding. The final ironic note, with the abstract diction, gives us the distance between the narrator and Maisie, as well as the subject of the novel.

The construction of the dialogues in *What Maisie Knew* follows the question-and-answer pattern already discussed in the earlier novels. In the present novel, however, that device is slightly less artificial, for asking questions is the natural child's way of trying to find out what the adults are thinking. The method is particularly noticeable in the final scenes of the novel as Maisie comes closer to adequate knowledge. The form is complicated, however, by two additional features of this novel. The first of these is that Maisie has learned to keep fairly quiet, not to knock on too many doors, and so her questions are for the most part few and cautious, spontaneous only when she is with Mrs. Wix. She early recognizes that many things are none of her business, "that questions were almost always improper; but she learned on the other hand soon to recognize how at last, sometimes, patient little silences and intelligent little looks could be rewarded by delightful little glimpses" (161). The ambiguity that results from *double-entendres* and Maisie's natural misunderstanding of adult affairs is another feature of the dialogues in the novel. She misinterprets Mrs. Beale's continuous allusions to her liaison with Sir Claude, and the result is both humor and more ambiguity, increased misunderstanding. In all, the question-and-answer technique emphasizes the distinction between the natural innocence of Maisie's world and the corruption of the adults'. The need to question focuses on her inability to communicate and keeps her always on the outside. Style and the construction of the dialogues in dramatic scenes are important aspects of James's experiment with a severely limited central consciousness—the awkward, passive little girl trying to understand a sordid world.

V

Character, central consciousness, and style all directly contribute to the structure of *What Maisie Knew*. The limited point of view is one of the main structural features of the novel, but several over-all structural patterns deepen our understanding of Maisie and give to her experience an organic unity that the simple unity of character does not provide. *What Maisie Knew* is a dramatic novel with the familiar Jamesian dialectic patterns and a novel of education with an almost mythic pattern of action. The development of each of these forms must be examined before it is clear just what and how Maisie knows.

What Maisie Knew in broad outline falls into three major movements in the action of the novel, each of which marks a significant stage in Maisie's education. After a short prologue, the first seven chapters describe Maisie's early childhood and the uses to which she is put by her parents. The Proustian overture presents the parents as grotesques and establishes Maisie as an object, "a bone of contention," "divided in two and the portions tossed impartially to the disputants" (4). In two pages James sounds the notes of "youth and innocence," education and Maisie's "little unspotted soul"; he presents the major themes of the novel. The body of the first act or phase of the action is given over to the introduction of the characters and to Maisie's peregrinations between Beale's and Ida's custody. She is the typical uncomprehending child caught in a failed marriage, and the whole question of her parents' use of her and of her education is raised.

The second movement of the novel, Chapters VIII-XXI, begins with the introduction of Sir Claude and the first hints of the liaison between Mrs. Beale and him. This section forms the complication of the action, the introduction of the second set of parents, the completion of the vicious circle surrounding Maisie, and the establishment of Mrs. Wix in her role as governess and post of safety. Throughout the section Maisie's knowledge increases as she moves between her step-parents and her governess and gives up her real parents; her perceptions begin gradually to become more alert and articulate. The last half of the act, Chapters XV-XXI, beginning with the meeting with Ida and the Captain in Kensington Gardens, marks the breakdown of the system to which Maisie has been subjected by the divorce. This second act has its own climax and denouement: the double failure of Maisie's real parents, Beale and Ida Farange, in balanced scenes of rejection in Chapters XVIII-XIX with Beale and Chapters XX-XXI with Ida. Both are disposed of forever in those scenes. The denouement, which includes Ida's failure, is a movement toward escape, the move from London to Folkestone. It is a flight from Maisie's earlier subjection toward a new freedom. The approach to freedom does not really begin, however, until the last vestige of the old system has been removed in the person of Ida Farange in the scenes at Folkestone.

Although flight from the complications of living is an important aspect of almost every novel of this period, only Maisie's is very successful; with the move to Boulogne and France, Maisie is in a sense freed. The last act, Chapters XXII-XXXI, is concerned with working out the conditions of this freedom. The final struggle for possession of Maisie, which brings about Maisie's first active part in her own life and active decision about her future, resolves the action. The abortive grand tour which makes up the section concludes with the partial triumph of Mrs. Wix and the complete triumph of Maisie, and the pair's return to England after the failure of Sir Claude and Mrs. Beale.

The main outlines of the action make these broad divisions fairly clear. The movement, however, between the second and third sections is not so abrupt as the change from one act to another would seem to indicate. Maisie's mental development reaches a peak at the beginning of Chapter XX when Sir Claude carries her off. Her reaction to her last meeting with her father and her total failure to communicate with him have been enough of a shock to lead to a new understanding. She does not react at all in the same way with Ida; she makes almost no effort to meet with her; she has learned from her previous mistakes with her father. When she finally does break her silence with a mention of the Captain, one of Ida's lovers, her mother "bolts," and Maisie has lost both her parents. James indicates the success of her understanding at the beginning of Chapter XX: "It was singular, but from this time she understood and she followed, followed with the sense of an ample filling out of any void created by symptoms of avoidance and flight" (202). But not until Ida has been disposed of can that understanding lead to further knowledge and action. These two chapters, XX and XXI, are in a sense transitional. They complete the action of the second part and forecast the action of the third.

Within this entire action Maisie grows up. The process of education is involved in the dialectical action of the forces that confront Maisie. She begins with one set of parents who fight for possession of her; she is seen characteristically "rebounding from racquet to racquet like a tennis-ball or a shuttlecock,"[15] or we have seen her described as the football in the midst of a furious struggle. Chapter divisions, within the act-structure, are also quite important, and the first chapters of the novel show Maisie alternately moving from one side, perhaps from one team, to the other: Chapter I—Beale's; Chapter II—Ida's; Chapter III—Beale's; Chapter IV—Ida's, and so forth. When Maisie becomes vaguely aware in Chapter VI that her parents, instead of trying to keep her from each other, are trying to force her on each other, the stage is set for the introduction of a new set of parents. The symmetry with which this is developed is typical of James in this novel, as well as in *The Awkward Age* and *The Sacred Fount* to follow. In Chapter VII, Sir Claude's marriage to Ida is announced and immediately countered by Miss Overmore's announcement of her own marriage to Beale. Maisie is now hemmed in by two sets of parents; the first, her real mother and father, try to reject her, and the second, her step-parents, try to gain possession of her. The motive for this last aim comes clear in Chapter VIII when James establishes the liaison between Mrs. Beale and Sir Claude. Maisie is their best excuse; she has "brought them together." As the first set of parents drifts away, the second comes closer to the center of Maisie's life. When Beale and Ida finally cast her away, the stage has been set for the split between the second two, a split caused initially by Sir Claude's scruples about "mixing up" Maisie in their illicit affair: "Mrs. Beale failed to share his all but insurmountable distaste for their allowing their little charge to breathe the air of their gross irregularity—his contention, in a word, that they should either cease to be irregular or cease to be parental" (205). Maisie again rebounds from one parent, Mrs. Beale, to another, Sir Claude, who in Chapter XX takes her away. The action recurs in the final chapters of the novel; Maisie returns to Mrs. Beale in Chapters XXVII and XXVIII, and then goes back to Sir Claude in Chapters XXIX and XXX. The last chapter of the novel brings the end of the cycle; Maisie escapes from all her parents and goes off on her own, accompanied by Mrs. Wix.

The rhythmic movement from one pole to another, the

balanced couples and opposites through which Maisie slalom-like makes her way, provide much of the dynamic force of the novel. Maisie moves from one sphere of influence to another in a kind of dialectic of action until she matures enough in this process to bring about her own synthesis of experience at the end of the novel.

The structure of *What Maisie Knew* is further enriched by the use of what James had learned from the drama. In the same way that the dialectic of action provides impetus, the alternation of dramatic scene with compressed "picture," or summary of the intervening action and Maisie's states of mind, gives a great deal of force to the drama of Maisie's growth, even though this alternation is not as symmetrical as the balanced movements in the action, or as the same alternation is in *The Spoils of Poynton*. James exhorts himself while writing *What Maisie Knew* in the familiar manner of his notebooks: "Ah this *divine* conception of one's little masses and periods in the scenic light—as rounded ACTS; this patient, pious, nobly "vindictive"* application of the scenic philosophy and method."[16] And again, "I realize—none too soon—that the *scenic* method is my absolute, my imperative, my *only* salvation. The *march of action* is the thing for me to, more and more, *attach* myself to . . . The scenic scheme is the only one that *I* can trust, with my tendencies, to stick to the march of an action."[17] James's "tendencies" were of course to develop a situation intensively and at a length out of proportion to his original intentions; scenes, he felt, controlled the excess as best he could. His use of scene in this novel is close to his most successful, and we need to look closely at this method of control and at the way in which the dramatic use of scene is fitted naturally into the structure of the novel.

The first scene of any length, only six pages although it comprises a full chapter, does not occur until Chapter X. In this respect, then, the novel corresponds quite closely to the initial form of *The Spoils of Poynton*, where totally scenic construction is absent from the first third of the novel; as in the earlier novel, the use of dramatic scenes increases in scope as the novel develops. Whether this is due, in the case of *What Maisie Knew*, to an initial short-story conception and the eventual forsaking of that intention, or whether the novel was initially planned this way cannot be said; brief notebook comments indicate that the first might be true.[18] Nevertheless, *What Maisie Knew* makes a greater success of the imposed form. The early stretches of narrative, of "picture," interspersed with only very brief scenes are quite appropriate to Maisie's infancy when the general impressions of her situation have a much greater significance than the very limited role she could possibly have in any scene; and an extended scene without her participation would shift the focus of the novel from Maisie herself. As Maisie matures in the second act of the novel, she becomes more articulate and thus better able to carry her part in a dramatic scene; James can then concentrate on the dramatic present and dramatize it in detail. The high points of the second act are Maisie's scenes with the Captain in Kensington Gardens and her scenes alone with her father and mother as they rid themselves of her. In these instances, considerable tension is achieved through the dramatic interplay of Maisie's innocence and her partial understanding. As Maisie becomes less passive and comes into conflict with others on her own, the dramatic scenes become more frequent and longer, until the last chapters of the novel are almost totally dramatic.

James also achieves greater variety in his handling of scenes in this novel. Where *The Other House* was almost totally scenic and *The Spoils of Poynton* settled into a symmetrical alternation between scene and meditation, *What Maisie Knew* uses, as noted earlier, suppressed scenes and indirect discourse, a variety of forms of narration between the scenes, and a greater variation in length of scene and picture. The balances are not quite so careful as in *The Spoils of Poynton* and chapters vary considerably in texture. The general movement, however, from nondramatic or suppressed and condensed dramatic narrative in the first act of the novel to extended and fully presented dramatic scene in the last act parallels Maisie's own growth.

As Maisie moves more directly into the action, the action becomes more dramatic. James can focus on the present; the last section of the novel occupies only a few days, where the first had covered several years. As perception grows, James concentrates on the moment of perception; earlier he had had to focus on scattered and more general responses. As the crisis in Maisie's life nears—"the death of childhood"—James moves in closer and we see her more clearly; she begins to take shape as an individual. The dramatic structure of the novel reinforces the growth of Maisie's mind and character; that structure is consequently more organic than that of *The Spoils of Poynton*.

The last half of *What Maisie Knew* embodies a form of myth which parallels the dramatic structure and gives added significance to Maisie's final actions. If one begins by noting the rather ambiguous need to get out of London at the beginning of Chapter XX, which Maisie realizes is something more than avoidance and flight from her parents, an explanation in terms of familiar myth offers it-

WHAT MAISIE KNEW

self. The pattern of withdrawal and return, of leaving the homeland in order to be educated and attain maturity, followed by the triumphant return home after achievement, is fully present in the novel and deepens the meaning of the last half of the action. Seen in this manner, each of the characters acts as a tempter. Beginning with Beale in his last scene, Chapters XVIII-XIX, each tempts Maisie in some way, offers her some overly simple or degrading way out of her situation: Beale and Ida demean her motives, suggest that money is the reward she seeks; Mrs. Beale offers beauty and a free, but immoral life; Mrs. Wix offers an excessively narrow vision of life in terms of the "moral sense"; and Sir Claude offers romance and love. All the temptations leave out the full life which Maisie knows is possible and which she is strong enough to want. Sir Claude's temptation is of course the most powerful; Maisie rejects it only because it cannot be had without also accepting Mrs. Beale's immorality. The withdrawal, which provides freedom in some inexplicable way (note Maisie's first responses to France and "abroad" in the first pages of Chapter XXII: "the great ecstasy of a larger impression of life" [231]), follows essentially the pattern of release from the systems and routines of normal life. This allows the heroine to achieve knowledge beyond the offerings of her tempters, and with that the myth is complete as she returns to normal life.

VI

In addition to its dramatic and mythic structures, *What Maisie Knew* is formed by the process of Maisie's education, and that education is a central theme of the novel, a point at which theme and structure merge. *What Maisie Knew* is a novel of education like *David Copperfield* (to which F. R. Leavis has compared it), Joyce's *A Portrait of the Artist as a Young Man,* the first parts of Proust's *A la recherche du temps perdu,* or *The Adventures of Huckleberry Finn.*[19] One critic, Marius Bewley, calls it "the most magnificent example in the language of the unfolding discretionary powers of a human being."[20] Education is both form and theme in the novel and a further examination of some aspects of it will lead to a consideration of the final meaning of the novel, the results of that education.

What Maisie Knew is, as noted earlier, filled with the imagery of education and learning, and further examples will show the prominence of this theme. Maisie's ever-present concern, as she rotates from one parent or stepparent or governess to another, is that she will miss out on her education, that she is too seldom in the schoolroom. Fine private schools for girls gleam on the horizon, but Maisie never enters one. Her education is taken care of mainly by Mrs. Wix and Mrs. Beale, and James treats both efforts ironically. Formal education, schoolbooks, and multiplication tables are not what Maisie profits from. References to "subjects" and "lectures" fill her with awe, but remain ironically inadequate, as, for example, when Mrs. Beale suggests some necessary subjects: "All the most important ones. French literature—and sacred history" (133). With Mrs. Beale the final achievement of this dream is attendance at lectures at the institution on "Glower Street . . . a pathway literally strewn with 'subjects,'" where "the fountain of knowledge, in the form usually of a high voice that [Maisie] took at first to be angry, plashed in the stillness of rows of faces thrust out like empty jugs" (164). The imagery heightens the silliness of the infant Maisie at college.

With Mrs. Wix "education" is no better. Mrs. Wix consistently avoids "subjects" and performs her tutelary role mainly "on the firm ground of fiction," "all about love and beauty and countesses and wickedness" (27), perhaps safer ground than Mrs. Beale's probable taste in "French literature." If not the romance of fiction, then the two spend their time talking about Sir Claude; the topic "constituted for the time the little girl's chief education" (73). James's ironic treatment of Maisie's "formal" education reaches a climax in the final scene of the novel, as Mrs. Wix "examines" Maisie on the subject of her "moral sense":

> "Your moral sense. *Haven't* I, after all, brought it out?" She spoke as she had never spoken even in the schoolroom and with the book in her hand.
> It brought back to the child's recollection how she sometimes couldn't repeat on Friday the sentence that had been glib on Wednesday, and she dealt all feebly and ruefully with the present tough passage. Sir Claude and Mrs. Beale stood there like visitors at an "exam." . . . She looked at her examiner; she looked at the visitors; she felt the rising of the tears she had kept down at the station. They had nothing—no, distinctly nothing—to do with her moral sense. The only thing was the old flat shameful schoolroom plea. "I don't know—I don't know." (353-54)

The passage points up the contrast between Maisie's real knowledge, which is connected with the tears, and the unreality of what she is supposed to have "learned in the schoolroom."

A related use of ironic, contrasting imagery points to the unreality of certain kinds of experience; this is the continual reference to "games," very appropriate to the child's vision of the world. We have already seen Maisie in her role as shuttlecock, tennis-ball, football, or perhaps one of her mother's billiard balls, like Mr. Perriam's eyes. Education, as we have also seen, is something of a game for her, but the focus of the imagery of games is on the distinction between real and unreal experience, one of Maisie's major lessons. This can readily be seen in her mother's one talent, billiards, in the constant changing of "sides" that Maisie tries to follow, and particularly in the continual references to Ida's "game" or Mrs. Beale's "game." Mrs. Wix draws together two main strands when she categorizes Mrs. Beale's motives as part of her "game" rather than her "moral sense." The contrast between play and seriousness is carried a step further when Maisie tries to convince Mrs. Wix that she does have a "moral sense" by describing her reaction to any unkindness Mrs. Beale might show Sir Claude: "Maisie met [Mrs. Wix's] expression as if it were a game with forfeits for winking. "I'd *kill* her!" That at least, she hoped as she looked away, would guarantee her moral sense" (288). The unreality of much of Maisie's world, including Mrs. Wix's "moral sense," is emphasized by James's ironic use of the imagery of formal education and games. Maisie must learn to know the real from the artificial and inadequate.

Maisie's real education, her development as an individual, is marked by her growing ability to distinguish between real and unreal, between true and false. As William Walsh has pointed out in an excellent discussion of Maisie's education, the major movement of the novel, its vitality, is "the growing correspondence between what Maisie sees and what she understands."[21] This aspect of Maisie's education is a process, a continual growth.[22] She moves from an age of mere sensation, of simple, unrelated perceptions and feelings to one of complexity of implication and interrelationship of meaning. James notes the "firsts" for Maisie throughout the novel: from "the age for which all stories are true and all conceptions are stories. The actual was the absolute, the present alone was vivid" (14), through her first passion (for Miss Overmore), her first recognition of a sense of responsibility (120), her first anger, and so forth. Gradually Maisie develops a set of images, memories, and a vocabulary which will allow her to formulate and relate her perceptions. James indicates repeatedly the pleasure with which she hears a new word; he describes "a high quickening of Maisie's direct perceptions, of her sense of freedom to make out things for herself" (99), and then her "sharpened sense for latent meanings" (243), her ability "to read the unspoken into the spoken" (269), and finally "a complication of thought that grew every minute" (325). With this developing sense of implication and the use of her memory, Maisie is increasingly able to understand what her elders are saying and doing, and able to relate that to possible actions of her own. She learns, in other words, to distinguish between the glamor of Sir Claude's appearance and the real weakness in his character. Maisie develops a sense of reality.

This is nowhere clearer than in her gradual discovery of the essential falseness of romance. For Maisie romance, as noted above, had started with Mrs. Wix's stories "all about love and beauty and countesses and wickedness" in "a great garden of romance" (27). Maisie learns the meaning of exactly the same terms in the real world, where romantic stories are false and the truth is utterly different. From Mrs. Wix's tales it is just a step to the two principal examples of romance in the novel. The lesser of these points out the unreality which Maisie is forced to learn about. Her visit to "the Countess," her father's mistress, is for her at first an Arabian-nights experience, a delightfully furnished fairytale world. In the presence of her father and later the countess, it rapidly becomes a nightmare. When Maisie is finally driven off by the two of them, her gold coins in hand, it is still, only now ironically and bitterly, "the Arabian Nights" (197).

With Sir Claude her experience is different. He is her romantic knight, the Prince Charming of Maisie's dreams. Her greatest struggle is to see beyond him, to understand the falsity of the dream he represents: "His presence was like an object brought so close to her face that she couldn't see round its edges" (139). In one scene Sir Claude encourages Maisie's romantic conception of him. As they walk in Kensington Gardens, he playfully describes it as the Forest of Arden, himself as the banished duke, and Maisie as "the artless country wench." The reference of course is to *As You Like It,* and the subtlety of James's irony is indicated by Sir Claude's pointing to a figure ahead of them as Rosalind, the banished Duke's lover—she turns out to be Ida Farange. But the point is that this is just the way Maisie does like Sir Claude and does conceive him. She rises above this only in the final pages of the novel when she tries to get her prince to go off with her. She realizes at the time the impossibility of the plan, but she tries anyway. When she is finally convinced of the futility of her desire, "the last flare of her dream" is extinguished and she faces reality (352).

Just as James opposes kinds of education, appearance and reality, and romantic and realistic visions, so the central themes of the novel are presented as balanced opposites, antitheses out of which Maisie must resolve some synthesis. As we have seen, Maisie learns to understand reality, to recognize false versions of life. But the major themes ask more than just how and what Maisie learns. They develop the quality and significance of what she learns and the effect of that learning on her. The dialectic begins in the opposition between innocence and knowledge. This tension results from the sordid conditions of the world Maisie faces, her growing knowledge of those conditions, and her resistance to corruption by that very knowledge. What James calls Maisie's "personal relation to her knowledge" is just this capacity for retaining her innocence as she grows in experience.

Maisie's innocence at first is a mixture of bewilderment and ignorance. She is innocent simply because she is too young to understand; she perceives details but not implications. This results in her typical conversational role—repeating the details of various promiscuous affairs without knowing what they mean. "There's nothing she hasn't heard. But it doesn't matter—it hasn't spoiled her," as Mrs. Beale comments (63). The tenuousness of her innocence is heightened by the fear that she is "only too much initiated" (161), that when she does begin to understand the implications of the behavior she observes, she will have been corrupted, "spoiled"; in other words, that she will know too much and have no standards for controlling her knowledge. The tension in the novel rests largely in the possibility that her "initiation" will give her knowledge of evil without a controlling knowledge of good. James makes the opposition between knowledge and innocence clear when Maisie confronts her father in his mistress's rooms; he describes "the small strange pathos on the child's part of an innocence so saturated with knowledge and so directed to diplomacy" (183).

Knowing so much, Maisie gives the appearance to those around her of not being innocent; her remarks are often *double-entendres,* but she is only aware for most of her life of the innocent half. Maisie finally becomes aware of this double impression she gives, of "all the years of her tendency to produce socially that impression of an excess of the queer something which had seemed to waver so widely between innocence and guilt" (232).

James's tone in the whole novel enforces Maisie's innocence. Her unconsciously ironic comments, the laughter of the adults, and the overly severe and prudish reactions of Mrs. Wix all point to the effects of the comic tone in keeping the corruption and promiscuity at a distance and making clear that it cannot touch Maisie. The society of unpleasant, immoral, pleasure-seeking people in which she moves remains apart from her, something she must learn enough about to understand in order to remain uncorrupted. James's treatment of the society and its representatives has a continual comic overtone; his attitude is like that present in much Restoration comedy which dealt with a similarly small and corrupt society.

The Jamesian innocent is in the midst of this, but stronger than any member of it. Maisie retains her innocence, or modifies it with experience and makes it strong, because she learns and can make serious moral use of her knowledge. That "queer excess" she gradually develops is a kind of knowledge that does not corrupt; none of the other characters, except Sir Claude, can understand this. Maisie's knowledge comes not from her schoolbooks, but from experience with the people in her life. All of them teach her something, and she gradually begins to understand the way of the world and how she can act in it. Near the end of the novel James presents

Maisie's vision of her growth and knowledge. Her vision is without particulars, she still has more conceptions than names; it is almost transcendental, and yet it is her response to her world and her experience as all of that comes back to her in the freedom of Boulogne; and it prepares her for understanding the final action of the novel:

> Mrs. Wix saw her as a little person knowing so extraordinarily much that, for the account to be taken of it, what she still didn't know would be ridiculous if it hadn't been embarrassing ... [Maisie] judged that if her whole history, for Mrs. Wix, had been the successive stages of her knowledge, so the very climax of the concatenation would, in the same view, be the stage at which the knowledge should overflow. As she was condemned to know more and more, how could it logically stop before she should know Most? It came to her in fact as they sat there on the sands that she was distinctly on the road to know Everything. She had not had governesses for nothing: what in the world had she ever done but learn and learn and learn? She looked at the pink sky with a placid foreboding that she soon should have learnt All. They lingered in the flushed air till at last it turned to grey and she seemed fairly to receive new information from every brush of the breeze. By the time they moved homeward it was as if this inevitability had become for Mrs. Wix a long, tense cord, twitched by a nervous hand, on which the valued pearls of intelligence were to be neatly strung. (281-82)

Maisie may not know "Everything" by the end of the novel, but she knows a pragmatic equivalent. After she has finally realized what she must do, and that she must do it herself, she meets her "great moment" for action with ease: "What helped the child was that she knew what she wanted. All her learning and learning had made her at last learn that; so that if she waited an instant to reply it was only from the desire to be nice. Bewilderment had simply gone or at any rate was going fast" (357). Knowledge for Maisie is knowing herself and knowing how to act with moral responsibility. As her vision grows more complex in the course of the novel, Maisie comes to terms with the people around her, the representatives of a decadent society. The conflict of innocence with knowledge results in an incorruptible knowledge that is morally strong and frees Maisie from the weaknesses of her elders. She has the strength finally to sacrifice the one she wants most—Sir Claude—and to accept the one who needs her most—Mrs. Wix.

Maisie is the center of the novel both structurally and thematically and never so firmly as in the questions of morality and responsibility that develop out of the clash of innocence and knowledge. We have already examined the results of that conflict, but let us look more closely at the moral vision and the meaning of the final chapters of the novel.

James again presents the theme through opposites, through seemingly irreconcilable principles. From Chapter XXVI to the end, Mrs. Wix continually questions Maisie's possession of a "moral sense." For Mrs. Wix this sense would enable Maisie to handle the knowledge of evil into which she has been initiated. It would enable her strictly to distinguish right from wrong. Maisie, however, has proposed in the previous chapter that the solution to all their problems is for all four, Maisie, Mrs. Wix, Mrs. Beale, and Sir Claude to live together. She has said that this is the way for them all to "take advantage of their freedom," but she senses that in saying this she "had never appeared so wanton" (271-272). A tension is immediately formed between the "moral sense" and freedom. For Mrs. Wix, Mrs. Beale's taking advantage of her freedom to live with Sir Claude would constitute a crime, "branded so in the Bible." For Maisie the action is natural. The theme develops in the last chapters as both Mrs. Beale and Sir Claude dramatically proclaim their freedom and Mrs. Wix returns again and again to Maisie's "moral sense."

Mrs. Wix tries to get Maisie to "condemn" the action of the other two. She cannot understand how Maisie can "know" without condemning. This effort only elicits a "vague sigh of oppression" from Maisie, a clear indication that she thinks differently, thinks that freedom is destroyed by the morality which "condemns." Thereupon James introduces an ironic note, for as Maisie wanders off to the window, to look out at life and escape Mrs. Wix's catechism, she hears "the drawl of a song about 'amour.' Maisie knew what 'amour' meant too, and wondered if Mrs. Wix did" (285). At the end of this chapter Maisie childishly tries to prove her moral sense by claiming she would kill Mrs. Beale, but it is a false note, given in the spirit of a game and indicating the unreality of Maisie's assertion. In the paragraph quoted above describing Mrs. Wix's final interrogation of Maisie, Maisie's answer is that she "doesn't know" what or where her "moral sense" is. In the final crescendo of what Maisie does know this is one of the few times she directly admits not knowing. It can, I think, only indicate that the question is meaningless. At this point Maisie is feeling the loss of Sir Claude—she says, "I feel as if I had lost everything"—and James makes clear that this is something other and more profound than the "moral sense": "As if she were sinking with a slip from a foothold, her arms made a short jerk. What this jerk represented was the spasm within her of something deeper than a moral sense" (354). What Maisie is experiencing is the extinction of her dream, of her romance, the death of her childhood. The "slip from a foothold" is a liberating one, although there are dangers implicit in it. Maisie has learned enough, however, to be free, free from the limits of her childhood, from the limits of her mind, and from the limits imposed by her elders. Sir Claude makes this clear later in the scene when he forces Mrs. Beale to release Maisie. He repeats the exultant cry that comes up again and again in the final pages: "You're free—you're free" (356).

But freedom for Maisie is also a removal of all the old safeties, the footholds, and she feels at first slightly frightened by it. There is no security in freedom; Fleda Vetch, for example, finds it isolating. It does, however, correspond to the "larger impression of life" that France has given her and to the vision of knowing All. It is the freedom not to have to appear stupid, not to have to exercise her "instant moral contraction," her cautious and politic silences around her elders. It is freedom to use her new-found intelligence, to benefit from what she knows. For Maisie this includes an understanding, without condemnation, of love, "amour," and the pathetic ends to which it has driven her elders. With freedom Maisie learns the responsibilities of life and the losses that are necessary. The final act that makes her truly free is her conscious effort to gain Sir Claude and her loss of him. She now has learned responsible choice, the only kind of freedom and knowledge worthwhile. It is broader than any "moral sense" that stifles life.

Out of this dialectic of theme has emerged the meaning

of Maisie's experience and the novel. Once we perceive what Maisie knows, our knowledge is complete. Her childhood dies as she begins to discover her identity and to realize that there are things within one which are to be feared. She has recognized this first in Sir Claude and then in herself—a fear of her own weaknesses, a fear of self. The final scenes embody the conventional recognition of the drama. When Sir Claude asks Maisie if she will give up Mrs. Wix and come to live with Mrs. Beale and him, Maisie "felt the coldness of her terror . . . She was afraid of herself" (338). Her terror increases as she tries to get Sir Claude to go off with her on the Paris train. But when the train leaves without them, she realizes that "she had had a real fright but had fallen back to earth" (345). What she fears is her romantic nature and the consequences of its possible triumph, the possibility that she will be just like the others. When her dream flares and goes out in her last effort to achieve romance, she finally is "afraid of nothing" (352). Maisie by then knows herself and her limits, and she realistically can accept herself. Romance would have denied this.

In this knowledge of self and triumph over fear, the return to reality, Maisie has learned to confront life. Mrs. Wix, at the end of the novel, accuses Sir Claude of having killed Maisie's moral sense, but he defends himself and one can hear James's approval of Maisie speaking through him: "I've not killed anything . . . On the contrary I think I've produced life. I don't know what to call it—I haven't even known how decently to deal with it, to approach it; but, whatever it is, it's the most beautiful thing I've ever met—it's exquisite, it's sacred" (354). In the fullness of this new life, Maisie can meet Sir Claude as an equal; she understands his weaknesses and does not condemn, for she has recognized them in herself. As she leaves, "their eyes met as the eyes of those who have done for each other what they can" (363). She has offered him her life in exchange for his fears, but he cannot rise to the offer, and she leaves to return to England with what she knows.[23] She is ready for the fulfillment that she had sensed her first day at Boulogne: "She recognized, she understood, she adored and took possession; feeling herself attuned to everything and laying her hand, right and left, on what had simply been waiting for her" (232).

All the patterns then are complete. Education has resulted in knowledge, the withdrawal to France has given new life, the temptations have been overcome, and Maisie returns uncorrupted. Mrs. Wix is still with her, but now only as companion, for Maisie knows so much more. The dramatic, mythic, and dialectic structures of the novel are completed with the return to England. *What Maisie Knew* is a triumphant novel both in meaning and form, a consistently fine example of James's own artistic values: "a deep-breathing economy and an organic form." All the forms and threads of the action, all the balanced thematic opposites are resolved at the end of the novel and the result is a profound, dramatic, and highly artistic vision of life.

6

The Awkward Age

The Awkward Age," James's next full-length novel, continues and elaborates upon many of the central themes of this period, and it is the equal of *What Maisie Knew* in richness and complexity of construction. The heroine of the novel is, in a sense, a slightly older Maisie—an innocent adolescent rather than an innocent child; and she is inside the "upper-class" world that the girl in James's contemporaneous story, *In the Cage*, could only look at from the outside. James's social concerns, present in the earlier novels, are more explicitly and fully treated here, particularly in a more detailed representation of a certain aspect of London life. The central themes are again moral explorations of innocence and knowledge, but because of the role that social convention, both traditional and modern, plays in the novel, the outcome is tragic rather than triumphant. In its final statement *The Awkward Age* echoes the waste and sacrifice at the end of *The Spoils of Poynton* rather than the possible fulfillment of *What*

Maisie Knew, although it unites the concerns of both. *The Awkward Age,* like *What Maisie Knew,* is also an artistic success, a fusion of substance and form; and James's pleasure in that achievement—"triumphantly scientific" and "scenic"—is obvious in his preface. He attempted a novel composed entirely in dramatic scenes, almost wholly in dialogue, like *The Other House;* but James's conception is much more radical than in the earlier novel for here he balances ten scenes symmetrically so that each will light a particular aspect of the central theme. The formal plan is extreme and experimental, yet perfectly consistent in the novel. Although the substance may perhaps tend to be lost sight of in the novelty of the technical experiment, especially on first reading, the two finally reinforce one another and emphasize the meaning of the novel.

After finishing *In The Cage* and *The Two Magics,* probably by late spring or early summer of 1898, James began *The Awkward Age.* Unfortunately James's notebooks do not record his progress on the novel; there is no mention other than an initial note on the "germ"[1] James does mention in several letters, however, his rush to complete the novel in December 1898, two months after serial publication had begun in *Harper's Weekly.*[2] The novel was finally published in book form in England in April 1899 and in America the following month.

Since James was, as usual, writing under pressure of serial publication and, as usual, in the belief that he was writing another short story (which by "an unforeseen principle of growth" rapidly became another of what he called his overtreated "comparative monsters"), the consistency of texture he achieves in the novel is remarkable. The controlling form is that of the drama, and the only analogues in his own works are *The Other House* and the plays. James restricts himself to the dramatic, objective present throughout the novel. As he says in a letter, there is no "going behind," no attempt to explore the psychology of the characters from the author's privileged position of subjective insight.[3] Psychological perceptions must come to the reader objectively, through the outward signs of speech, tone, gesture, and action. The foundation of this technique is in the drama.

In his preface to the novel, however, James indicates a more immediate source. He chose the form, he says, "in which the ingenious and inexhaustible, the charming philosophic 'Gyp,' casts most of her social studies."[4] "Gyp" was the pseudonym of a French social satirist, Martel de Janville, who, together with another writer, Henri Lavedan, parodied French manners in witty dialogues which were novel-length but were printed like plays with names of characters prefixed to speeches and with no authorial comment, a form known as *roman dialogué*.[5] James's reference to this model is significant, for it points to a major concern of his novel, social criticism. Embodied in *The Awkward Age* is an extensive analysis of the damaging effects on the individual of changing social conventions. The great success of James's analysis and of his portrayal of Mrs. Brook's circle is in his accomplishing it almost entirely through social conversation; he lets them reveal themselves. Social criticism in the form of dramatic comedy adhering strictly to the objectivity of drama is the most obvious feature of *The Awkward Age*. James combines "Gyp" with his deeper knowledge of the dramatic form developed during this experimental period. After the scenic experiments in his three preceding novels,

James is well able to experiment more drastically with the form of the novel.

The length to which James pushed his experiment is mirrored in some of the critical reactions to the novel. Although F. R. Leavis and F. W. Dupee, among others, have recognized the success and importance of the novel,[6] many have found it difficult to read, vague, and tenuous. Both Percy Lubbock and Joseph Warren Beach, though ardent Jamesians, considered it too experimental, the far end of the line.[7] That *The Awkward Age* does carry the totally dramatic novel about as far as it can go is true, but this should not deter us from recognizing James's success with the form. A far more serious criticism, although unsupported by any analysis, is made by Edmund Wilson in his well-known essay on "The Ambiguity of Henry James." The difficulties of reading the novel are made clear, although exaggerated, in Wilson's description of it: "The innocent Nanda Brookenham . . . has a whole host of creepy creatures around her . . . James has relapsed into a dreamy, inner world where values are often uncertain and where it is not even possible for him any longer to judge the effect of his stories on his audience . . . James could never have known how we should feel about the gibbering, disembowelled crew who hover about one another with sordid, shadowy designs in *The Awkward Age*."[8] The virtue of Wilson's attack is that it points out the problems an experimental and unusual novel presents to the reader, and *The Awkward Age* is, as Percy Lubbock notes, quite unlike any other novel.[9] That a careful reader should know what to make of the characters and values of *The Awkward Age,* and that in some way James's intentions are made clear, will, I hope, be evident in the analysis of an admittedly difficult novel.

THE AWKWARD AGE

II

The basis of any drama is the conflict of character in motive, speech, and action. In *The Awkward Age* James develops in detail half a dozen major characters and a number of minor ones; he carefully delineates the relationships among them and their significance for the themes of the novel. Of course many of them are "disembowelled" and more of them occasionally "gibber," but that is the way of the world; all novels of social criticism give us examples of such people, as does life. There are others, as always, who do not gibber, who speak seriously and purposefully and attempt to discover the meaning of their experience. Both the foolish and the praiseworthy, perhaps the "fools" and the "free spirits," come from the same level of society, and many of them are unusually articulate and mental creatures, which accounts in some of them for a seeming lack of emotion and physical response. Within the limits of this particular group, however, using it almost as a convention, James constructs a human society as important as any other he created. The small, unique group stands for the society as a whole.

In *The Awkward Age* the central figures in the group are Mrs. Brookenham and her daughter Nanda, the two young bachelors, Mitchett and Vanderbank, an older gentleman, Mr. Longdon, and the Duchess and little Aggie, her niece. Part of the group, but less central to the action of the novel, is a ring of relatives, aristocrats, and friends: Petherton, Cashmore, Lady Fanny, Tishy Grendon, Edward and Harold Brookenham. Many of these characters are given nicknames—Fanny, Tishy, Mitchy, Van—which may perhaps reflect James's attitude toward the society and which can, if repeated often enough, begin to sound pretty silly; I hope the reader will bear with this in the following discussion—the concentration of names is greater here than in the novel. All of the characters represent various aspects of the themes of the novel, and all are placed in a variety of relationships with each other which provide the tensions of the drama and even the form of it.

James, as usual, works in balances and symmetries; one character is paired off with another, usually to show contrasting versions of a general type. The six major characters (if we exclude for a moment little Aggie, whose role is more symbolic than dramatic) fall into three pairs: Nanda and Mrs. Brookenham, Mitchett and Vanderbank, and Mr. Longdon and the Duchess. Nanda, Mitchett, and Mr. Longdon are the generally praiseworthy characters in the novel, the ones who gain the greatest share of our sympathy. The "evil" ones, or those who obstruct the good characters, are Mrs. Brookenham, Vanderbank, and the Duchess. The good are characterized by genuineness, sincerity, and a general lack of pretence; the bad, on the other hand, continually disguise their motives and present a false appearance. There are further gradations on either side, however. Mrs. Brook, as she is called, alone of all the characters, is consciously and inveterately hypocritical. Van, on the other hand, is generally unaware of the hypocrisies inherent in his nature.

Similarities bind the pairs together. Nanda and her mother, Mrs. Brook, both appear to be humorless, sad, knowing, and innocent. Nanda is self-possessed and "unnaturally grave," "at once so downright and yet of so fresh and sweet a tenderness of youth."[10] Van and Mitchy in her first scene conclude that she is "tragic." All Nanda's external characteristics are direct reflections of similar ones in Mrs. Brook, but in her mother they are slightly exaggerated and comic. Mrs. Brook has "the pure light of youth," although she is forty-one, and her "youth" is commented on throughout the novel. She also suggests, in James's initial description, "the luxury, the novelty of woe, the excitement of strange sorrows and the cultivation of fine indifferences. This was her special sign—an innocence dimly tragic" (42). She perpetually rolls her eyes "as if from the extremity of martyrdom or the wistfulness of some deep thought" (45). And, like Nanda, she never laughs. The final resemblance between mother and daughter is in name only; Nanda is named after her mother, Fernanda. The terms of these descriptions are important both in the comic tone of the novel and in preparation for the tragic conclusion, as well as in characterization.

The two young bachelors who form the core of Mrs. Brook's circle are Mitchett and Vanderbank, "Mitchy" and "Van" throughout. They both are witty, humorous, and attracted to Mrs. Brook; they have enough intelligence to appreciate the hidden form of her wit. They have a similar situation in the circle and are friends. They are both suitors for Nanda. From this point the contrasts begin. Mitchy is tremendously wealthy; Van is a civil servant with no independent income. Van is handsome, attractive to women, socially adept; Mitchy is ugly, unattractive, and socially adept mainly because he is wealthy and clever. Van's attentions are generally to his appearance, his looks; while Mitchy has "little intrinsic appearance" and his clothes are usually treated as slightly comic. Mitchy is *nouveau riche,* "the son of a shoemaker and who might be the grandson of a grasshopper" (62), while Van is generally of the Establishment. Mitchy has no egoism, while Van's vanity is his main characteristic; he cannot escape his self-concern.

Mr. Longdon and the Duchess, our third pair, are alike in only a few ways. They are both outsiders and somewhat older. They stand for traditions that exist or existed elsewhere, on the Continent for the Duchess or in the past for Mr. Longdon. Mr. Longdon twice describes himself as Rip Van Winkle; he feels as if he had been "disinterred—literally dug up from a long sleep" (8). And he plays this role in the novel; he is the visitor from fifty years earlier, a representative of an older set of social customs and manners which contrasts with the newer conventions he finds on his return to the present. The Duchess is also a visitor; she comments often on contemporary English manners and contrasts them with her own continental ones, where the young are completely protected and the elders may do whatever they like. The Duchess, however, in spite of her foreignness and her role as critic of English manners, also presents a front to disguise her essential type. She has an air of distinction which "corresponded superficially with her acquired Calabrian sonorities, from her voluminous title down, but the colourless hair, the passionless forehead, the mild cheek and long lip of the British matron, the type that had set its trap for her earlier than any other, were elements difficult to deal with and were at moments all a sharp observer saw. The battleground then was the haunting danger of the bourgeois" (52). The bourgeois side links her with Mr. Longdon's old-fashioned aspect, and this tie gives her the occasion several times in the novel to confer at length with him and try to advise him, as, for example, when in Book Five, Chapter IV, she advises him to try to get Van to marry Nanda. Generally

THE AWKWARD AGE

he takes her advice, and she is often proved right in her judgments of the other characters. At the same time, however, her motives are selfish (she wants Mitchett rather than Van for her niece Aggie), and her personal life is immoral, in direct contrast to Mr. Longdon's. She is the only character in the novel who unquestionably is involved in an illicit affair.

These various characters all reflect familiar Jamesian types that we have examined in the earlier novels. There are expansions and certain idiosyncratic differences, but on the whole James draws on a handful of types for the basis of his characterizations. Nanda, of course, we have met before in Fleda Vetch—the young innocent, hopelessly in love, and a voluntary martyr. And like Maisie, she knows too much, her innocence is suspect; but also like Maisie she is stronger than her knowledge, uncorrupted by it, even though convention finally defeats her because of it. Vanderbank is the handsome, socially successful young man whom the women "like too much," whose looks inspire "the sacred terror." He closely resembles Tony Bream and Owen Gereth; he is intelligent (more so than Owen) but not as tolerant as Sir Claude. James goes so far, in the preface to *The Princess Casamassima*, as to call Vanderbank one of his "intense *perceivers*," and describes him as "the divided Vanderbank . . . the extreme pinch of whose romance is the vivacity in him, to his positive sorrow and loss, of the state of being aware."[11] Mitchy, on the other hand, has Sir Claude's tolerance, general ease, and intelligence, but few of his weaknesses. We must go back to Ralph Touchett in *The Portrait of a Lady* for a parallel to Mitchett. They both love the heroine selflessly, both can only be her friend, both try to help, both are very wealthy, and neither inspires "the sacred terror." Mrs. Brookenham is somewhat like many other middle-aged, match-making ladies in James's novels, particularly Mrs. Gereth and Mrs. Beever. Idiosyncracies, however, place her completely apart and allow James to "think Mrs. Brook the best thing I've ever done."[12] For a parallel to her falseness and hypocrisy no one is closer than Madame Merle in *The Portrait of a Lady*. Mrs. Brook, however, is essentially a new departure. Mr. Longdon is also a character somewhat new for James, although there are perhaps resemblances to Mr. Touchett. As an older man, an outsider confronted with a new morality, a representative of the unlived life with some tragic loss in the past, he is perhaps closer to James himself and especially to later heroes like John Marcher and Lambert Strether. All these are, of course, only general types particularly congenial to James; in the novel, he develops the idiosyncracies mentioned above and in the details of the action makes each of the characters a fully presented individual.

One of the most significant features of *The Awkward Age* is the static quality of the characters; none of them changes very much. To return to terms used in earlier chapters, all the characters in *The Awkward Age* are "fixed"; none of them is free. Although the situation changes and the conditions of their existence change, what Nanda says of herself might be true of everyone in the novel: "I shall never change—I shall always be just the same . . . What I am I must remain. I haven't what's called a principle of growth" (214). Relationships between the characters change—Van in particular draws away from the others—but the characters themselves go on in the same way, and Van's change is simply a change in our view of him and his reaction to the situation into which he has been forced. This static quality is in part a result of the duration of the action; the novel covers only a little over a year (from just before Easter until a year from the following June), so that there is not the long period of growth and change observed in Maisie. For a novel conceived almost entirely dramatically, however, this lack of change is peculiarly undramatic. The plot has almost none of the recognition and reversal essential to a character's growth. There is even little growth in self-knowledge; Nanda "knows" a great deal, but she comments that it seems as if it had always been so. This fixity of character is central to the meaning of the novel. None of them can change because they are all limited by the society in which they exist, the customs of which dictate their actions—approving or denying, aiding or stultifying. *The Awkward Age* portrays a closed world; there is no way to change, no way out even, except withdrawal, exile. One of James's main assertions in the novel, and his strongest criticism of the society, is just that it is constrictive; customs change, in history, but human beings cannot. This is precisely the tragic quality of the world that James creates in *The Awkward Age*.

The Awkward Age, then, is essentially a static novel. For all its drama and scene, it is really a picture, a revelation of a situation. The novel follows the course of an action, a plot which has some elements of suspense in the possibility that Van may marry Nanda, but as the plot develops this suspense is rather quickly disposed of. Mr. Longdon's proposal that Van marry Nanda, and his offer of a dowry, which comes only after half the novel, is countered immediately by Van's hesitant, ambivalent response. The question then becomes why Van will not marry Nanda, an examination of inaction rather than the course of an action. Similarly, the central problem of the novel, the effect on Nanda of "coming down" into the adult world of the drawing room, is static because she is unaffected; she knows as much before as after, and interest is thereby turned toward the other characters' assumptions, true or false, about the effect. Compared to *What Maisie Knew* the moral concern in *The Awkward Age* is never really in doubt; our interest is in the effects of the moral problem on all the characters, not so much in the possible contamination of one central figure. What we are confronted with, then, is a moral drama in which static characters are presented objectively, and in which the main focus is on a total social situation as it affects those characters and their interrelationships.

Changing relationships among static figures point to a final aspect of characterization in *The Awkward Age*. We have seen how James pairs off the major characters in opposite reflections of certain common central features. Character is integral to the structure of the novel in just this same way, and an additional example of the static quality can be seen in James's structural intentions. Each of the ten books of the novel is named for one of the characters, who bears a special relationship to the events of that particular book. James describes the construction in his preface in a way that suggests the unity of character and form:

> I drew on a sheet of paper—and possibly with an effect of the cabalistic . . . the neat figure of a circle consisting of a number of small rounds disposed at equal distance about a central object. The central object was my situation, my subject in itself, to which the thing would owe its title, and the small rounds represented so many distinct lamps, as I liked to call them, the function of each of which would be to light

with all due intensity one of its aspects . . . Each of my lamps would be the light of a single "social occasion" in the history and intercourse of the characters concerned, and would bring out to the full the latent colour of the scene in question and cause it to illustrate, to the last drop, its bearing on my theme. I revelled in this notion of the Occasion as a thing by itself, really and completely a scenic thing . . . The beauty of the conception was in the approximation of the respective divisions of my form to the successive Acts of a Play."[13]

Before returning to the notion of acts and scenes, we must examine the role which character plays in this conception. Because each of the books bears the name of one of the characters, certain relationships are established between various characters and the central situation. For convenience in the following discussion, I will list the books in order: I, Lady Julia; II, Little Aggie; III, Mr. Longdon; IV, Mr. Cashmore; V, the Duchess; VI, Mrs. Brook; VII, Mitchy; VIII, Tishy Grendon; IX, Vanderbank; X, Nanda. The direction of the whole, from I to X, is from old conceptions of innocence to new innocence, from Lady Julia to Nanda, who so closely resembles her physically, with the two central books serving as prime examples of experience and corruption. James's plan also involves a set of parallels between corresponding books in the first and second halves of the novel. So we have, as noted, Nanda paired with Lady Julia, their remarkable similarity yet extreme difference made clear, at the beginning and end of the novel. Working inward from the extremes, Little Aggie and Vanderbank likewise form a pair, in this case of ignorant, unconscious corruption. Van's attraction to Aggie blinds him to her lack of moral character; for him she fits the social standards and is therefore pure. His jealousy of Mitchy, who marries little Aggie, is exemplary of this;

he, Van, should have been her husband. Tishy Grendon and Mr. Longdon are also balanced structurally, early and late. They are both outsiders, both ignorant of the right way to behave in the new society—Tishy through stupidity and Mr. Longdon through unfamiliarity. Mitchett and Mr. Cashmore are set up nearer the center of experience. Both are knowing, both aware of social implications, but Cashmore is vulgar and corrupt in his attraction to Nanda, while Mitchy's experience does not affect his essential purity of motive; he is naturally good. At the center are the Duchess and Mrs. Brook, disguised corruption and pretended innocence, in one a corruption purely physical and in the other, Mrs. Brook, a corruption not at all physical, almost mental. The Duchess is something of a pagan, but Mrs. Brook is too modern and intellectual for that simplicity.

Through this arrangement of characters as "lamps," James illuminates his subject progressively from old innocence to new innocence through varying, not always continuous stages of experience. Integral to it all is a quest for a balance between innocence and knowledge. True and false innocence and true and false experience are exemplified in various books under the "lamp" (sign or symbol) of one of the characters. The symmetry and balance with which James constructs his novel and interrelates his characters reinforces the static quality of the whole, the aspect of the closed circle, and at the same time multiplies the implications inherent in his subject. The novel takes on a formal arrangement appropriate to the highly civilized and restricted society it pictures.

III

As James remarks in his preface, "the beauty of the conception" is in the correspondence between his "occasions"

THE AWKWARD AGE

and the acts of a play. The formality of *The Awkward Age* is achieved in part by James's use of the drama as a model. *The Awkward Age* is the most successfully and completely "scenic" of James's novels, and this is the basic feature of the structure of the novel. If *The Awkward Age* were to be printed as a play or after the fashion of "Gyp," the main themes and the body of the novel would be retained. Certain features, however, would be lost. James's departures from totally scenic presentation are slight, but essential to his novel; and they are in their way consistent with his dramatic model. The novel is cast almost entirely in dialogue, but James uses several devices from the drama to supplement the speeches. As may have been apparent, much of the description of character quoted earlier comes not from dialogue, but from the author. Somewhat in the manner of Shaw, and many others, in the printed texts of his plays, James gives a full physical and characterizing description when a character first appears. The other intrusions into the dialogue of the novel are of this order: James indicates the tone of speeches, the unspoken but visible reactions of other characters, and the placement and movement of the figures on his stage. The careful notations of tone, gesture, and response are little more than ideal acting would give to the dialogue.

The attention to placement and movement in a given scene carefully reinforces the relationships among the characters. It may give a "picture" of a scenic moment which is almost symbolic. This technique can be seen in the long scene between Mr. Longdon and Vanderbank in which the former reveals his intention of giving Nanda a dowry and in effect proposes that Van marry her. James indicates all the features of the room—the raised sofa, the billiard table below, the one bright light over the table—as the two men shift back and forth from table to sofa, nervously shoving the billiard-balls around, or one sitting above the other on the sofa. Van first sits above with "a little the look of some prepossessing criminal who, in court, should have changed places with the judge" (259-60). Later, immediately after he has asked Van if he loves Nanda, Mr. Longdon "mounted to the high bench and sat there as if the judge were now in his proper place" (267), while Van remains below under the bright light. In Book Eight, Chapter IV, one can again see the playwright carefully constructing a scene, placing characters in meaningful relationships. When everyone comes together at Tishy Grendon's in this climactic scene of the novel, the symbolic picture is clear. Mrs. Brook and the Duchess are seated together on the sofa, and the others are arranged in a circle in front of them. Mitchy is on Mrs. Brook's left, and reading around the circle we find Van, Edward and Harold Brookenham, Lady Fanny, Nanda, Mr. Cashmore, Tishy, and Mr. Longdon, who is next to the Duchess. Some of the relationships examined above are repeated in this circle. Mrs. Brook and the Duchess are at the center; Mr. Longdon and Tishy are together, as are Van and Mitchy. Nanda, however, is flanked by Mr. Cashmore and his wife, Lady Fanny, the two most profligate characters in the novel; they represent her greatest danger and point to the final implications of the scene when Mrs. Brook draws out in front of them all Nanda's knowledge of the supposedly corrupting French novel. I will return to the scene later, but it is clear at this point that James employs simple stagecraft to emphasize Nanda's exposure, to put characters into meaningful relationships, and to heighten the drama of his novel.

Cutting himself off from the novelist's customary resources of direct narrative to establish theme and situation, James instead uses various characters to present the central themes of the novel, and in some cases to describe at some length the central situation in the novel. For example, much of what Mrs. Brook says about Nanda's plight is true, although she herself is ironic about it. She describes Nanda as "my innocent and helpless, yet somehow at the same time, as a consequence of my cynicism, dreadfully damaged and depraved daughter" (84), which is a fairly apt description of the central theme of Nanda's danger. The Duchess also presents this theme clearly when she describes society's attitude toward the problem of the young girl as "a muddle, a compromise, a monstrosity" (55), almost the same terms that James himself uses in his preface. The Duchess also plays the role of adviser to Mr. Longdon and gives him a clearer understanding of the social scene; in explaining the situation to him her speeches are generally quite long, contrasting, as we shall see, with the usual brief speeches in the dramatic conversations.

James, then, employs a number of devices to supplement the bare outline of the dialogue. These effects do enrich the novel, but dialogue remains the principal vehicle—"really constructive dialogue, dialogue organic and dramatic, speaking for itself, representing and embodying substance and form" as James presents his ideal in his preface to the novel.[14] The dialogue in *The Awkward Age* is perhaps James's best. Speeches are mostly quite short, often a few words, seldom over ten or twelve lines long, keeping the pace of the novel quite rapid. James has progressed considerably from the longer speeches and spellings-out of *The Other House*. He retains, however, some of the principal techniques that he experimented with in that novel. He uses the question-and-answer technique, particularly when one of the central characters is trying to enlighten one of the lesser, for example in scenes between Mrs. Brookenham and her husband (very much like the conversations of the Assinghams in *The Golden Bowl*), or when two opposing characters, such as Nanda and her mother, try to understand each other's motives and actions. And, as usual, the technique indicates some failure in communication. The debate is also used between two opposing characters and with an effect of high irony when Mrs. Brook and the Duchess clash.

The main form of the dialogue, however, is less specialized and in a way more natural. Between two similar or sympathetic characters, such as Mrs. Brook and Mitchy or Van, or Nanda and Mr. Longdon, dialogue becomes an allusive shorthand broken only by longer analytical statements, or summaries, by one or the other speaker. As we shall see, this can also lead to some of the ambiguities and difficulties of James's "late style" of which dialogue is an essential feature. The last page of the novel will indicate the general character of the kind of dialogue James develops to a high art in *The Awkward Age*. Nanda is describing her final situation to Mr. Longdon:

"We're many of us, we're most of us—as you long ago saw and showed you felt—extraordinary now. We can't help it. It isn't really our fault. There's so much else that's extraordinary that if we're in it all so much *we* must naturally be." It was all obviously clearer to her than ever yet, and her sense of it found renewed expression; so that she might have been, as she wound up, a very much older person than her friend. "Everything's different from what it used to be."

"Yes, everything," he returned with an air of final indoctrination. "That's what he [Van] ought to have recognized."

"As *you* have?" Nanda was once more—and completely now

THE AWKWARD AGE

—enthroned in high justice. "Oh he's more old-fashioned than you."

"Much more," said Mr. Longdon with a queer face.

"He tried," the girl went on—"he did his best. But he couldn't. And he's so right—for himself."

Her visitor, before meeting this, gathered in his hat and stick, which for a moment occupied his attention. "He ought to have married—!"

"Little Aggie? Yes," said Nanda.

They had gained the door, where Mr. Longdon again met her eyes. "And then Mitchy—!"

But she checked him with a quick gesture. "No—not even then!"

So again before he went they were for a minute confronted. "Are you anxious about Mitchy?"

She faltered, but at last brought it out. "Yes. Do you see? There I am."

"I see. There we are. Well," said Mr. Longdon—"Tomorrow." (544-45)

The allusive quality, the quick understanding without lengthy explicit statement, the way in which the speaker's thought is completed by the listener, is an integral part of the social scene and of the high intelligence of James's characters. The mark of stupidity in the novel is an inability to follow rapid transitions of the sort quoted above, an inability especially clear in Edward Brookenham, Mr. Cashmore, or Tishy Grendon, or a need to ramble on, as in the bourgeois Duchess. William James describes the conversation of intelligent people in a way that distinctly fits the dialogue in this novel by his brother:

When two minds of a high order, interested in kindred subjects, come together, their conversation is chiefly remarkable for the summariness of its allusions and the rapidity of its transitions. Before one of them is half through a sentence, the other knows his meaning and replies. Such genial play with such massive materials, such an easy flashing of light over far perspectives, such careless indifference to the dust and apparatus that ordinarily surround a subject and seem to pertain to its essence, make these conversations seem true feasts for gods to a listener who is educated enough to follow them at all.[15]

James's dialogue is not necessarily that of the highly educated, but it is appropriate to the social sphere that he is describing. It is used, as in the above passage, to represent a kind of communion between individuals that very seldom happens, in fiction or life; it marks the greatest success of the high consciousness that James is always concerned with. At the same time it is perhaps the only sort of dialogue which could keep so intensely objective a novel as *The Awkward Age* interesting and moving rapidly. The technique is not easy on the reader, as William James indicates about his listener, for if his mind is not of the order of the characters', he may miss what is happening in the rapidity of the conversation. What James achieves in this novel, nevertheless, is worth all the difficulty.

IV

James in his preface brings up this question of difficulty in the context of a discussion of the drama. He describes at some length a critic's reaction to the poverty and simplicity of the dramatic form; to be at all clear the drama must deal with lightweight subjects, for any complexity would result in obscurity. James does not deny this; he merely asks for "the very greatest attention" to his complexities. He then goes on to describe writing *The Awkward Age* "as if I were in fact constructing a play."[16] The rest of his comments on the dramatic art help us under-

THE AWKWARD AGE

stand what he wanted his novel to be, what in addition to scenic construction in dialogue he hoped the dramatic novel would exemplify:

I may doubtless appear now not less anxious to keep the philosophy of the dramatist's course before me than if I belonged to his order. I felt, certainly, the support he feels, I participated in his technical amusement, I tasted to the full the bitter-sweetness of his draught—the beauty and the difficulty (to harp again on that string) of escaping poverty *even though* the references in one's action can only be, with intensity, to each other, to things exactly on the same plane of exhibition with themselves. Exhibition may mean in a "story" twenty different ways, fifty excursions, alternatives, excrescences, and the novel, as practised in English, is the perfect paradise of the loose end. The play consents to the logic of but one way, mathematically right . . . We are shut up wholly to cross-relations, relations all within the action itself; no part of which is related to anything but some other part—save of course by the relation of the total to life.[17]

James once again is primarily a dramatist, and in *The Awkward Age* he redeems his failure on the stage. We have seen the multiple cross-references in character; now let us look at the development of the action itself, "the logic" of the "one way," through the series of ten "Occasions" or acts. The cross-references here are equally complex and "difficult," make for anything but poverty, and yet form an ordered whole out of the course of an action and the illumination of a situation.

The plot of *The Awkward Age* follows a single action viewed from two different angles. The question of Nanda's exposure, which is involved with Mrs. Brook's social circle, Nanda's love for Van, and her friendship with Mr. Longdon and Mitchy, is the central thread of the novel. It is a peculiar, individual question as it affects Nanda and her life; and it is a social, public question as it touches on the social set and its leader, Mrs. Brook. The novel shifts between these two poles—Mrs. Brook and Nanda; there are really two heroines and two separate, but intricately related questions. The duality is further indicated in that the two heroines are present at the same time only twice in the novel, and only once are they alone together. Mrs. Brook is the center of the action in Books Two, Four, Six, and Nine; Nanda holds the stage in Books Three, Five, Seven, and Ten; they both occupy the center in Book Eight; and they meet only in Book Six, Chapter III and Book Eight, Chapter IV. The swing from one to the other is quite apparent. The purpose of this will become more obvious as we follow the course of the action.[18]

In Book One, "Lady Julia," neither of the central figures is present, after the conventions of the drama. In a section that is somewhat like the overture to *What Maisie Knew*, the prologue to *The Other House*, and perhaps even the first chapter of *The Spoils of Poynton*, Mr. Longdon and Vanderbank discuss the two central characters and all the major themes of the novel. Mr. Longdon's romantic past, his undying and unrequited love for Lady Julia, Nanda's grandmother, is placed in contrast to the "fast" modern set to which he has just been introduced. Past and present, London life, the tone of the circle, Nanda's age (which her mother says is sixteen; she's really almost nineteen), and the problems she presents to her elders—all are taken up at some length. Personal relationships are central; the contrast between friendship, as Mr. Longdon understands it, and the loser intimacies of the modern set is the focus of the development of relationships to follow. Van's rather perverse desire to be thought immoral is in sharp contrast to his sense of what is wrong with the group—"we keep giving each other away" (19)—and he wants Mr. Longdon to condemn him, glories in his exposure, hopes to shock in an almost prurient way. By the end of Book One the reader and Mr. Longdon are fully prepared for the kinds of action which follow.

Book Two, "Little Aggie," introduces Mrs. Brook under the two signs of social climbing and money. Harold's petty thievery is a reflection of his mother's more sophisticated avarice. As the book progresses, the whole question of Nanda's exposure is brought out in conversations with the Duchess regarding the problems that arise with two mature girls, Nanda and little Aggie. We finally have the social circle displayed almost in full when Lord Petherton and Mitchy join the group. The subject of the conversation throughout the last few chapters of the book is the illicit, promiscuous relations involving Lady Fanny, Carrie Donner, Lord Petherton, and the Duchess—the first clear example of what really endangers Nanda. Mrs. Brook throughout glories in the liaisons, meeting, consoling, and advising the various lovers.

Nanda is presented in Book Three, "Mr. Longdon." Van's social ease, Mitchy's infatuation with Nanda, and Nanda's gravity and self-possession point up the developing relationships among the three. Nanda soberly holds Mitchy off, tries to be friends, while Van is obviously most interested in passively observing Nanda's effect on Mr. Longdon. The core of the book is the establishment of the relationship between Nanda and Mr. Longdon on the basis of both her similarity to and her difference from her grandmother, Lady Julia.

Book Four, "Mr. Cashmore," forcibly acquaints Mr.

Longdon with Nanda's exposure and peril. Cashmore's crude and obvious desire to seduce Nanda reveals the kind of circle into which she might move, and Mr. Longdon's hatred of Mrs. Brook expresses his growing sense of danger. The relationships among the characters become even more intricate, and Mrs. Brook's selfish desire to draw Mr. Longdon to Nanda in order to get his money combines with Cashmore's vulgarities to make vivid the portrait of Mrs. Brook's circle.

Book Five, "The Duchess," introduces the actual machinery that will carry the plot through to the end. Nanda reveals her love for Van in a conversation with him in the first chapter. In the second there is an example of what exposure to her mother's circle means for her; in talking with Mr. Longdon she reveals her knowledge of the illicit relationships among the characters. Finally, in the last three chapters of the book, the Duchess gives a summary account of Nanda's danger to Mr. Longdon, and on the basis of what he has heard and seen he decides that Nanda should marry as soon as possible. He tries to bring this about by telling Van that the girl will receive a large sum of money when she marries. In effect, he tries to bribe him. The social situation is given added dimensions by the portrayal of a weekend visit to a rented country-place.

Book Six, "Mrs. Brook," follows the course of the action begun in the previous book. Van reveals to Mrs. Brook the terms of Mr. Longdon's offer, but, while telling Mitchy of the offer, she tells Van that he will never marry Nanda. The book displays Mrs. Brook's circle most clearly through its three inner members. They assert that they are "one beautiful intelligence" (297), and comment on the "extraordinary freedom and good-humour of our intercourse" (301); but the artificial, game-like quality of their behavior is shown when we discover that a fine of five pounds is imposed for a "cheap paradox." The last chapter of the book presents Nanda and her mother together for the first time. James describes the conversation between "these good friends" as diplomatic and "nice," and it is little more than that until Mrs. Brook introduces the subject of Mr. Longdon. After some discussion of "working" Mr. Longdon for what can be gotten out of him, she commands Nanda to go off with him. The complete failure in communication between the two becomes obvious in the contrast between Nanda's interest in personal relationships— "He makes one enjoy being liked," "It's so charming being liked . . . without being approved" (323-324)—and her mother's fear of social failure and desire for money—"Your father and I have most to think about . . . when we have to turn things round and manage somehow or other to get out of town, have to provide and pinch, to meet all the necessities, with money, money, money at every turn running away like water" (326). When Nanda speaks of doing something for Mr. Longdon by going to him, her mother replies that she wants her "still more to have some idea of what you'll get by it" (329). The book ends as Harold, his mother's son, nips another five-pound note off the table.

Book Seven, "Mitchy," gives the clearest picture of Nanda. She talks first with Van, in a pathetic attempt to win him, and then with Mitchy, in an equally hopeless effort to discourage him. In the first chapter, with Van, Nanda's knowledge, her exposure, is emphasized throughout— "Don't I know everything," "I must take in things at my pores," "Girls understand now. It has got to be faced" (340, 341). And her perception that Van is in his way as old-fashioned and sensitive about her knowledge as Mr.

Longdon establishes the final, undeniable split between herself and Van. With Mitchy she takes even greater control of the situation and makes him promise to save little Aggie from becoming like the Duchess. The focus of the scene is on the affinity between the two; she tells him, "*You're* one who, in perfect sincerity, doesn't mind one straw how awful . . . one's knowledge may be. It doesn't shock you in a single hereditary prejudice" (357). An even deeper insight into Nanda's character comes when she admits that she likes to love in vain, that she can only love the kind of man who cannot approve of her. The book ends with a conversation between Van and Mitchy which hovers around the topics of Mr. Longdon's money and Nanda's exposure; the appeal and the scruple which confront Van. He tacitly admits that he will not marry her, and his reason is that "everything, literally everything, in London, in the world she lives in, is in the air she breathes —so that the longer *she's* in it, the more she'll know" (378).

Book Eight, "Tishy Grendon," is the climax of the novel, bringing all the characters together after several months' separation, and foreshadowing the disintegration to come in the last two books. The Duchess again warns Mr. Longdon of dangers, and Nanda's exposure is examined once more in a scene with Van and herself. The climactic scene, however, is in Chapter IV. All the characters are seated together around a circle, described and discussed above, when Mrs. Brook makes her final move. She publicly demands that Nanda, who has been staying with Mr. Longdon, return to her family, hoping that this will force Mr. Longdon to commit himself fully to Nanda, give her money, and secure her future. And in front of them all she ironically plays with the details of little Aggie's (now married to Mitchy) flirtation with Lord Petherton (her aunt's

THE AWKWARD AGE

lover). In showing no concern for Nanda's presence, she obviously shocks Mr. Longdon. The climax of the scene comes when she hypocritically condemns Nanda for having read a French novel which she herself admits reading, but claims to think "hideous." Nanda comments that "One hardly knows now, I think, what is and what isn't" and Van adds, "I think I agree with Nanda that it's no worse than anything else" (433). With this Nanda's exposure is complete, accomplished directly by her mother, and Mr. Longdon immediately leaves.

The ninth and tenth books explore the disintegration of Mrs. Brook's circle and the final disposal of Nanda. In Book Nine, "Vanderbank," Van visits Mrs. Brook after several months' absence. Nanda's situation is discussed and, when Mrs. Brook slyly tells Van that Mr. Cashmore visits Nanda, he leaves without paying his intended call on Nanda. The remainder of the book takes up Mrs. Brook's plan to get Mr. Longdon to take Nanda permanently, and describes Van's jealousy of Mitchy's marriage to the "proper" girl, little Aggie, who is spotless before her marriage but quickly becomes too "knowing." With Chapter III, Mrs. Brook's last appearance, the original circle is completely destroyed. As Mitchy departs, we hear more about Harold's petty thievery and about his new liaison with Lady Fanny. In Chapter IX, the last of the book, James turns to Mitchy and Mr. Longdon and the subject of Nanda's love.

Book Ten, "Nanda," continues with this subject, and one by one the remaining characters are disposed of. Van gives up both Mrs. Brook and Nanda, too conscious of the guilt of the mother and of his guilt toward the daughter. Mitchy visits Nanda and discusses what her mother's circle has become and what her knowledge has led to. He leaves knowing that she will not abandon her friendship for him. Mr. Longdon comes to take Nanda out of it all, in spite of his awareness of what she knows. And Nanda finally breaks down under the tragedy of her loss of Van, the only time she loses self-control in the novel. She leaves, however, in full knowledge of what her environment has done to her; she sacrifices all life for peace with Mr. Longdon.

Book Ten returns to the themes and ideas introduced in Book One, gives the themes final statement, and completes the action. London life, the effect of the social situation, Nanda's exposure to it and her knowledge, the fact that, though changed, Mrs. Brook's circle goes on (she is now adviser to little Aggie in her affairs) all recur to the initial themes of the novel. Very little has changed, but knowledge, our knowledge and the characters' knowledge of themselves and others, has deepened. Even the details of the last book, such as the photographs in Nanda's room, parallel the setting of the first book, in which photographs of the same people were in Van's room. The novel, moving through ten books, comes full circle. The visitor to the new society whom we met at the start leaves, taking with him its tragic victim.

The variety of incident and the interrelationship of character in *The Awkward Age* is ordered by the structure of the novel. The intricate set of cross-references examined earlier in terms of character and arrangement of books is paralleled by the ordered movement of the action. There is, however, really very little overt action in the novel; most of the actions which do occur are verbal: Mr. Longdon makes his offer, Nanda encourages Mitchy to marry, Mrs. Brook verbally exposes Nanda. The novel is almost all talk, all dialogue, all superficially placid conversation. This peculiar form of action, in which no one "does" anything, points to the deepest concern of the novel. James is examining a static social situation in which nothing can be done. Thus the balances and symmetries in the structure of the novel, the circular, closed nature of the form, both reinforce the static formality of the situation and provide the only method by which James can give depth to his drama. The intricate turning-in upon itself of the structure of the novel reflects the society.

The circle in Book Eight, Chapter IV, which includes all the characters and through their talk brings the novel to a climax, is a model of the whole book, the image, in miniature, of a structure based on a circle which begins with the old confronting the new and ends with the best of the new returning to the old. The organic form James most admired is achieved in *The Awkward Age*. It is a form within which there is life of depth and significance, and the stylized aspect of the structure, the truly intricate circle of characters and books, at once reflects and is justified by the struggling life and formal society within it. "In *The Awkward Age* the multiplicity yields to order," as James contends in his preface.[19] In this analysis of the structure I hope one can begin to see "the exemplary closeness" of the novel which James asserted was a fusion of form and substance. Before evaluating that fusion, we must examine more closely the themes and meaning of the novel, the substance within the form.

V

Character, of course, is part of the substance and is intricately worked into the structure. Themes arise from the relationships among characters, include smaller details of character in a larger meaning, and draw significance from the grouping of the characters into a social entity which includes and affects all the people in the novel. This social entity in *The Awkward Age* is, as James says, "a particular, even a 'peculiar' one," Mrs. Brook's circle, and yet it stands for modern society, for London and English social life in the nineties. The particularities of the group, its peculiar and special nature, merely individualize it; it belongs also to a general social type. James's repeated references in the novel to London life in general make this clear; James says in his preface that "there are more things in London, I think, than anywhere in the world,"[20] and calls the city "that vast nursery of sharp appeals and concrete images which calls itself, for blest convenience, London."[21] In Book One Van describes London life in a way which establishes the contrast between Mrs. Brook's circle, with its concern for social position and money, and Nanda's and Mr. Longdon's search for some valuable personal relationship in the midst of it all: " 'It strikes you that right and left, probably, we keep giving each other away. Well, I dare say we do . . . What's London life after all? It's tit for tat.' [Mr. Longdon:] 'Ah but what becomes of friendship? . . .' 'I never really have believed in the existence of friendship in big societies—in great towns and great crowds. It's a plant that takes time and space and air; and London society is a huge "squash," as we elegantly call it —an elbowing pushing perspiring chattering mob' " (19-20). It is typical of the cross-references in the novel that Van returns to the same theme in Book Ten when he visits Nanda in her "tower" over the "great wicked city" (495), for down below is Mrs. Brook's drawing room. London life is only an extension of Mrs. Brook's circle, and Nanda's exposure is often referred to in this larger context: "Of course she's supposedly young, but she's really any age you like: your London world so fearfully batters and bruises them" (248). We often see Nanda in danger in places outside her mother's circle but which have the same features of London life that the smaller group does. The events of the novel move from place to place: small *tête-à-têtes* in Van's rooms or Mrs. Brook's, larger gatherings at Mrs. Brook's and Tishy Grendon's, a typical weekend at a rented country estate (the society is urban, owns no land), and a contrasting visit to Mr. Longdon's country place. *The Awkward Age* is a varied picture of a social world, an expressly "modern" one of the 1890's.

Typical of this modernity and the center of Nanda's dangers is the circle of which her mother is the leader. The keynote of the group is "talk": "I happen to be so constituted that my life has something to do with my mind and my mind something to do with my talk. Good talk: you know—no one, dear Van, should know better—what part for me that plays" (284). All the talk is extremely, even self-consciously, clever and it becomes something of a game with its own rules and fines imposed for breaking them. When Mrs. Brook asks Mr. Longdon why he hates her, Van breaks in: "I should warn you, sir . . . how little we consider that—in Buckingham Crescent certainly—a fair question. It isn't playing the game—it's hitting below the belt. We hate and we love—the latter especially; but to tell each other why is to break that little tacit rule of finding out for ourselves which is the delight of our lives and the source of our triumphs. You can say, you know, if you like, but you're not obliged" (407). This is not quite real, merely a game with the counters of human intercourse and normal motives. Conversation becomes a sort of intellectual puzzle, a game of hide-and-seek the motive. All the talk is of course part of the purely dramatic, verbal aspect of the action noted above, but within the group this feature is carried to an extreme.

The nature of Mrs. Brook's circle, then, is twofold. Any mention of it includes as principal descriptive term something relating to the mind—intelligence, intellect, idea—but there is also always detachment—at its most praiseworthy, freedom, but shading with Mrs. Brook into artifice and indifference. This quality, which has already been noted in her character, pervades the whole circle. Mrs. Brook describes her group as "one beautiful intelligence" and there is much talk of "tremendous perceptions," "intellectual elbow-room," and "freedom of talk." The intellectual quality of the talk is reflected primarily in its cleverness, in its concern "for each other's vibrations," in attempts to discover motives and feelings without being told. But it tends too often to be "mere talk"; the effect of detachment is clear in Van's judgment and Mrs. Brook's reaction: "[Mrs. Brook:] 'And yet to think that after all it has been mere *talk!*' ... [Van:] 'Mere, mere, mere. But perhaps it's exactly the "mere" that has made us range so wide.' Mrs. Brook's intelligence abounded. 'You mean that we haven't had the excuse of passion?'" (313). The truth is that their passions do not often engage their "talk," their minds. They are detached observers, selfish in thought and action; for others they have only their "tremendous perceptions" and the thrill the game gives them. They are essentially passive.[22]

Van's joyful guilt at Mr. Longdon's implied condemnation in Book One sets the tone for the whole circle. Mr. Longdon is unfamiliarly and old-fashionedly moral; for those in the circle he is someone to watch and glean pleasure from for the new perceptions he brings. Mrs. Brook delights in observing the promiscuities of

Lady Fanny, "the ornament of our circle," and she encourages Mr. Longdon to "show" them his passion for Lady Julia, her mother, and tells him of "our positive delight in your being exactly so different; the pleasure we have in talking about you, and shall still have—or indeed all the more—even if we've seen you only to lose you" (190). The circle glories in its perceptions, particularly if they are detached from any emotional involvement; the group is the apotheosis of all that is frightening and sterile in James's many detached spectators (unless the narrator of *The Sacred Fount* should surpass them). Mitchy reveals the true nature of their perversions, a kind of *fin-de-siècle* decadence: "Nothing is more charming than suddenly to come across something sharp and fresh after we've thought there was nothing more that could draw from us a groan. We've supposed we've had it all, have squeezed the last impression out of the last disappointment, penetrated to the last familiarity in the last surprise; then some fine day we find that we haven't done justice to life" (350). There can be no more damning comment. The people in the circle are always close to boredom, always titillating themselves with a grasped freshness in an attempt to escape their anhedonia, their exceptional inability to feel. That is Mrs. Brook's greatest fear, and so she maintains her group for the sensations she can gain from them, drawing Aggie to her when the others have failed her, "working" Van to keep him for herself, and "working" Mr. Longdon for the new perceptions he may give, and of course for the money to be gotten out of him.

In addition to the cultivation of her perceptions, money and social position are the two values in Mrs. Brook's life. She tells Van that money is "usually, with people, the very first thing I get my impression of" (179). Most of her actions in the novel are directed to getting Mr. Longdon's money for Nanda, after it has become apparent that Nanda will not accept Mitchy, who has even more money. Money is also one appeal to Van; he cannot respond to Nanda's love, but Mr. Longdon's offer attracts him. Almost every one of Mrs. Brook's scenes ends with some reference to money, to Mr. Longdon's worth or to her son Harold's acquisitive habits. Mr. Longdon's criticism of the rented country place can stand for a criticism of the whole cash-value basis of Mrs. Brook's society: "What are people made of that they consent, just for money, to the violation of their homes?" (219).

Nanda's home is violated in this way as a matter of course. Her mother's society, the nature of the small circle, imposes itself directly on her, and this imposition creates the central problem of the novel: the effect of social convention on the individual. This relationship is also more personal and affects the action. As the Duchess says, Mrs. Brook "must sacrifice either her daughter or what she once called to me her intellectual habits" (255). The alternatives are clear, and although there is much talk of a compromise between the English and the "continental" custom, there really is none. Mrs. Brook continues the same; Nanda is sacrificed figuratively in the continual talk of what to do about her, and literally in the climactic scene at Tishy Grendon's. Van has the intelligence to see what has happened, to see clearly the relation between Nanda and the circle; he is able to judge though unable to act: "What stupifies me a little . . . is the extraordinary critical freedom—or we may call it if we like the high intellectual detachment—with which we discuss a question touching you, dear Mrs. Brook, so nearly and engaging so your most private and sacred sentiments. What are we playing with, after all, but the idea of Nanda's happiness?" (306). Van of course mistakes the direction of Mrs. Brook's private and sacred sentiments; they are directed more toward him than Nanda and more toward herself than him. Just a few moments after she has learned of Mr. Longdon's offer of a dowry if Van will marry Nanda, Mrs. Brook fails to mention either the offer or Van to her daughter; their discussion stays on what can be gotten out of Mr. Longdon or Mitchy. The group violates Nanda's innocence precisely because they are unwilling to sacrifice their own pleasures to save it. Nanda must, regardless of knowledge or innocence, fit into their patterns of social and monetary striving, and she must not conflict with their enjoyment of "talk." In the one example of Mrs. Brook's "talk" in Nanda's presence, Book Eight, Chapter IV, she alludes, as we have seen, to Aggie's impurity and Nanda's knowledge of the "hideous" French novel. Nanda has no protection from her mother. Social convention, in the person of her mother and the people around her, destroys her chances for life.

The central, personal themes of the novel are familiar ones. They are essentially the same questions of innocence and knowledge that James explored in *What Maisie Knew*. The principal difference in *The Awkward Age* is that here the subject, Nanda, is older, closer to adult life, and the surrounding adult society is conceived in the terms of the social history of convention, based on a radical contrast between old and new mores. Nanda's innocence is of the same inviolability as Maisie's. Her knowledge does not corrupt, for James distinguishes between innocence and ignorance. In contrast to Nanda, little Aggie's protected position and her genuine ignorance give her the appearance of innocence, which is shattered as soon as she gains knowledge after marrying Mitchy. Nanda, on the other hand, is innocent and knowing; she cannot help knowing, because of her exposure, but knowledge and innocence are separate and uncontradictory. Nothing affects her essential purity; she is never shocked, always sober and controlled: "There was always in Nanda's face that odd preparedness of the young person who has unlearned surprise through the habit, in company, of studiously not compromising her innocence by blinking at things said" (232). The acceptance of knowledge for Nanda means being true to herself, not pretending not to know, in short acting the reverse of her mother's hypocrisy. Mr. Longdon warns her against trying "to *appear* to be anything," and Nanda replies with remarkable self-knowledge: "Anything different, you mean, from what I am? That's just what I've thought from the first. One's just what one *is*—isn't one? I don't mean so much . . . in one's character or temper—for they have, haven't they? to be what's called 'properly controlled'— as in one's mind and what one sees and feels and the sort of thing one notices" (229-30). Nanda's character and temper make her inviolable; her knowledge cannot corrupt because her morality will not let it. She recognizes that what is "right is for one not to pretend anything else" (356). In this way she can control a life in which "there was never a time when I didn't know *something* or other" (528). Nanda sees herself as "a sort of a little drainpipe with everything flowing through" (358).

The image is perfect, for Nanda is subjected to the sewage of society and knows it. The awareness, however, destroys her. The society insists that the maiden be pure in mind as well as body before marriage, no matter what sort of harlot she may become after; and Nanda does not qualify. Her knowing innocence displaces her, makes her impossible for her mother and Van, acceptable only to Mitchy and Mr. Longdon who will ignore the standards. She is sacrificed, a martyr to false convention and a rapidly changing society. This accounts for her inevitable gravity. Whereas there was some hope for Maisie, and she was fresh and cheerful in it, there is none for Nanda, and she has no cheer. The sterility and sacrifice that seemed to be voluntary in Fleda Vetch are imposed on Nanda. It is her one way out. Only when Mr. Longdon, near the end of the novel, forces her to admit her own impossibility, her love for Van, does she give way to "a passion as sharp and brief as the flurry of a wild thing for an instant uncaged" (540). In the rest of the novel, Nanda is in the cage: "It's I who am the horrible impossible and who have covered everything else with my own impossibility" (541). She has been put to uses which she does not fit by the morality of her mother's world, and she still remains as innocent as Lady Julia, only displaced in time; because the world is thirty years older, she knows too much but is morally too strong to pretend otherwise. Innocence and knowledge are held by her integrity; Nanda cannot be her mother's hypocrite.

The themes are resolved in the ultimate meaning of the title of the book. Nanda herself is almost never awkward; she only makes others so. But she is at "the awkward age," neither child nor woman. She is also neither in the world nor out of it; she is awkwardly thrust into some limbo because she is unplaceable in the changed customs and artificial conventions of the world. The age itself is awkward, a period when moral conventions do not correspond to the manners of the society, when knowledge of the one hinders observance of the other. In such a period of anarchy, when the society is divorced from its morality, the good, like Nanda, Mitchy, or Mr. Longdon, are displaced persons, awkwardly existing out of the full stream of life.

The Awkward Age is finally tragic, for the best are sacrificed to the worst. Mrs. Brook's salon goes on, Van will continue to charm, but Mitchy is cursed with a false marriage, Mr. Longdon must retire once more, and Nanda is lost. Halfway through the novel, in a rare departure from James's dramatic objectivity, Mr. Longdon has an unspoken vision of the end of it all: "Both girls [Aggie and Nanda] struck him as lambs with the great shambles of life in their future; but while one, with its neck in a pink ribbon, had no consciousness but that of being fed from the hand with the small sweet biscuit of unobjectionable knowledge, the other struggled with instincts and forebodings, with the suspicion of its doom and the far-borne scent, in flowery fields, of blood" (239). He perceives the true meaning of Nanda's innocence. One must have consciousness, but in the society James portrays one cannot have objectionable knowledge and remain innocent, for society will reject the awkwardness this imposes for the smooth compatibility of a Harold Brookenham, who has grown up in the image of his mother. Nanda's final, naive "everything's different from what it used to be," is more than simple nostalgia. It is James's outcry at the human predicament in the society he has portrayed. The scent of blood in flowery fields is James's and Mr. Longdon's imagination of disaster.[23]

The tragedy of Nanda Brookenham is her alienation; her integrity cuts her off from life. There is significance in the gibbering, disembowelled crew that surrounds her; it

THE AWKWARD AGE

is the same crowd that inhabits *The Cherry Orchard.* Nanda cannot communicate with anyone of that world. She is accepted by Mr. Longdon, but understood only by Mitchy. Henry James's tragic vision was nowhere more intense than in *The Awkward Age,* outwardly a comic social novel, actually an exploration of a diseased society. He had found the form which would truly express the predicament of his disinherited, innocent girls; and he equalled it only in *The Wings of the Dove.*

The circumscription of the form of *The Awkward Age* matches the closed society embodied in it. It is essentially a sterile society, but a complex one. James achieves his circle by creating a small group to represent his larger criticism of London life. Within the circle the relations are multiplied and made complex. James fuses the structure with the substance of the novel to produce a tragic work of art in which meaning is mirrored in that structure; Nanda's only escape is withdrawal, breaking out of the circle. The whole is achieved by the effective use of what James had learned in his "theatrical exercises," strict attention to form and careful objectivity of presentation.

In *The Awkward Age* James redeemed his dramatic years and wrote his greatest "scenic" novel. He also brought to full artistic expression his vision of English life, a vision finally and almost totally damning. After one more novel, he returned to the international theme. But in *The Awkward Age* he had successfully shown the relationship between the self and society and perhaps demonstrated why so many of his novels deal with so limited a society. He saw no hope for the self in it.

The dramatic texture of *The Awkward Age* is built on a social comedy close to Restoration comedy; James's objectivity is one of tolerant wit. His final judgment, however, is tragic.[24] By moving away from the central consciousness for this one novel, James was able to give dramatic objectivity to the social group he pictured. The drama of dialogue, wit, and gesture enabled him to remain above the society and simply let it reveal itself. The dramatic novel as represented by *The Awkward Age* is one of James's major achievements, for it is objective and at the same time tragic. What sort of hell should we have experienced if we had seen it all represented on Nanda's grave sad consciousness?

7

The Sacred Fount

> We work in the dark—we do what we can—we give what we have. Our doubt is our passion and our passion is our task. The rest is the madness of art.
>
> Henry James, "The Middle Years"

NO SINGLE WORK by Henry James is more strikingly experimental than *The Sacred Fount*. It may at times appear to be little more than the "technical exercise" that Joseph Warren Beach first called it.[1] It does not attain the fullness of *What Maisie Knew* and *The Awkward Age;* the experimental, the even game-like aspects of the novel, are never quite transformed, as they are in the two previous novels, to the successful, the proven. The degree of tenuousness and questioning, of hesitation and ambiguity in structure and meaning, suggests a new departure, but one made in the dark and toward an uncertain destination. *The Sacred Fount* is a trying-out, a final experiment before the achievements of the major phase. Since it was written, however, at the height of James's artistic powers, just after two successes and just before *The Wings of the Dove* and *The Ambassadors,* his obsessions and skills at this moment in his career inform it and give it a strong claim on our attention. Much critical effort has been applied to the novel, particularly to its final meaning and to its literary value.[2] I believe that a clearer idea of that meaning and value can be attained by looking at the experimental aspects of the novel, especially in the light of this whole period of experiment. Technique, structure, and theme in the novel itself need to be seen in the context of the other novels of the nineties.

An important fact in the history of *The Sacred Fount*, which has played a part in its evaluation, is that James did not include the novel in the New York Edition of 1907-9. His apparent rejection of the novel has led critics also to reject it. We must, however, form our judgment of the novel primarily on the novel itself. James was attempting in that collected edition to give a clear picture of his career as he saw it, and certain novels did not fit the plan. As Leon Edel notes, "The exclusions were not merely matters of 'taste' but related distinctly to the 'architecture' of the Edition."[3] That *The Sacred Fount* cannot be rejected simply because it did not fit into this edition is also apparent from a glance at the other novels excluded: *Watch and Ward, The Europeans, Confidence, Washington Square, The Bostonians,* and *The Other House*, at least three of which have central places in the James canon.

Since it was not included, there is no preface in which James could provide us with information about his intentions and methods of composition; and there are only very brief notebook entries on the novel.[4] Nevertheless, certain features of its composition are similar to those of the other novels of the period and provide an initial insight. The notebooks are of some help here. James's first notebook entry on *The Sacred Fount*—February 17, 1894

THE SACRED FOUNT

—comes in the middle of that dramatic period when he jotted down the subjects for most of his later novels. He mentions the novel again in February and May of 1899 and evidently began the novel some time after that. It is probable that he spent much of 1900 writing the novel. Never serialized, it was published in February 1901. As usual, James conceived the idea of *The Sacred Fount* as the subject of a short story, an "anecdote" and a "concetto," or conceit. And, again as usual, the novel expanded during composition, which will help account for certain structural features considered below. The short-story conception also helps somewhat to explain the use of a first-person narrator, for the technique is common in James's short stories, particularly when that narrator is a detached observer, usually a critic or some kind of literary man, who objectively relates the story. The technique is often found in James's stories of artists and writers.[5]

In *The Sacred Fount* we find the same kind of observer, but James has transferred his attention to the subjective response of the man, rather in the manner of his use of the third-person central consciousness in *The Spoils of Poynton* and *What Maisie Knew*. This transfer complicates story and theme, for the narrator's objectivity comes into doubt. *The Sacred Fount* is the only full-length novel in which James employs a first-person narrator; only short novels like *The Aspern Papers* and *The Turn of the Screw* are comparable, and they have posed similar problems for the reader. The results of the use of this particular narrator and of James's focus on him are just those uncertain qualities which mark the novel as experimental, that mystification which the reader feels throughout. So our analysis must be concerned primarily with the peculiar problems of first-person narration, especially as that affects the style of the novel, and with the structure within which that narrator moves. Theme and meaning follow from these. What has been learned of James's techniques and ideas in the earlier novels should be of great value in seeing the pattern in this carpet.

II

The Sacred Fount has a simplicity of outline which is somewhat like that of *The Other House*, the initial novel of this experimental period. There is none of the elaboration of character and society that can be found in *What Maisie Knew* or *The Awkward Age*. James again limits his characters to a handful. There are two perhaps symmetrically arranged couples: Mr. and Mrs. Brissenden, Gilbert Long and May Server; there is the narrator who observes the action and speculates on the arrangement; a painter, Ford Obert, with whom he discusses his ideas; and a subordinate figure, Lady John, who may or may not have some relation to one of the couples. None of the characters is developed at length, most have very little to say and are given only one or two individualizing traits. For the most part, they follow generally the Jamesian types found in the other novels of the period.[6] Gilbert Long, like Owen Gereth, is a hearty, robust gentleman, "a fine piece of human furniture"; Guy Brissenden has all the helplessness of that type with none of its strength; Grace Brissenden combines traits of Mrs. Gereth and Mrs. Brookenham, intelligent, forceful, and somewhat suspect; and May Server is the charming, beautiful, red-haired ingénue, with some unaccountable tragic quality about her. May is like Jean Martle, Fleda Vetch, Nanda Brookenham, and all those heroines of Henry James who are reputed to be modeled on his cousin Minny Temple.

In spite of the vagueness of outline, she clearly points ahead to Milly Theale. All of these characters, however, do very little; they exist as types. And this brings us to an essential difference between *The Sacred Fount* and a novel like *The Other House*.

In *The Sacred Fount* there is almost no external action; more even than *The Awkward Age* the novel is static, an exploration of a situation. The story itself is extremely simple. The narrator, taking a train to the country for a weekend at a house called Newmarch, meets two acquaintances, Mrs. Brissenden and Gilbert Long. Mrs. Brissenden seems younger than he remembers her, and Gilbert Long seems cleverer. When he arrives at Newmarch, the narrator meets Guy Brissenden, who seems to have aged unnaturally, and he conceives the theory of the sacred fount—that one partner to a couple will draw on the gifts of the other, thus depleting the other's vitality. Mrs. Brissenden draws on her husband's youth and becomes younger while he ages too rapidly. To prove the theory and to provide symmetry, there must also be some woman who is giving Long his new intelligence. The remainder of the novel is taken up with the narrator's thirty-six-hour search for the woman and his effort to prove the theory. All of this search takes place in conversations with the other characters and in the narrator's solitary meditations. When Mrs. Brissenden denies his theory late the second night, the novel ends with the narrator's resolve to return to London early the next day. That is the extent of the action. The novel moves through a series of conversations which attempt to explore the central situation, the relations among these people, in much the same manner that conversation is the method of *The Awkward Age*.

This simplicity is merely on the surface, however, and

considerable complexity is introduced by James's narrative technique. All of the details of character and all the elements of the story come to us through the narrator, the "I". His theory of the sacred fount unifies the novel, brings all the conversations into focus; and his meditations on his theory, his sensitive response and endless intellectualizing upon that response, make up the major part of the subject matter. For the first-person narrator in *The Sacred Fount* is not a detached observer, conveying to the reader as objectively as possible the details of what he observes. His subjective experience of those objective details becomes the focus of the novel, just as Fleda Vetch's responses become the subject, rather than merely the recording consciousness of *The Spoils of Poynton*. In *The Sacred Fount* the mind of the narrator intrudes between the reader and the experience. The first-person narrator has, as James says, in the preface to *The Ambassadors*, "the double privilege of subject and object."[7] The impressionism which results has a direct bearing on both the difficulty and the meaning of the novel.

James also discusses in his preface to *The Ambassadors* his rejection of the first-person technique for that novel, and his comments surely reflect on *The Sacred Fount,* its immediate predecessor: "Had I meanwhile made [the central figure—Strether] at once hero and historian, endowed him with the romantic privilege of the 'first person'—the darkest abyss of romance this, inveterately, when enjoyed on the grand scale—variety, and many other queer matters as well, might have been smuggled in by a back door."[8] He goes on to describe the "looseness" of the technique and "the terrible fluidity of self-revelation."[9] Looseness, fluidity, and romance are directly related to James's distinctions between the romantic and the real in the preface to *The American,* distinctions which are of exceptional value in understanding *The Sacred Fount,* for they are central to perceiving the narrator's role in the novel:

> The real represents to my perception the things we cannot possibly *not* know, sooner or later, in one way or another; it being but one of the accidents of our hampered state, and one of the incidents of their quantity and number, that particular instances have not yet come our way. The romantic stands, on the other hand, for the things that, with all the facilities in the world, all the wealth and all the courage and all the wit and all the adventure, we can never directly know; the things that can reach us only through the beautiful circuit and subterfuge of our thought and our desire.[10]

James goes on to describe the kind of experience with which the romantic deals: "Experience liberated, so to speak; experience disengaged, disembroiled, disencumbered, exempt from the conditions that we usually know to attach to it . . . and operating in a medium which relieves it . . . from the inconvenience of a *related,* a measurable state, a state subject to all our vulgar communities."[11] The separation of the first-person narrator from his material, the subjective isolation of consciousness, is exactly the romantic nature of the form; the danger is that he will be cut off entirely from the real, that isolation will lead to "the darkest abyss of romance." The final meaning of the novel is directly involved in this dichotomy, and we can only get at that meaning through the narrator. The narrator of *The Sacred Fount* is one of James's most elaborate and disturbing characterizations, for he is a romantic confronting the materials of reality. James's innocents, Fleda Vetch especially, are in a similar situation; but in *The Sacred Fount* the technique places the reader in the narrator's mind, cut off from the "vulgar community." We see only his thought and his desire and share his inability to determine what is real.

The first-person narrative technique limits the reader to what the narrator tells him. Placed in this position, the reader is forced to concern himself with the characteristics of the mind within which he is confined. By understanding its nature we can better understand its special relation to the external world and the material it presents us. In this novel, James focuses directly on the mind of the narrator, and that mind is so individualized, even eccentric, that it must have some effect on the material that passes through it. James's primary interest is with that effect, that subjective, romantic coloration and even transformation of reality.

The narrator of *The Sacred Fount* is a highly idiosyncratic figure. We learn early that he is an older man, that he is not attached to any of the people at Newmarch; he is in much the same relation to his society as Mr. Longdon in *The Awkward Age*. He is a detached observer of those around him. He is outwardly passive; we catch him at times lurking outside windows, overhearing conversations, watching people from a distance. He speaks of his "general habit—of observation."[12] Part of his separateness is his sensitivity, his unusual response to nuance and detail, to implication; he is almost hyper-observant. His shyness and careful privacy are also part of the role of outsider or observer. He has a horror of exposing his thoughts to the world. He does, however, have a great curiosity about other people, and he is an inveterate theorizer about their behavior. He speaks of his "extraordinary interest in my fellow-creatures. I have more than most men. I've never really seen anyone with half so much. That breeds observation and observation breeds ideas" (147). In addition to noting his habit of observation, two aspects of this speech are remarkable: his extreme egotism and his commitment to "ideas." Halfway through the novel he exults in his theory, describes it as "an undiluted bliss, in the intensity of consciousness that I had reached. *I alone was magnificently and absurdly aware*—everyone else was benightedly out of it" (177). His egotism is grandiose; he thinks of his theory and the other characters as his "creations": "to see all this was at the time, I remember, to be as inhumanly amused as if one had found one could create something" (104). Throughout he tends to see himself as god or artist—Lady John at one point tells him to give up "the attempt to be providence" (176).

His ideas are behind all his interests; he is drawn into the affairs of others, "though always but intellectually." As his theory of the sacred fount begins to form, he describes his feelings and thoughts as those of the philosopher (and, interestingly, partly in the language of the detective):

> I felt from the first that if I was on the scent of something ultimate I had better waste neither my wonder nor my wisdom. I was on the scent . . . I was just conscious, vaguely, of being on the track of a law, a law that would fit, that would strike me as governing the delicate phenomena—delicate though so marked—that my imagination found itself playing with. A part of the amusement they yielded came, I daresay, from my exaggerating them—grouping them into a larger mystery (and thereby a larger "law") than the facts, as observed, yet warranted; but that is a common fault of minds for which the vision of life is an obsession. (22-23)

The result of this obsession is "the joy of the intellectual mastery of things unamenable, that joy of determining, almost of creating results" (214). Two characteristics stand out in addition to his intellectual bent: his imagination and his obsession. The whole novel is a testament to the obsession; only an obsession could build so much on so slight a base. But to understand that obsession, his "private madness," we must look further into his character.

His imagination combines with his intellect to give a compelling force to his vision. The artistic, creative nature of his hypothesis about the people around him is in part his imaginative coloration of the "laws" of human behavior. The clearest indication of how his imagination enhances what he sees comes during a moment he spends alone in the gardens, away from people and the need to observe and theorize:

> There was a general shade in all the lower reaches—a fine clear dusk in garden and grove, a thin suffusion of twilight out of which the greater things, the high tree-tops and pinnacles, the long crests of motionless wood and chimnied roof, rose into golden air. The last calls of birds sounded extraordinarily loud; they were like the timed, serious splashes, in wide, still water, of divers not expecting to rise again. I scarce know what odd consciousness I had of roaming at close of day in the grounds of some castle of enchantment. I had positively encountered nothing to compare with this since the days of fairy-tales and of the childish imagination of the impossible. *Then* I used to circle round enchanted castles, for then I moved in a world in which the strange "came true." It was the coming true that was the proof of the enchantment, which, moreover, was naturally never so great as when such coming was, to such a degree and by the most romantic stroke of all, the fruit of one's own wizardry. I was positively—so had the wheel revolved—proud of my work. I had thought it all out, and to have thought it was, wonderfully, to have brought it. (128-29)

THE SACRED FOUNT

The passage touches on all his characteristics: intellect, egotism, sensitivity. But it is even more revealing of the narrator's romantic imagination, his painting of reality with strokes of beauty, strangeness, enchantment, wizardry. Characteristically, he has this romantic vision in solitude, just as later in the novel, he moves out into the night alone and finds "the breath of the outer air a sudden corrective to the grossness of our lustre and the thickness of our medium, our general heavy humanity" (199). The house then becomes "our crystal cage." The narrator's intellect and his imagination enable him to escape from this cage of reality into a romantic world which will accommodate his pure and elegant theory of the sacred fount.

At the same time, however, his imagination does not entirely free him from the "grossness" and "thickness" of "heavy humanity." Intellectually, it remains pure and light, but humanly it is often "the imagination of atrocity" (173) or, as it is also for Fleda Vetch, "the imagination of a disaster." The odd and remarkable metaphor in the center of the passage quoted above is a brilliant example of that; the quiet notation of the "divers not expecting to rise again" is an indication of this aspect of the narrator's imagination. The theory of the sacred fount, for all the symmetry and beauty it embodies for the narrator, is a theory of vampirism, the destruction of one human being by another, the drawing out of life. Although quieter and less explicit, it is much like Hawthorne's representation of evil in *The Scarlet Letter*.[13]

The narrator, then, is a romantic egotist with an intellect of some power and an imagination of great force, capable of giving him joy but at the same time profoundly, though perhaps unconsciously, morbid. For him humanity offers little more than material for the pleasures of the mind, although a bleaker vision hides beneath joy. As he notes, "Light or darkness, my imagination rides me" (276).

The nature of the man is reflected in his language; we cannot escape his character for we must read his words. And one of the principal difficulties in reading this at times obtuse work is the style. As the narrator himself comments, when one of the characters accuses him of being crazy, of not being understandable: "No, I daresay, to do you justice, the interpretation of my tropes and figures *isn't* 'ever' perfectly simple" (283). The variety of his figures runs from those suicidal divers to the sacred fount itself, a horror under its sacredness, and to his conception of himself in the final scene with Mrs. Brissenden as "an exemplary Christian" watched by "a Roman lady at a circus."

"Tropes and figures" do provide one of the major vehicles of the narrator's thought, but even more prominent and finally more difficult in its sheer volume is his intellectual, abstract, elaborate prose style. The whole of Chapter VI is an almost impenetrable example of his mental activity, an extreme form of the style found in the meditations of Fleda Vetch, but a few shorter passages must represent the quality of his mind and the nature of his expression. The narrator "reflects" in the following manner: "What was none of one's business might change its name should importunity take the form of utility. In resisted observation that was vivid thought, in inevitable thought that was vivid observation, through a succession, in short, of phases in which I shall not pretend to distinguish one of these elements from the other, I found myself cherishing the fruit of the seed dropped equally by Ford Obert and by Mrs. Briss" (93-94). And again, later: "If there had been, so to speak, a discernment, however feeble, of *my* discernment, it would have been irresistible to me to take this as the menace of some incalculable catastrophe or some public ugliness. It wasn't for me definitely to image the logical result of a verification by the sense of others of the matter of my vision" (174). This is James's prose at its densest and most abstract, and comprehending it takes some effort. Above all, the prose shows the density, the convolutions and intricate intellectual movements, of the narrator's mind. The style mirrors the man in this first-person narrative, and we finally agree with his own judgment: "I daresay that . . . my cogitations —for I must have bristled with them—would have made me as stiff a puzzle to interpretative minds as I had suffered other phenomena to become to my own" (92). The intricate prose style presents the character and forms throughout the novel an abstract, almost unreal medium in which the drama of the novel takes place.

III

The drama and the style are present in the opening paragraph of the novel, a meditative passage in which the narrator reveals details of his character that will gain in significance as the "action" progresses: "It was an occasion, I felt—the prospect of a large party—to look out at the station for others, possible friends and even possible enemies, who might be going. Such premonitions, it was true, bred fears when they failed to breed hopes, though it was to be added that there were sometimes, in the case, rather happy ambiguities" (1). The narrator's logical turn of mind and his tendency to think in rather melodramatic blacks and whites is evident, although this is modified by the added third alternative, ambiguities—which he will not always find "happy."[14] A few lines below the narrator mentions, only to disclaim, what will be his greatest weakness: "The wish was father to the thought." His sensitivity, even his fear of others, is noted as he chooses to avoid one of the other members of the party.

In that opening moment the character and mind of the narrator are hinted at, and we move on to be intensely present in each of his impressions and in his obsessions with the behavior of other people. *The Sacred Fount* is subtly dramatic, a further example of James's experimentation with the possibilities of the dramatic novel. Much of the novel is given over to conversations between the narrator and usually only one of the other characters, scenes in dialogue which are typically in the manner of *The Awkward Age* and the other novels of this period. Balancing this, however, is the dramatic immediacy of the meditations that go on in the mind of the narrator, and this is peculiar to *The Sacred Fount*. These passages can best be described as interior monologues which are controlled and intellectualized in a way that stream of consciousness usually is not. While they bear some similarity to passages of meditation involving centers of consciousness like Fleda Vetch or Maisie Farange, the analysis and abstraction is more extreme, as noted above, and at the same time the use of the first person strongly increases the sense of the dramatic present. Although he is recounting the story from a later time, the narrator seldom breaks the illusion of the present and tells more than he knows at a particular moment; James uses this to create drama and suspense, and to keep the reader moving at the pace of the narrator, mystified and expectant.

The quality of suspense in the drama of the novel is partly that of the mystery story, and James from time to time, as noted in one of the passages above, uses imagery

THE SACRED FOUNT

from the detective story. One of the other characters, Ford Obert, warns the narrator about prying and searching for "material clues," but Obert assures the narrator that it can be an "honorable" game—when it relies on "psychologic signs alone, it's a high application of intelligence. What's ignoble is the detective and the keyhole" (66). The narrator takes this for assurance of his own purity of motive, although he still longs for a material clue. Moreover, scents, clues, false scents, covering one's tracks, and evidence of various sorts are all part of the narrator's vocabulary.

The suspense and immediacy of the drama are an integral part of the structure of the novel. James immerses us in the mind of the narrator as he wanders through his weekend at Newmarch. Each impression, each reflection, is carefully recorded in its place, each conversation as it occurs. A good deal of the intensity of the drama is the result of this closeness to the present and the narrow limits of the duration of the action. James stays close to chronological time. The whole of the action takes about thirty-six hours; most of it occurs between morning and midnight of the second day. And James observes the other traditional dramatic unities of place and action.[15]

The drama of *The Sacred Fount* falls into phases typical of James's construction during this period. There are four or perhaps five "acts" in the novel, and each serves a particular purpose in the development of the action and the narrator's thought. The first act or phase of the action, Chapters I and II, is a prelude which introduces the characters and gives an initial exposition of the narrator's theory and the themes of the novel. The act takes place the afternoon before the day of the main action. Act two begins the next morning, establishes the relationship between the narrator and Mrs. Brissenden, and complicates the action and theme in the series of conversations and the scene before the picture of the man with the mask (Chapters III-V). Chapter VI is partly transitional; it carries the action over a time interval until late afternoon and summarizes the narrator's mental and imaginative progress. It begins the third phase of the action, which continues through Chapters VII and VIII. This third act concentrates on the two depleted figures in the formula of the sacred fount, Guy Brissenden and May Server. It also marks the narrator's closest approach to emotional involvement with the other characters. As the center of the novel, it illustrates the highest complication of his theory and his greatest confidence. After another time interval, the fourth act begins with the narrator's decision to give up his inquiry, partly because of his emotional identification with the depleted pair. The whole of the fourth phase, however, (Chapters IX-XI) contains the narrator's gradual return to the theory, revealed mostly through his mental reactions to what he observes during an evening of wandering and watching. The section ends with a conversation with Ford Obert, who, through his own partial enthusiasm for the theory, is able to reinforce the narrator's obsession. The fifth phase (which might perhaps be considered part of the fourth, since there is no time interval) is the long scene with Mrs. Brissenden and the narrator (Chapters XII-XIV). Here the narrator's theory is apparently destroyed, and the focus of the action is on the irreconcilable split between his mind and reality, on his inability ever really to know the truth about the people he has been observing.

The over-all pattern in the action is simply a deepening of the narrator's consciousness and a more and more intense participation in the present. The first three phases take up the first half of the novel; the final two phases, the last evening, comprise the last half; and the final long scene with Mrs. Brissenden, although it takes but one hour in the time of the action, occupies fully a quarter of the novel. This slowing of the pace actually marks a gradual increase in the drama, and the form is in this sense quite similar to that of *The Spoils of Poynton* or *What Maisie Knew*. It is as if James's further penetration into a subject means closer and closer attention to the present, to the immediate and dramatic. James gradually draws closer to the situation in order to explore every possible aspect; at the same time he moves slowly toward a complete recording of everything that transpires in a given moment. The effect of this movement in *The Sacred Fount* is progressively to heighten the intensity of the narrator's obsession and to emphasize in detail the final contrast between Mrs. Brissenden and himself.

The dramatic structure of *The Sacred Fount* also parallels some of James's earlier experiments in the combination of scene and meditation. The scene presents the objective view and the meditation the subjective, with the qualification that the narrator's consciousness is to some extent present throughout most of the scenes; the continual alternation from scene to meditation keeps the structure of the novel balanced. The first two phases are made up of very short scenes followed by short meditations in which the narrator attempts to account for the objective details. This alternation continues through the third phase, although a predominance of meditation, especially in Chapters VI and VIII, indicates the narrator's increasing subjective involvement. In the scene with the narrator and May Server, for example, in Chapter VIII, the woman says almost nothing; everything is given to the reader through the subjective filter of the narrator's speeches and thoughts. This subjective, meditative movement continues into the fourth section, broken only by the brief conversation with Lady John in Chapter IX, until Ford Obert once more brings an objectivity into this almost stifling engrossment in the narrator's subjective speculations. The brilliant final scene with the narrator and Mrs. Brissenden, one of the longest sustained scenes in the novels of this period, marks a balance between subjectivity and objectivity and reveals James's mastery of the scenic technique. The narrator's thoughts are continually present, but they are repeatedly pierced by Mrs. Brissenden's assertions. The subjective is presented in a balanced war with the objective, and the result is a stalemate. The pendulum swing from scene to meditation is finally balanced in a scene where both are fully present, as they were at times in *What Maisie Knew* and as they will be in *The Ambassadors*.

The dialogue of these scenes and the thought-patterns of the meditations follow forms common to the novels of this period, and they enhance the artistic construction of James's novel. The dramatic structure of acts divided into scenes and meditations is paralleled and reinforced by the balanced logic of the narrator's mind. One rather exaggerated example must serve to indicate his logical insistence: "Lady John and Guy Brissenden, in the arbour, were thinking secludedly together; they were together, that is, because they were scarce a foot apart, and they were thinking, I inferred, because they were doing nothing else" (101). His mental patterns follow this deductive form; he invariably applies logic and reason to human behavior.[16] The theory of the sacred fount is an absolute,

THE SACRED FOUNT

once the narrator has first propounded it, to which all evidence is submitted, then accepted if it fits or rejected if it does not. The conclusion of the novel results from this kind of thinking; the narrator's theory meets only with Mrs. Brissenden's denial. The dichotomy remains unresolved, open. His theory is also formalized and balanced in a manner similar to the structure of the novel, although he can recognize, but not give up, the dangerous artificiality of his formula: "These opposed couples balanced like bronze groups at the two ends of a chimney piece, and the most that I could say in lucid deprecation of my thought was that I mustn't take them equally for granted merely *because* they balanced. Things in the real had a way of not balancing; it was all an affair, this fine symmetry, of artificial proportion. Yet . . . it was vivid to me that, 'composing' there beautifully, they could scarce help playing a part in my exhibition" (183). Opposition, balance, symmetry are opposed to "things in the real," and they have all played a part in James's conceptions, as for example in the balanced form of *The Spoils of Poynton* or the intricate oppositions and symmetries of the couples in *What Maisie Knew* or *The Awkward Age*. In *The Sacred Fount* James uses the same kind of structure, yet the balance and symmetry, as we can see in the passage above, are also objectified by James and made a part of the mental bias of the narrator who insists on finding symmetries.

The dialogue in the novel also reinforces the form. When the narrator is not tracing out his syllogisms in his mind, he is trying them out on others. The question-and-answer technique in conversation, used in earlier novels in the period, is extremely valuable here in sustaining the mystery and heightening the quest for a solution. The conversations are much like the inquiries of a detective, in which the narrator attempts continually to gain information from the others, or in which they occasionally try to understand what he is getting at. The submerged effect, as usual in James's novels, is of a total failure of communication between, in this case, the narrator and every other person. In a similar fashion, James uses the technique of the debate in the last scene to point up elaborately the difference between Mrs. Brissenden's and the narrator's visions of the world. The careful balance between assertion and admission of points only heightens the split between the two. The debate is a draw. The narrator is still unable to bridge the gap between himself and "things in the real."

IV

The balances, symmetries, and oppositions in the structure are paralleled by the thematic patterns which often exist as dialectical tensions. The final words of the novel, the narrator's statement that "It wasn't really that I hadn't three times her method. What I too fatally lacked was her tone" (319), set up a dichotomy which in retrospect informs all the themes of the novel. The narrator attempts, using the methods of reason, to establish order, to find a theory which will account for the behavior of the observed characters. Mrs. Brissenden finally contradicts this theory with a flat denial and a crude assertion of the realities of the social world.

The social situation is at the base of all this. In its way *The Sacred Fount* is as strong a criticism of James's society as *The Awkward Age* or *What Maisie Knew*. The narrator's theory is abstract, pure, and beautiful, as he maintains, but these qualities are a mask for the reality from which it derives. It raises to the level of apologue or parable, to metaphor, the corrupt conditions of life in the world of Newmarch. The masked assumption is of couples and coupling, of hidden liaisons and immoral arrangements. The sacred fount in itself is a euphemism for some sort of sexual depletion or vampirism; but the narrator sees in all these arrangements a purity and elegance. He sees them all as people "deeply in love," with "a great pressure of soul to soul" and "the seal of passion" (16, 17). The one unquestionable example of a liaison, however, is "that Mrs. Froome and Lord Lutley were in the wondrous new fashion—and their servants too, like a single household—starting, travelling, arriving together" (4). Newmarch itself (as the name tells us) is in that "wondrous new fashion," "a funny house . . . I'm not sure that anyone *has* gone to bed. One does what one likes" (244-45). The new fashion here is the same modern morality that James found repellent in *What Maisie Knew* and *The Awkward Age;* it is a newness that James represents as "moral squalor," to use F. R. Leavis's term for it. The narrator is reacting to the same situation that confronted Mr. Longdon and that endangered Maisie. His reaction is to try to enhance it, romanticize it, draw from it what beauty he can; but it remains squalid. He never judges the outside world morally in any direct way; all his moral judgments are usually turned on himself. But when he comes closest to being drawn in emotionally, he reveals the horror that has been masked by his intellectual joy. The atrocities he can imagine are then apparent. When he sees May Server, he sees the viciousness of the sacred fount: "I saw as I had never seen before what consuming passion can make of the marked mortal on whom, with fixed beak and claws, it has settled as a prey. She reminded me of a sponge wrung dry and with fine pores agape. Voided and scraped of everything, her shell was merely crushable. So it was brought home to me that the victim could be abased" (136). The hollowness of the drained victim, the images of the scraped shell, the dry sponge, all this overwhelms any beauty; and the passion is one which consumes. Whether or not the narrator is right about May Server's place in his scheme, through his vision James gives us a profound comment on the effect of the fashionable love-game all these couples are engaged in. The society in *The Sacred Fount* is as corrupt as in *The Awkward Age*, but the narrator's romantic theory keeps him from seeing this very often.[17]

His theory also tends to cover up any difference between appearance and reality, a second major theme in the novel.[18] For the narrator, and to some extent even for the reader, there is finally no way of distinguishing between true and false, real and unreal. The narrator must, not knowing the truth, attempt to guess at it through the appearance of the other characters. When Mrs. Brissenden asserts different relationships among the characters, the narrator has no way of knowing whether she is lying to protect herself or telling the truth. He has no way of knowing whether or not he is deceived by appearance, perhaps even crazy, as she says. Reality remains hidden to him.

This is nowhere better shown than in the symbolic portrait of the man with the mask in Chapter IV. The narrator examines the portrait with May Server, Ford Obert, and Gilbert Long (a scene that is repeated in the same form and for some of the same purposes in *The Wings of the Dove*):

The figure represented is a young man in black—a quaint, tight black dress, fashioned in years long past; with a pale, lean, livid face and a stare, from eyes without eyebrows, like that of some old-world clown. In his hand he holds an object that strikes the spectator at first simply as some obscure, some ambiguous work of art, but that on second view becomes a representation of a human face, modelled and coloured, in wax, in enamelled metal, in some substance not human (55).

May Server says that the object is "the Mask of Death," but the narrator insists that it is "much rather the Mask of Life," that it is the face of the man that is dead. Customary symbolism would indicate that May Server is right, that the mask is appearance, lifeless, while the face is reality, life. But the sort of reality that is hidden behind the narrator's theory of the sacred fount is death-in-life, as is evident from his description of May Server (quoted above), and this is the effect of the pale, livid man in black. The mask then has perhaps the quality of life that he attributes to it. It is, he says, "blooming and beautiful," but it has a "grimace" which the narrator cannot see. It is an "obscure," "ambiguous work of art," which is just what his theory is, for he can perceive only intermittently the grimace that is embodied in his theory, the horror that is transformed to art by his imagination. The portrait is consciously ambiguous itself. It represents both death and life, the reality of death-in-life of the face and the artifice of life-in-art of the mask, the appearance which masks reality. This central ambiguity is what keeps the narrator's romantic, artistic vision separate from the vision of all the others, as that is finally represented by Mrs. Brissenden.[19]

In *The Sacred Fount*, as in *The Spoils of Poynton*, art and life are separate, and the artistic individual is divorced from life.[20] The narrator in this novel has some of the same innocence and inviolability of Fleda Vetch or

Nanda Brookenham, and it keeps him apart from life. His essential sterility is the same as that which James objectified in other ways in all his tales of unlived life and half-dead, middle-aged men like John Marcher in "The Beast in the Jungle." The divorce between life and the individual in the novel is combined with the epistemological theme, the effort to detect the difference between appearance and reality. The effort here, however, ends in total failure. There is no way of distinguishing true and false. Out of these various themes and the narrator's speculations develops the final meaning of the novel, James's vision of truth in *The Sacred Fount*.

We have seen that the narrator has method, obsession, and an intense interest in his fellow-creatures. Out of this he spins a beautiful theory about the relationships among them. It is a theory with symmetry and balance, based on incessant observation and a belief in passionate love. At the heart, however, it is a theory of the destruction of one individual by another, for James as for Hawthorne the greatest of human sins. Based as it is on the appearances of people, there is no way of telling how accurate the theory is for the particular case. The narrator is so isolated from the rest of humanity that he has no way of verifying his hypothesis through experience or through getting the "objective proof" for which he longs. His proof must remain subjective, based on his general knowledge of human nature. In this, the theory does point to a truth, reinforced as it is by the nature of the society and by the symbolic portrait of the man with the mask. But it remains a general, unparticularized truth. For all the narrator's observations and ratiocination, the truth remains intuitive and comes to him through his "imagination of atrocity." He had as much of it early in the novel as at the finish, perhaps more. What finally defeats him, refuses to accept either him or his theory, calls him crazy, is the tone of the society which he observes, represented at the end by Mrs. Brissenden, a tone of harsh, insolent reality. This is perhaps truly life, but it is disordered and meaningless. The narrator's vision, on the other hand, is art, ordered and beautiful. The two are separate worlds, united only by a general truth to human nature, the conditions of existence. James carefully introduces the allegory of the cave late in the novel to suggest that the narrator's theory is perhaps a way to reality. Obert, using the narrator's vision, has "blown on my torch . . . till, flaming and smoking, it has guided me, through a magnificent chiaroscuro of colour and shadow, out into the light of day" (222). The narrator is "dazzled" by the metaphor. It represents the possible triumph of his vision, the discovery of reality through art.

But the narrator's paradoxically intuitive and logical approach, his artistic and intellectual vision, comes up against Mrs. Brissenden immediately after this. She denies, as we have seen, any truth to his theory of the sacred fount, and tells him that he may be insane. And so perhaps he finally is. *The Sacred Fount* may stand as a parable for Henry James's difficulties and beliefs as an artist, for his vision of the relationship between art and reality. But, if so, it is conceived in a moment of despair. For the whole structure of the novel points to the same meaning inherent in the themes. There is a final and total split between the vision of Mrs. Brissenden and that of the narrator, between life and art.[21] We must, however, look further; there is a distinction to be made between the narrator's potential insanity and James's meaning.

The narrator's spirits have been high throughout the

novel. His intellectual joy is marred only by fears of failure and, briefly, by his feelings for May Server. The last phase of the novel, however, is a movement further and further into doubt, until the narrator finally feels that he will never again "quite hang together." The effects on his intellectual egotism are even stronger, and he admits his alienation from life at the moment he most clearly recognizes the implications of his position: "I could only say to myself that this was the price—the price of secret success, the lonely liberty and the intellectual joy. There were things that for so private and splendid a revel—that of the exclusive king with his Wagner opera—I could only let go, and the special torment of my case was that the condition of light, of the satisfaction of curiosity and of the attestation of triumph, was in this direct way the sacrifice of feeling . . . I was there to save my priceless pearl of an inquiry and to harden, to that end, my heart" (296). The recognition of the price of art is complete. The divorce between art and life, even between the individual and the world, imposes sacrifices. Like Fleda Vetch and Nanda Brookenham, the narrator is left free, but it is a "lonely liberty," a freedom provided by isolation. And the isolation means not only the death of the heart, but also never truly knowing the world, never being able to verify his intuitions. Any conception then is a dream, a vision, a madness.

But even if the narrator is left isolated, there is still some connection with the world through his theory. His egotism and his intellect contribute to his isolation, but his romantic imagination explains what kind of connection he has with the world he still lives in. The "private and splendid revel," the Wagner opera, the "priceless pearl of an inquiry" are all romantic visions of the real world. The ambiguous mask of life or death is separate from but contains some truth about the real world. The narrator at the end of the novel has come up against "things in the real," "the things we cannot possibly *not* know," the accidents of the world we live in—in this case the disordered, promiscuous relationships in the society which the narrator inhabits. These are, for James, the real. But the narrator cannot conceive or cannot admit promiscuity or chaos; he is obsessed with order. And so he discovers only the things "we can never directly know; the things that reach us only through the beautiful circuit and subterfuge of our thought and our desire."[22] He discovers the essence of the world through the romantic, which for James is "experience disengaged," which is not "a state subject to all our vulgar communities."[23] *The Sacred Fount* points finally to the distinction between the romantic and the real. James's achievement is that he goes beyond the narrator and gives us, in the balanced structure of the novel, a vision of both states, of the romantic and the real, of the essence and accident of the world.

James achieves this, however, only with considerable sacrifice. *The Sacred Fount* is an obtuse, difficult novel, and the form is almost too limited a vehicle for James's vision. The confusions and limitations of the first-person narrator almost mask the success of the author. For the novel is one of despair; the final balanced vision means a loss of purity. The narrator disintegrates before us as a corrupt world imposes itself on his artistic vision, leaving doubt as the only possible attitude. *The Sacred Fount* has an undercurrent of despair that is not controlled by our final realization of the meaning of the narrator's experience. This kind of despair is controlled in a novel like *The Awkward Age*. The society may reject Nanda, but she remains intact; the narrator of *The Sacred Fount* does not.

The undertones of *The Sacred Fount* show a tragic vision of life which points forward to the twentieth century, to James's next novels, and to other novelists who follow him. For what we are confronted with is a finely, complexly constructed novel in which the main sensations are of failure: the failure of perception, of communication, of belief. What remain most strongly with us are madness, alienation, the inability to feel, and the loneliness of freedom, central themes in many novels of this century. *The Sacred Fount* exhibits James's mastery of his dramatic techniques, his use of a kind of interior monologue, and his careful attention to structure, which almost results in that organic form so many novelists were consciously to work for. The form of the novel, with its restriction to the subjective, individual consciousness, is one best understood in comparison to novels of a later period. At the same time James is also close to offering one of the major twentieth-century solutions to the chaos of life—salvation through art. Proust, Joyce, and Virginia Woolf all offered this as an answer to the conditions James presents in *The Sacred Fount*. The narrator's theory of the sacred fount is an artistic vision for ordering experience similar in nature to Proust's vision in the last volume of *A la recherche du temps perdu,* when the narrator of that novel decides that only by recreating his experience in a work of art can he make it meaningful. James's narrator has not had and never will have this final vision, for James in his synthesis of the romantic and the real has ruled out the separate artistic vision which is all the narrator can achieve; he rules out systems of the sort by which his contemporary Henry Adams attempted to explain the same kind of experience. Perhaps James's novel

THE SACRED FOUNT

is closer in theme, in the delineation of the relationship between the romantic and the real, to a novel by one of his contemporaries published only a year before his—Joseph Conrad's *Lord Jim;* for James's art is always of the world he lives in, of the individual alienated from but struggling with his world. It is the true novelist's vision.

The close of *The Sacred Fount* marks the end of five years of experiments in the novel for Henry James, and he moves on to broader visions of the individual struggling with the world in *The Ambassadors, The Wings of the Dove,* and *The Golden Bowl.* The achievement of the period of experiment in the form of the novel is best represented in *What Maisie Knew* and *The Awkward Age;* but in the final novel of that period, James again demonstrates his mastery of form and the value of experiment in the novel. The complexity and vision in this experiment point ahead. *The Sacred Fount* is of 1901.

Notes

Index

NOTES

1: Introduction: The Context of Experiment

1. F. W. Dupee, *Henry James* (Garden City, N. Y., 1956); Oscar Cargill, *The Novels of Henry James* (New York, 1961); Joseph Wiesenfarth, F.S.C., *Henry James and the Dramatic Analogy: A Study of the Major Novels of the Middle Period* (New York, 1963), focuses specifically on this period and on these novels (except for *The Other House*), but I find his theory of the "qualities" of the "dramatic novel"—intensity, economy, objectivity—rather too general and not entirely adequate for a full analysis and understanding of the novels. The relationship to the drama is only a part of James's experiments, and his analyses of the individual novels are rather brief and are limited to following up one part of his "analogy"—intensity in *The Spoils of Poynton*, and so on. In a more extensive analysis of each novel I am interested in tracing all the relevant aspects of the achievement of form in a particular novel.

2. Marius Bewley, *The Complex Fate: Hawthorne, Henry James and Some Other American Writers* (London, 1952); Dorothea Krook, *The Ordeal of Consciousness in Henry James* (Cambridge, 1962); Laurence Holland, *The Expense of Vision: Essays on the Craft of Henry James* (Princeton, 1964); J. A. Ward, *The Imagination of Disaster: Evil in the Fiction of Henry James* (Lincoln, 1961).

NOTES TO CHAPTER 1

3. Richard Poirier, *The Comic Sense of Henry James: A Study of the Early Novels* (New York, 1960); F. O. Matthiessen, *Henry James: The Major Phase* (New York, 1944).

4. Henry James, *The Letters of Henry James*, ed. Percy Lubbock (London, 1920), I, 66. Hereafter cited as *Letters*.

5. "I am not sure that Henry James had not secretly dreamed of being a 'best-seller' in the days when that odd form of literary fame was at its height; at any rate he certainly suffered all his life—and more and more as time went on—from the lack of recognition among the very readers who had most warmly welcomed his early novels." Edith Wharton, *A Backward Glance* (New York, 1934), p. 191.

6. *Letters*, I, 165.

7. *Ibid.*, I, 159.

8. *Ibid.*, I, 168.

9. Henry James, *The Art of the Novel: Critical Prefaces*, introd. R. P. Blackmur (New York: Charles Scribner's Sons, 1934), p. 336. Hereafter cited as *The Art of the Novel*.

10. Henry James, *The Notebooks of Henry James*, edd. F. O. Matthiessen and K. B. Murdock (New York: Oxford University Press, 1955), p. 348. Hereafter cited as *Notebooks*.

11. Henry James, *Notes on Novelists with Some Other Notes* (New York, 1916), pp. 441, 442. The comments were made in 1897 about the novels of George Gissing.

12. I use the term in somewhat the sense defined by Austin Warren, *Rage For Order* (Chicago, 1948), pp. 145-147, and by Morton Dauwen Zabel when he calls Henry James "a major exponent in our literature" of "the dialectic intelligence," *Craft and Character: Texts, Method, and Vocation in Modern Fiction* (New York, 1957), p. 127.

13. What John Holloway calls the "'trajectory' of a narrative work" in *The Charted Mirror* (London, 1960), p. 117.

14. *Ibid.*, p. 109; see also Dorothea Krook, *The Ordeal of Consciousness*, Chap. 1.

15. Graham Greene, *The Lost Childhood and Other Essays* (New York, 1951), p. 25. Cf. also his comparison of *The Awkward Age* with Elizabeth Bowen's *The Death of the Heart* in "Two Novels," *The Spectator*, 161:578 (October 7, 1938).

16. Mark Schorer, "Foreword," *Critiques and Essays on Modern Fiction: 1920-1951*, selected by John W. Aldridge (New York, 1952), p. xix.

17. R. P. Blackmur, *The Lion and the Honeycomb: Essays in Solicitude and Critique* (London, 1956), p. 286.

2: The Early Nineties and the Drama

1. Greene, *The Lost Childhood*, pp. 45-50.

2. *Notebooks*, p. 133; see also Leon Edel's full biographical account of James's experiences in the theater in *Henry James, The Middle Years: 1882-1895* (Philadelphia and New York, 1962), esp. pp. 279-389; Henry James, *The Complete Plays of Henry James*, ed. Leon Edel (Philadelphia and New York, 1949); Henry James, *Guy Domville*, ed. with biographical chapters by Leon Edel (Philadelphia and New York, 1960), pp. 13-121.

3. Entry for 23 January 1895, *Notebooks*, p. 179.

4. *Ibid.*, pp. 126-127, 130-131, 136-141, 150-151, 169-176, 178-179.

5. *Ibid.*, pp. 192-194, 225-229.

6. Krishna Baldev Vaid, *Technique in the Tales of Henry James* (Cambridge, 1964), argues persuasively in his introduction that James's tales have been neglected or underrated by the emphasis on his novels. Following this line of argument one might suggest that the tales of the early nineties are much more significant in James's career than his futile efforts in the drama. The drama, however, is I believe as important (if not more) for the later experiments in the novel.

7. All dates are those of initial publication in either periodical or book.

8. *Notebooks*, p. 180.

9. *Letters*, I, 66.

10. Henry James, *The Selected Letters of Henry James*, ed. Leon Edel (Garden City, N. Y., 1960), pp. 169-170.

11. Leon Edel's editions of *The Complete Plays* and *Guy Domville*; Henry James, *The Scenic Art, Notes on Acting and the Drama: 1872-1901*, ed. Allan Wade (New York, 1957).

12. Francis Fergusson, "James's Idea of Dramatic Form," *Kenyon Review*, 5:498 (Autumn 1943).

NOTES TO CHAPTER 2

13. *Letters*, I, 216.
14. *Complete Plays*, pp. 347-351.
15. F. W. Dupee, *Henry James*, p. 145; see also Leo B. Levy, *Versions of Melodrama: A Study of the Fiction and Drama of Henry James: 1865-1897* (Berkeley and Los Angeles, 1957), p. 70.
16. Henry James, *The Scenic Art*, p. 232.
17. R. P. Blackmur, *The Lion and the Honeycomb*, p. 274.
18. Quote in Henry James, *The Complete Plays*, p. 346.
19. Stephen S. Stanton, ed., *Camille and Other Plays* (New York, 1957), pp. xii-xiii.
20. C. E. Montague, *Dramatic Values* (New York, 1911), p. 70.
21. Eric Bentley, *The Life of the Drama* (New York, 1964), pp. 22, 23.
22. Eric Bentley, *What is Theater?* (Boston, 1956), p. 67.
23. Henry James, *The Scenic Art*, p. 245.
24. *Ibid.*, p. 255.
25. *Ibid.*, p. 250.
26. *Ibid.*, p. 255.
27. *Ibid.*, p. 252-253.
28. Cf. Leon Edel's introduction to *The Other House* (London, 1948), pp. xvi-xvii, for a discussion of James, Ibsen, and the drama; and Laurence Holland, *The Expense of Vision*, p. 85, on James, Ibsen, and the well-made play.
29. *Letters*, I, 241.
30. Bentley, *The Life of the Drama*, pp. 170-171.
31. *Notebooks*, p. 188.
32. Eric Bentley, *Bernard Shaw, 1856-1950,* amended edition (Norfolk, Conn., 1957), pp. 117-118.
33. Henry James, *The Art of the Novel*, p. 323.
34. *Notebooks,* pp. 253, 188.
35. F. O. Matthiessen, *Henry James, The Major Phase*, p. 16.

3: *The Other House*

1. *Notebooks,* p. 147.
2. *Ibid.*, p. 348.
3. Joseph Warren Beach, *The Method of Henry James* (Philadelphia, 1954), pp. 87-97.

4. Edwin Muir, *The Structure of the Novel* (London, 1954), p. 47.

5. *Notebooks*, p. 140. See also Oscar Cargill, *The Novels of Henry James*, pp. 209-212, for a discussion of the novel in relation to Greek tragedy. Cargill sees Dr. Ramage and Mrs. Beever in the role of chorus.

6. See Maurice Valency, *The Flower and the Castle* (New York, 1963), p. 79, for a discussion of the family doctor as *raisonneur* in the plays of Dumas *fils*.

7. Henry James, *The Other House*, ed. Leon Edel (New York: New Directions, 1948), p. 95. All further references will be to this edition and will be included in the text.

8. *Ibid.*, pp. xv-xviii, and Oscar Cargill, *The Novels of Henry James*, pp. 208-211. Edel also compares Rose with other Ibsen heroines, Rebecca West and Hilda Wangel, and finds some aspects of the plot similar to that of *Rosmersholm*.

9. James, *The Other House*, p. xvi.

10. Henry James, *The Scenic Art*, p. 256.

11. Discussion of James's use of dialogue can be found in Beach's *The Method of Henry James*, pp. 72-86. I am indebted to him, although my discussion follows a slightly different tack.

12. Cf. Valency, *The Flower and the Castle*, p. 82: "In the thesis play, the crucial choice is neither tragic nor inevitable, but only problematical, a juridical matter to be decided in accordance with juridical considerations. Thus, in tragedy everything leads to the disaster, but in the thesis play, to the debate—the obligatory scene is a discussion, and the denouement, a verdict." I believe that *The Other House* combines the two forms, as I hope the analysis will show.

13. Austin Warren, *Rage For Order*, pp. 145-147.

14. I am indebted here to Francis Fergusson's discussion of the plot of *Ghosts* in *The Idea of a Theater* (Garden City, N. Y., 1949), pp. 161-170.

15. *Notebooks*, pp. 138-141.

16. Eric Bentley, *In Search of Theater* (New York, 1953), p. 345.

4: *The Spoils of Poynton*

1. *Notebooks*, pp. 81, 136-138, 198-200, 207-212, 214-220, 247-256.

NOTES TO CHAPTER 4

2. See Edwin Muir, *The Structure of the Novel* for a discussion of the novel of character and the dramatic novel.

3. D. W. Jefferson in *Henry James* (Edinburgh and London, 1960), p. 69, has referred briefly to this dual approach. See also Laurence Holland, *The Expense of Vision*, p. 58, for a discussion of the differences between *The Portrait of a Lady* and *The Spoils of Poynton* as due, respectively, to the approach of the painter and the dramatist, and pp. 85-87 for an analysis of the relationships among *The Spoils of Poynton*, Ibsen, and the well-made play.

4. Henry James, *The Art of the Novel*, pp. 127-128.

5. *Ibid.*, p. 129.

6. *Ibid.*, p. xxiv.

7. Henry James, *The Novels and Tales of Henry James* (New York: Charles Scribner's Sons, 1908), X, 9. All subsequent references are to this volume of this edition and will be included in the text.

8. *The Art of the Novel*, p. 131.

9. *Ibid.*, p. 123.

10. For additional discussion of the "spoils" as "things" see Cargill, *The Novels of Henry James*, pp. 227-230, and Holland, *The Expense of Vision*, pp. 91-92.

11. Richard Poirier, *The Comic Sense of Henry James*, p. 249.

12. *The Art of the Novel*, pp. 129-130.

13. *Ibid.*, p. 130.

14. In the original edition (London, 1897), the passage reads: "dodged and dreamed and romanced away the time."

15. *The Art of the Novel*, p. 128.

16. *Notebooks*, p. 215.

17. *Ibid.*, pp. 198-200.

18. *Ibid.*, p. 208.

19. *Ibid.*, p. 209.

20. *Ibid.*, p. 208.

21. *Ibid.*, p. 219.

22. *Ibid.*, p. 249.

23. *Ibid.*, p. 251.

24. *Ibid.*, p. 198.

25. Cf. Charles G. Hoffmann, *The Short Novels of Henry James* (New York, 1957), pp. 55-70, who divides the novel into a prologue of two chapters, three acts of six chapters each, and an epilogue of two chapters.

WHAT MAISIE KNEW

26. Alan H. Roper, "The Moral and Metaphorical Meaning of *The Spoils of Poynton*," *American Literature*, 32:182-196 (May 1960).

27. *Ibid.*

28. Eliseo Vivas, *Creation and Discovery* (New York, 1955), pp. 19-20.

29. The fire in Ibsen's *Ghosts* when "the orphanage, symbol of a lying society, goes up in flames" as G. Wilson Knight, *Ibsen* (New York, 1962), p. 52, describes it, may have given James a hint for this scene. The burning of Lovborg's manuscript in *Hedda Gabler* may indirectly be related.

30. Roper, "The Moral and Metaphorical Meaning," 191.

5: *What Maisie Knew*

1. *The Art of the Novel*, pp. 144-145.
2. *Notebooks*, pp. 126-127, 134.
3. *Ibid.*, pp. 236-240.
4. *Ibid.*, pp. 256-265.
5. Ward S. Worden in "A Cut Version of *What Maisie Knew*," *American Literature*, 24: 493-504 (September 1953), has some interesting observations on James's abridgement of the last parts in the English serial publication.
6. Henry James, *The Art of the Novel*, p. 129.
7. *Ibid.*, p. 147.
8. Henry James, *The Novels and Tales of Henry James* (New York: Charles Scribner's Sons, 1908), XI, 8. All subsequent references are to this edition and will be included in the text.
9. It is significant that one of James's next tales, *The Turn of the Screw*, is also about a governess. Miss Overmore and Mrs. Wix both have some traits which are developed in the later tale.
10. In this interpretation of Mrs. Wix's attraction to Sir Claude I am agreeing with Marius Bewley's recognition of the sexual elements in it. F. R. Leavis has expressed disapproval and insisted that Maisie's and Mrs. Wix's "adorations" are the same. Maisie herself realizes that they are not on pp. 288-290. Cf. Marius Bewley, *The Complex Fate*, pp. 100-101, 128-129. See also Sister M. Corona Sharp, *The Confidante in Henry James: Evolution and Moral Value of a Fictive Character* (Notre Dame, Ind., 1963),

pp. 127-149, for the view that Mrs. Wix evolves "from simple confidante . . . through an active championship, to the final stage of potential corrupter and rival of the child."

11. *The Art of the Novel*, p. 145.

12. An interesting analysis along these lines can be found in Ian Watt, "The First Paragraph of *The Ambassadors:* An Explication," *Essays in Criticism*, 10:250-274 (July 1960).

13. *The Art of the Novel*, pp. 145, 146.

14. Short discussions of the social comedy in *What Maisie Knew* can also be found in D. W. Jefferson, *Henry James*, pp. 72-75, and in F. R. Leavis's comments in Marius Bewley, *The Complex Fate*, pp. 119-124.

15. *The Art of the Novel*, p. 140.

16. *Notebooks*, p. 258.° "vindicating" (James's note).

17. *Ibid.*, p. 263.

18. Throughout the notebooks James continually underestimates the possible length of his novels and tales.

19. For developed comparisons of *What Maisie Knew* and *Huckleberry Finn* see Glauco Cambon, "What Maisie and Huck Knew," *Studi Americani*, VI (1960), 203-220 and Tony Tanner, *The Reign of Wonder* (Cambridge, 1965), pp. 279-281.

20. Bewley, *Complex Fate*, p. 111.

21. William Walsh, *The Use of Imagination* (London, 1959), p. 150.

22. For some closely relevant comments see James's "The Art of Fiction," in *The Future of the Novel*, ed. Leon Edel (New York, 1956), pp. 23-24.

23. For the view that Maisie is in some way corrupted by her environment see Cargill, *The Novels of Henry James*, pp. 256-258, Harris W. Wilson, "What *Did* Maisie Know," *College English*, 17:279-282 (February 1956), and John C. McCloskey, "What Maisie Knows: A Study of Childhood and Adolescence," *American Literature*, 36:485-513 (January 1965).

6: *The Awkward Age*

1. *Notebooks*, p. 192.

2. Leon Edel and Dan H. Laurence, *A Bibliography of Henry James* (London, 1957), pp. 115-116 and *Letters*, I, 300; *The Selected Letters of Henry James*, ed. Leon Edel, p. 145.

THE AWKWARD AGE

3. *Letters*, I, 341-342.
4. Henry James, *The Art of the Novel*, p. 106.
5. For comment on the form in France see Cargill, *The Novels of Henry James*, pp. 263-264.
6. F. R. Leavis, *The Great Tradition* (Garden City, N. Y., 1954), pp. 205-208; F. W. Dupee, *Henry James*, pp. 170-176.
7. Percy Lubbock, *The Craft of Fiction* (New York, 1945), pp. 189-202; Joseph Warren Beach, *The Method of Henry James*, pp. 243-249.
8. Edmund Wilson, "The Ambiguity of Henry James," *The Question of Henry James*, ed. F. W. Dupee (New York, 1945), pp. 180-181.
9. Lubbock, *The Craft of Fiction*, pp. 194-195.
10. Henry James, *The Novels and Tales of Henry James* (New York, Charles Scribner's Sons, 1908), IX, p. 137. All subsequent references are to this edition and will be included in the text.
11. *The Art of the Novel*, p. 71.
12. *Letters*, I, 341-342.
13. *The Art of the Novel*, p. 110.
14. *Ibid.*, p. 106.
15. William James, *The Principles of Psychology* (New York, 1904), II, 370-371. Quoted in Jacques Barzun, *The House of Intellect* (New York, 1959), p. 68.
16. *The Art of the Novel*, p. 113.
17. *Ibid.*, pp. 113-114.
18. For a somewhat different analysis of the structure which sees the first book as prologue to the nine which follow, see Eben Bass, "Dramatic Scene and *The Awkward Age*," *PMLA*, 79:148-157 (March 1964). Ian Gregor also sees the first book as prologue, although his structural analysis is not as elaborate as Bass's, in Ian Gregor and Brian Nicholas, *The Moral and the Story* (London, 1962), p. 157.
19. *The Art of the Novel*, p. 117.
20. *Ibid.*, pp. 104-105.
21. *Ibid.*, p. 99.
22. Cf. Dorothea Krook, *The Ordeal of Consciousness*, pp. 152-153 and Gregor, *The Moral and the Story*, p. 158.
23. Cf. the general discussion of this aspect of the novel in J. A. Ward, *The Imagination of Disaster*, pp. 90ff.

24. Dorothea Krook, *The Ordeal of Consciousness*, p. 138, also mentions the combination of comedy and tragedy in the novel.

7: *The Sacred Fount*

1. Joseph Warren Beach, *The Method of Henry James*, pp. 250-254.

2. The output begins to equal that dealing with *The Turn of the Screw*. The most valuable essay remains Leon Edel's introduction to his edition of *The Sacred Fount* (New York, 1953). Other rewarding essays are Dorothea Krook, *The Ordeal of Consciousness*, pp. 167-194; Laurence Holland, *The Expense of Vision*, pp. 183-226. Most of the other essays of value will be cited in the notes below.

3. Leon Edel and Dan H. Laurence, *A Bibliography of Henry James*, p. 168.

4. *Notebooks*, pp. 150-151, 275, 292.

5. For an analysis of the background of the novel in the short story see Claire J. Raeth, "Henry James's Rejection of *The Sacred Fount*," *ELH*, 16:308-324 (December 1949).

6. For a discussion of character types in James's fiction of this period see J. A. Ward, *The Imagination of Disaster*, pp. 86-87.

7. Henry James, *The Art of the Novel*, p. 321.

8. *Ibid.*, p. 320.

9. *Ibid.*, p. 321.

10. *Ibid.*, pp. 31-32.

11. *Ibid.*, p. 33.

12. Henry James, *The Sacred Fount*, ed. Leon Edel (New York: Grove Press, 1953), p. 89. All subsequent references are to this edition and will be included in the text.

13. Various comparisons with Hawthorne have been made. Cf. Leo B. Levy, "What Does *The Sacred Fount* Mean?" *College English*, 23:381 (February 1962); James K. Folsom, "Archimago's Well: An Interpretation of *The Sacred Fount*," *Modern Fiction Studies*, 7:141 (Summer 1961).

14. Cf. Robert J. Andreach, "Henry James's *The Sacred Fount*: The Existential Predicament," *Nineteenth-Century Fiction*, 17:198-199 (December 1962).

15. Cf. R. P. Blackmur, "The Sacred Fount," *Kenyon Review*, 4:347 (Autumn 1942).

THE SACRED FOUNT

16. See Andreach, p. 203, for a discussion of the narrator's method of thought.

17. In *The Novels of Henry James*, p. 287, Oscar Cargill argues that the narrator is corrupted by the society.

18. For a discussion of appearance and reality in the novel see Edel, "Introduction," pp. xvi-xx.

19. See also Edel, pp. xviii-xx; Krook, p. 177n; Holland, pp. 197-198; James Reaney, "The Condition of Light: Henry James's *The Sacred Fount*," *University of Toronto Quarterly*, 31:143-144 (January 1962), for other discussions of the portrait.

20. The classic identification of the narrator with James is in Wilson Follett, "Henry James's Portrait of Henry James," *New York Times Book Review* (August 23, 1936), 2, 16.

21. This recurrent theme in James's work finds its classic statements in the preface to *The Spoils of Poynton* in James, *The Art of the Novel*, p. 120: "Life being all inclusion and confusion and art being all discrimination and selection"; life is "nothing but splendid waste"; and in James's letters to H .G. Wells in *The Portable Henry James*, ed. Morton Dauwen Zabel (New York, 1951), pp. 482-489. See also Landon C. Burns, "Henry James's Mysterious Fount," *Texas Studies in Language and Literature* (Winter 1960-61), 524-526.

22. *The Art of the Novel*, p. 32.

23. *Ibid.*, p. 33.

INDEX

Adams, Henry, 232
Andreach, Robert J., 246, 247
Archer, William, 28
As You Like It, 156
Augier, Emile, 28

Balzac, Honoré de, 3
Bass, Eben, 245
Beach, Joseph Warren, 43, 45, 168, 205, 240, 241, 245, 246
Beckett, Samuel, 3, 94
Bentley, Eric, 29, 34-35, 37, 74, 240, 241
Bewley, Marius, 3, 152, 237, 243, 244
Blackmur, R. P., xiii, 17, 28, 82, 239, 240, 246
Bowen, Elizabeth, 4, 238
Burke, Kenneth, xiii
Burns, Landon C., 247

Cambon, Glauco, 244
Cargill, Oscar, 3, 53, 237, 241, 242, 244, 245, 247
Chekhov, Anton, 32, 74-75, 76, 203
Compton-Burnett, Ivy, 4
Conrad, Joseph, 3, 8, 14, 16, 92, 233

Dickens, Charles, 132, 151
Dumas *fils,* Alexandre, 28, 241
Dupee, F. W., 3, 27, 168, 237, 240, 245

Edel, Leon, 24, 25, 28, 53, 206, 239, 240, 241, 244, 246, 247
Eliot, George, 4, 8, 16

Faulkner, William, 3
Fergusson, Francis, 24, 28, 239, 241
Fitzgerald, F. Scott, 4
Flaubert, Gustave, 8
Follett, Wilson, 247
Folsom, James K., 246

Gissing, George, 59, 238
Greene, Graham, 13, 19, 238, 239
Gregor, Ian, 245
Gyp (Martel de Janville), 167, 179

Hardy, Thomas, 14, 16
Harper's Weekly, 166
Hawkes, John, 3
Hawthorne, Nathaniel, 49, 70, 215, 228, 246
Hoffmann, Charles G., 242
Holland, Laurence, 3, 237, 240, 242, 246, 247
Holloway, John, 11, 13, 238
Howells, William Dean, 6, 14

Ibsen, Henrik, 30-33, 37, 53-54, 56, 74, 76, 240, 241, 242, 243
Illustrated London News, 39

JAMES, HENRY, WORKS:
  "After the Play," 27
  The Album, 25
  "The Altar of the Dead," 77
  The Ambassadors, 2, 4, 6, 20, 36, 38, 51, 94, 96, 97, 174, 205, 210, 222, 233
  The American, 26, 211
  The American (play), 25
  "The Art of Fiction," 1, 57, 244
  The Art of the Novel, 6-7, 38, 78, 81-82, 121, 124, 134, 136-137, 167, 176-177, 184-185, 210-211, 238, 240, 242-247 *passim*
  The Aspern Papers, 7, 207
  The Awkward Age, xiii, 2, 7, 9, 10, 12, 13, 14, 15, 20, 22, 25, 36, 37, 38, 40, 41, 43, 45, 49, 51, 54, 59, 60, 63, 70, 84, 88, 96, 118, 129, 132, 133, 147, *165-204,* 205, 208, 209, 212, 218, 223, 224, 225, 226, 228, 230, 231-232, 233, 244-246

INDEX

JAMES HENRY WORKS: (con't.)
"The Beast in the Jungle," 174, 228
The Bostonians, 2, 12, 49, 206
"The Chaperon," 20
Confidence, 206
Covering End, 41
"The Coxon Fund," 22, 77
Daisy Miller, 26
"The Death of the Lion," 21, 22
Disengaged, 25
The Europeans, 7, 206
"The Figure in the Carpet," 21, 22-23, 77
The Golden Bowl, 2, 4, 6, 18, 20, 36, 49, 54, 94, 97, 117, 182, 233
Guy Domville, 2, 19, 21, 25, 26, 34, 39
In The Cage, 2, 165, 166
The Ivory Tower, 4, 7, 40
"The Lesson of the Master," 21, 77
A London Life, 7, 13, 49, 122
"The Middle Years," 19, 21, 22-23, 205
New York Edition, 79, 206
"The Next Time," 21, 22
The Notebooks of Henry James, 19-20, 21, 36, 65-66, 78, 93-94, 95-97, 121-122, 148, 166, 206-207, 238-246 *passim*
Notes on Novelists, 59
The Other House, xii, 2, 6, 7, 9, 10, 13, 20, 25, 31, 32, 37, 39-76, 77, 78, 79-81, 82, 84, 91, 92, 94, 97, 99, 102, 103, 120, 122, 126, 127, 129, 150, 166, 167, 173, 174, 181, 186, 206, 208, 209, 237, 240-241
The Other House (play), 42, 57-58
The Outcry, 41
The Portrait of a Lady, 41-43, 50, 81, 173-174, 242
The Princess Casamassima, 2, 6, 12, 13, 173

JAMES HENRY WORKS: (con't.)
"The Private Life," 20
"The Pupil," 20
"The Real Thing," 21
The Reprobate, 25
The Sacred Fount, xiii, 2, 6, 9, 12, 13, 17, 20, 22, 23, 37, 42, 46, 94, 147, 197, 205-233, 246-247
The Scenic Art, 24, 31-33, 54, 239, 240, 241
The Sense of the Past, 4
The Spoils of Poynton, xii, 2, 6, 9, 11, 12, 13, 15, 20, 23, 36, 39, 40, 42, 46, 49, 51, 63, 77-119, 120, 121, 122, 123, 125, 129, 134, 135, 136, 138, 139, 148, 149, 150, 162, 165, 173, 174, 186, 201, 207, 208, 210, 211, 215, 216, 218, 221, 223, 227, 230, 237, 241-243
Tenants, 25
Theatricals: Second Series, 25, 26
Theatricals—Two Comedies, 25
The Tragic Muse, 2, 5, 6, 12, 13, 17, 23
The Turn of the Screw, 2, 9, 14, 20, 70, 94, 207, 243, 246
The Two Magics, 166
Washington Square, 7, 206
Watch and Ward, 206
What Maisie Knew, xii, 2, 7, 8, 9, 11, 12, 13, 14, 15, 20, 23, 36, 37, 40, 42, 45, 46, 49, 51, 54, 59, 84, 88, 97, 118, *120-164*, 165, 166, 173, 176, 186, 199, 205, 207, 208, 218, 221, 222, 223, 224, 225, 233, 243-244
The Wings of the Dove, 2, 4, 6, 20, 36, 45, 49, 50, 51, 54, 88, 91, 94, 97, 117, 129, 132, 203, 205, 209, 226, 233
James, William, 4, 26, 34, 183-184, 245
Jefferson, D. W., 242, 244
Jones, Henry Arthur, 33
Joyce, James, ix, 3, 121, 152, 232

INDEX

Knight, G. Wilson, 243
Krook, Dorothea, 3, 237, 238, 245, 246, 247

Lavedan, Henri, 167
Leavis, F. R., 4, 152, 168, 225, 243, 244, 245
Levy, Leo B., 240, 246
Lubbock, Percy, 168, 245

McCloskey, John C., 244
Matthiessen, F. O., 3, 38, 238, 240
Meredith, George, 16
Montague, C. E., 29, 240
Muir, Edwin, 45, 57, 241, 242

Pinero, Arthur Wing, 33
Poirier, Richard, 3, 32, 87-88, 238, 242
Proust, Marcel, ix, 141, 144, 152, 232

Raeth, Claire J., 246
Reaney, James, 247
Robins, Elizabeth, 54
Roper, Alan H., 103, 243

Sarcey, Francisque, 27
Sardou, Victorien, 28
Schorer, Mark, xiii, 16, 239
Scribe, Eugène, 28, 29
Sharp, Sister M. Corona, 243-244

Shaw, George Bernard, 32, 33, 34, 37, 74-75, 179
Stanton, Stephen S., 240
Stevenson, Robert Louis, 5

Tanner, Tony, 244
Temple, Minny, 208
Turgenev, Ivan, 3, 8
Twain, Mark, 120-121, 136, 152, 244

Vaid, Krishna Baldev, 239
Valency, Maurice, 241
Vivas, Eliseo, 110, 243

Walsh, William, 154, 244
Ward, J. A., 3, 13, 237, 245, 246
Warren, Austin, 63, 238, 241
Watt, Ian, xiii, 244
Wells, H. G., 247
Wharton, Edith, 4, 238
Wiesenfarth, Joseph, FSC, 237
Wilson, Edmund, 168, 245
Wilson, Harris W., 244
Worden, Ward S., 243
Woolf, Virginia, ix, 3, 232

Yellow Book, The, 21, 22, 121

Zabel, Morton Dauwen, 238
Zola, Emile, 14

SHENANDOAH UNIVERSITY LIBRARY
WINCHESTER, VA 22601